The Political Economy of Poverty, Equity, and Growth

Series editors
Deepak Lal and Hla Myint

A World Bank
Comparative Study

*The Political
Economy of Poverty,
Equity, and Growth*

Brazil and Mexico

Angus Maddison
and Associates

Published for the World Bank
Oxford University Press

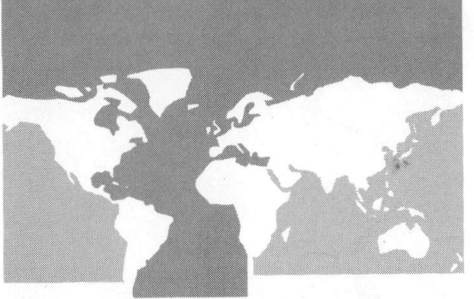

Oxford University Press

OXFORD NEW YORK TORONTO DELHI
BOMBAY CALCUTTA MADRAS KARACHI
KUALA LUMPUR SINGAPORE HONG KONG
TOKYO NAIROBI DAR ES SALAAM
CAPE TOWN MELBOURNE AUCKLAND
and associated companies in
BERLIN IBADAN

© 1992 The International Bank for
Reconstruction and Development / THE WORLD BANK
1818 H Street, N.W., Washington, D.C. 20433

Published by Oxford University Press
200 Madison Avenue, New York, N.Y. 10016

Oxford is a registered trademark of Oxford University Press.

All rights reserved. No part of this publication
may be reproduced, stored in a retrieval system,
or transmitted in any form or by any means,
electronic, mechanical, photocopying, recording,
or otherwise, without the prior permission
of Oxford University Press.

Manufactured in the United States of America
First printing July 1992

The findings, interpretations, and conclusions expressed in
this study are entirely those of the authors and should not
be attributed in any manner to the World Bank, to its
affiliated organizations, or to members of its Board of
Executive Directors or the countries they represent.

Library of Congress Cataloging-in-Publication Data

Maddison, Angus.
   The political economy of poverty, equity, and growth, Brazil and Mexico /
Angus Maddison and associates.
      p.   c. — (A World Bank comparative study)
   Includes bibliographical references and index.
   ISBN 0-19-520874-9
   1. Brazil—Economic policy. 2. Income distribution—Brazil. 3. Mexico—Economic
policy. 4. Income distribution—Mexico.
   I. Title. II. Series: World Bank comparative studies.
   HC187.M3823   1992

92-15645
CIP

HC
187
.M2823
1992

Foreword

This volume is the fourth of several emerging from the comparative study "The Political Economy of Poverty, Equity and Growth," sponsored by the World Bank. The study was done to provide a critical evaluation of the economic history of selected developing countries in 1950–85. It explores the *processes* that yielded different levels of growth, poverty, and equity in these countries, depending on each country's initial resource endowment and economic structure, national institutions and forms of economic organization, and economic policies (including those that might have been undertaken).

The Scope of the Comparative Study

The basic building block of the project is a coherent story of the growth and income distribution experiences of each country, based on the methods of what may be termed "analytical economic history" (see Collier and Lal 1986) and "political economy." Each country study provides both a historical narrative and a deeper explanation of how and why things happened. Each study also seeks to identify the role of ideology and interest groups in shaping policy.

Our comparative approach involved pairing countries whose initial conditions or policies seemed to be either significantly similar or significantly different. Although initial impressions of similarity or difference may not have been borne out on closer inspection, this binary approach offered a novel and promising way of reconciling in-depth case studies with broader comparative methods of analysis.

To provide this in-depth study of individual cases, a smaller number of countries was selected than is conventional in comparative statistical studies. We have serious doubts about the validity of inferences drawn from such cross-sectional regression studies about historical processes (see Hicks 1979). Therefore this project, by combining qualitative with quantitative analysis, has tried instead to interpret the nature and significance of the usual quantifiable variables for each country in its historical and institutional context.

To provide some unifying elements to the project, we presented the authors of the country studies with several provisional hypotheses to be considered in the course of their work. These concern the determinants of growth, the importance of historical and organizational factors in determining alternative feasible paths of growth to redress poverty, and the relative roles of ideas, interests, and ideology in influencing decisionmaking.

Our synthesis volume in this series discusses the extent to which these hypotheses were or were not substantiated in each of the country studies. The following list of the country studies and their principal authors suggests the range of the overall comparative study:

Malawi and Madagascar	Frederic L. Pryor
Egypt and Turkey	Bent Hansen
Sri Lanka and Malaysia	Henry Bruton and Associates
Indonesia and Nigeria	David Bevan, Paul Collier, and Jan Gunning
Thailand and Ghana	Oey A. Meesook, Douglas Rimmer, and Gus Edgren
Brazil and Mexico	Angus Maddison and Associates
Costa Rica and Uruguay	Simon Rottenberg, Claudio Gonzales-Vega, and Edgardo Favaro
Colombia and Peru	Antonio Urdinola, Mauricio Carrizosa Serrano, and Richard Webb
Five Small Economies: Hong Kong, Singapore, Malta, Jamaica, and Mauritius	Ronald Findlay and Stanislaw Wellisz

Many of these volumes will be published in this series by Oxford University Press. In addition, a volume of special studies on related topics, edited by George Psacharopoulos, will also be published.

Brazil and Mexico

This study of Brazil and Mexico covers two of the largest middle-income developing countries. They are both rich in natural resources and had some of the highest rates of growth among developing countries in the postwar period until about 1980, when both were hit by the debt crisis. Since then the economic performance of both countries has been dismal. Both countries are also similar in having high population growth rates and long histories as independent nations. But whereas the polity in Mexico has been dominated by a single party, the Partido Revolucionario Institucional (PRI), since the 1920s Brazil's political history has been more chequered, with a limited democracy having been twice replaced by military dictatorships. Both countries had substantially similar growth experiences, but Mexico enjoyed a lengthy period of price stability in contrast with the high endemic inflation in Brazil.

Both are countries with high degrees of inequality by international standards, although Maddison and his associates conclude that income distribution in Mexico is somewhat more equal than in Brazil and that absolute poverty has been reduced in both countries.

The authors provide a careful accounting of the sources of growth in the two countries for 1950–80 and find that capital accumulation and a rapidly growing labor supply were major sources of growth and, surprisingly, that increases in total factor productivity, which measures the efficiency of resource allocation, were quite respectable by international standards.

This is particularly surprising because the authors detail a panoply of dirigiste economic policies that have damaged growth performance. They give several reasons why they think this dirigisme was less damaging than in many other countries, such as India or Nigeria. Both countries remained open to foreign technology because of substantial inflows of foreign direct investment. Market forces continued to operate in the large domestic markets because the vigor of the private sector helped to maintain competition. Brazil maintained relatively realistic exchange rates, and Mexico remained free from exchange control. It was not until the debt crisis hit that the distortions created by past policy made it more difficult to manage the economy efficiently. The authors find over-expansionary macroeconomic policies preceding the second oil price rise at the end of the 1970s as the common cause of the two countries' subsequent debt crises.

The authors also provide an account of the political history of the two countries and suggest that conventional political economy models based on class conflict or on the rent seeking of interest groups do not provide good explanations for the growth outcomes, although they partially explain the distributional outcomes.

All in all, the study provides a concise account of the policies and outcomes relating to growth and distributional issues, which should be of general interest to both development economists and economic historians.

Deepak Lal and Hla Myint
Series editors

Authorship Note

The overall responsibility for the volume in its final form rests with Angus Maddison, the principal author. Annibal Villela wrote the section on the political element in Brazilian macroeconomic policy in chapter 2, on agricultural and industrial policy in Brazil in chapter 3, and on the distributive impact of the Brazilian social welfare programs in chapter 4. Victor Urquidi wrote the section on the political element in Mexican macroeconomic policy in chapter 5, Paul Lamartine Yates wrote the section on Mexican agricultural policy in chapter 6, and Nora Lustig wrote the section on the distributive impact of the Mexican social welfare programs in chapter 7. The final draft was completed in July 1989.

Background papers and material on Brazil were provided by Claudio Contador, Sonia Maria Rocha, Luiz V. Villela, and Renato A. Z. Villela and on Mexico by Gerardo Bueno, Jesus Reyes Heroles G. G., and Saul Trejo.

Contents

Foreword   *v*

Authorship Note   *viii*

Part I. Comparative Analysis   1

1. Introduction   3

   Comparing Growth Outcomes and Policy in Brazil and Mexico   4
   The Crisis of the 1980s   7
   A Comparative View of Distribution and Redistribution   10
   Note   16

Part II. Brazil   17

2. Interests, Ideology, and the Exercise of Power   19

   The Political Element in Macroeconomic Policy, 1929–87   25
   Notes   42

3. Brazilian Growth Performance since 1950   43

   Overall Economic Performance   43
   Agricultural Policies   63
   Policies toward Industry and Services   71

4. Brazilian Outcomes in Terms of Equity and Alleviation of Poverty   79

   Income Distribution   79
   The Distributive Impact of Social Welfare Programs   96
   The Fiscal Structure and Its Distributive Impact   106
   Note   110

Part III. Mexico   111

5. The Mexican Polity, Institutions, and Policy   113

Interests, Ideology, and the Exercise of Power   113
The Political Element in Macroeconomic Policy, 1940–85   122

6. Mexican Growth Performance since 1950   143

The Overall Growth Accounts   143
Agricultural Policies   161
Policies toward Industry and Services   176

7. Mexican Outcomes in Terms of Equity and Alleviation of Poverty   185

The Dimensions of Income Inequality and Poverty   185
The Distributive Impact of Social Welfare Programs   191
Overall Distributive Impact of Government Spending and Revenue   205

Statistical Appendix   209

Reliability of GDP Estimates for Brazil   209
Reliability of GDP Estimates for Mexico   219

Bibliography   231

Index   241

Tables

1-1. Comparative Levels of GDP per Capita in Ten Economies, 1950, 1980, and 1987   5
1-2. Annual Average Compound Growth Rates of Ten Economies, 1929–87   6
1-3. Rates of Inflation and Importance of External Finance, Brazil and Mexico, Selected Periods, 1950–88   8
1-4. Crude Petroleum Production in Seven Countries, 1973, 1980, and 1986   9
1-5. Relative Price Movements, Brazil and Mexico, 1978, 1981, and 1986   9
1-6. Inequality of Before-Tax Income of Households in Eleven Countries, Various Years, 1961–73   11
1-7. Distribution of Arable Land Ownership, Mexico in 1970 and Brazil in 1980   12
1-8. Education Standards in Brazil and Mexico, 1980   13
1-9. Income Differentials by Level of Education, in Brazil, Mexico, and the United States, in the 1970s   14

2-1. Presidents of Brazil and Percentage of the Population That Voted for Them, 1919–90   20
2-2. Finance Ministers, Planning Ministers, and Governors of the Central Bank, 1964–90   32
2-3. Economic Indicators, Selected Years, 1929–85   41

3-1. Main Expenditure Categories of GDP, Selected Years, 1950–87   44
3-2. Basic Indicators of Growth Performance, Selected Years, 1940–80   44
3-3. Indexes of Basic Indicators of Growth Performance, Selected Years, 1940–80   45
3-4. Sources of Growth by Decade, 1940–80   45
3-5. Distribution of Population and Per Capita Income, by Region, Selected Years, 1819–1980   47
3-6. Structure of Brazilian Employment and Gross Value Added, 1950, 1980, and 1985   48
3-7. Share of Leading Primary Commodities in Total Exports, Selected Periods, 1821–1983   49
3-8. Per Capita Food Supply in Six Countries, 1975–77   52
3-9. Foreign Equity Capital in Brazil, by Country of Origin, 1930, 1975, and 1983   55
3-10. Brazilian External Debt and Foreign Direct Investment Assets, Selected Years, 1889–1984   56
3-11. Brazilian Foreign Trade Indicators, Selected Years, 1929–87   60
3-12. Key Indicators for Brazilian Agriculture, Forestry, and Fishing, Selected Years, 1950–80   64
3-13. Index of Output per Person Engaged in Agriculture, Forestry, and Fishing, in Ten Countries, 1975   64
3-14. Production of Main Crops, Selected Years, 1950–85   68
3-15. Evolution of Rural Credit, 1969–84   69
3-16. Levels of Manufacturing Productivity in Five Countries Compared with the United States, 1975   72

4-1. Social and Economic Indicators for the Northeast and Southeast, 1960 and 1980   80
4-2. Population and Income per Capita by Region, State, and Territory, 1950 and 1980   81
4-3. Personal Income Distribution by Decile, 1960, 1970, and 1980   82
4-4. Average Personal Income by Decile, 1960, 1970, and 1980   83
4-5. Miscellaneous Social Indicators for Brazil, Selected Years, 1950–80   84
4-6. Variation in Levels of Education between Persons in Brazil and Six Other Countries   88
4-7. Dependency Ratios in Four Countries, Selected Years, 1950–80   89
4-8. Total Fertility Rates, Selected Years, 1950–80   90
4-9. Ethnic Characteristics and Income of Employed Persons, 1976   92
4-10. Distribution of Agricultural Landownership, 1950 and 1980   92
4-11. Number of Families below the Poverty Line, 1960, 1970, and 1980   95
4-12. Social Security Contributors and Value of Receipts, Selected Years, 1971–83   98

xii Contents

4-13. Social Security Expenditure, Selected Years, 1971–83   99
4-14. Life Expectancy at Birth, by Region, Selected Years, 1950–80   99
4-15. Number of Social Security Beneficiaries in Various Categories, 1975 and 1983   100
4-16. Social Charges as a Percentage Addition to Wage Costs   102
4-17. School-Age Population and Enrolment, 1960, 1970, and 1980   103
4-18. Distribution of Public Expenditures on Health Services, Selected Years, 1949–82   104
4-19. Outstanding Loans of the Housing Financial System, by Government and Private Institutions, 1974 and 1984   106
4-20. Categories of General Government Revenue, Total Expenditure, and Overall Balance, 1970, 1982, and 1984   107
4-21. Incidence of Major Taxes, by Level of Disposable Income, 1975   108
4-22. Categories of General Government Current and Capital Expenditure, 1970, 1982, and 1984   109

5-1. Presidents of Mexico, Percentage of the Population That Voted for Them, and Percentage of Poll They Obtained, 1920–88   114
5-2. Ministers of Finance, 1927–86   122
5-3. Directors General of the Bank of Mexico, 1925–86   123
5-4. External Debt and Stock of Foreign Direct Investment Assets, Selected Years, 1889–1986   126
5-5. External Debt and Debt Service, 1970 and 1975–88   134
5-6. Economic Indicators for the Adjustment Period, 1981–88   138

6-1. Main Expenditure Categories of GDP, Selected Years, 1950–87   144
6-2. Indicators of Growth Performance, Selected Years, 1940–85   144
6-3. Indexes of Basic Indicators of Growth Performance, Selected Years, 1940–85   145
6-4. Sources of Growth, by Period, 1940–85   146
6-5. Growth of Real GDP, by Major Sector, Selected Periods, 1910–85   147
6-6. Structure of Employment and Gross Value Added, 1950 and 1986   148
6-7. GDP per Employed Person, by Region, 1950 and 1980   149
6-8. Public and Private Gross Fixed Investment as a Proportion of GDP, Selected Years, 1930–85   150
6-9. Annual Yield of Various Financial Instruments, 1985 and 1986   152
6-10. Ratio of Labor Force to Total Population in Three Countries, 1950 and 1980   153
6-11. Elements in the Current Balance of Payments, Selected Years, 1950–85   155
6-12. Evolution of Import Licensing, 1956–85   155
6-13. PEMEX Finances, 1973 and 1980   157
6-14. PEMEX Subsidies to Domestic Consumers, 1980   157
6-15. Indicators of Macromanagment Performance, 1941–87   159
6-16. Public Expenditure as a Share of GDP, Selected Years, 1965–82   159
6-17. Government Employment, 1975–86   160
6-18. Government Share of Value Added and Employment, by Sector, 1975 and 1983   160

Contents   xiii

6-19. Ejidos and Ejidatarios, by Decade, 1930–70   163
6-20. Number of Families Mainly Dependent on Farming, 1960 and 1970   165
6-21. Number and Arable Area of Parcelas and Arable Farms, by Size and Type of Tenure, 1970   167
6-22. Distribution of Parcelas and Arable Farms, by Size, 1940 and 1970   168
6-23. Indexes of Producer Prices, Nominal and Real, Selected Years, 1950–84   173
6-24. Annual Growth Rates of Agricultural Output, at 1970 Prices, Selected Periods, 1940–85   174
6-25. Value of Agricultural Production at 1970 Prices, Selected Years, 1950–85   176
6-26. Crude Petroleum and Natural Gas Production, Selected Years, 1901–87   177
6-27. Net Fixed Tangible Capital Stock in Mining and Manufacturing, 1970 and 1982   178
6-28. Growth of Subsectors within Manufacturing, 1950–85   179
6-29. Implicit Nominal Protection for Manufactured Goods, 1960, 1970, and 1980   180
6-30. Evolution of Direct Foreign Investment, 1973–86   181
6-31. Government Employment, by Sector, 1975 and 1986   182

7-1. Three Summary Measures of Inequality of Income, Selected Years, 1950–75   186
7-2. Social Indicators for Mexico, Selected Years, 1940–85   187
7-3. Average Annual Family Income after Taxes, 1950 and 1975   188
7-4. Locus of Mexican Poverty, by Occupation of Household Head, 1975   189
7-5. Link between Education and Poverty, by Education of Family Head, 1975   189
7-6. Share of Population Covered by Social Security, Selected Years, 1965–80   193
7-7. Rural and Urban Population Covered by Social Security, 1960, 1970, and 1976   194
7-8. Population Covered by Social Security, by State, 1978   195
7-9. Expenditures of IMSS, by Type of Benefit, 1980   196
7-10. Public Current and Investment Expenditure on Education, Selected Years, 1935–80   197
7-11. Federal Educational Spending per Student, 1976   198
7-12. Number of Students per Teacher, Selected Years, 1950–81   199
7-13. Share of Students and Teachers in Public and Private Educational Institutions, 1970 and 1985   200
7-14. Government Expenditure per Capita on Health, by Client Group, 1972, 1978, and 1983   202
7-15. Fiscal Cost of Food Subsidies, 1969–82   204
7-16. Categories of Government Expenditure, 1975 and 1982   205
7-17. Categories of General Government Revenue, Total Expenditure, and Overall Balance, 1975 and 1982   206

xiv Contents

7-18. Tax Incidence, by Level of Income, 1968   206
7-19. tax Incidence, by Type of Tax, 1980   207

A-1. Brazilian Population, GDP, and GDP per Capita, Selected Years, 1900–50   212
A-2. Brazilian GDP, Population, and GDP per Capita, 1950–88   212
A-3. Brazilian Gross Domestic Project by Sector at Factor Cost, Selected Years, 1950–88   214
A-4. Value of Brazilian Commodity Exports and Imports, Selected Years, 1950–87   214
A-5. Brazilian Exchange Rate, Internal and World Prices, and Real Exchange Rate, Selected Years, 1889–1967   215
A-6. Brazilian Multiple Exchange Rates, by Category, 1953–66   216
A-7. Brazilian Exchange Rate, Internal and World Prices, and Real Exchange rate, 1967–88   217
A-8. Active Labor Force and Labor Force with Monthly Earnings below One Minimum Rate, Selected Years, 1960–83   218

B-1. Mexican Population, GDP, and GDP per Capita, Selected Years, 1895–1950   220
B-2. Mexican GDP, Population, and GDP per Capita, 1950–88   220
B-3. Mexican Gross Domestic Product, by Sector, Selected Years, 1895–1985   222
B-4. Mexican Employment by Sector, Selected Years, 1900–84   222
B-5. Value Added per Person Employed in Mexico, Selected Years, 1900–84   223
B-6. Population by Age and Sex, Selected Years, 1950–80   224
B-7. Economically Active Population in Mexico, by Age and Sex, 1950, 1960, and 1980   225
B-8. Mexican Activity Rates, by Age and Sex, 1950 and 1980   226
B-9. Mexican Exports, Total and per Capita, and Exchange Rates, Selected Years, 1801–1988   227
B-10. Mexican Exchange Rates, Internal and World Prices, and Real Exchange Rates, 1950–87   228
B-11. Mexican GDP Deflator, Selected Years, 1950–88   229
B-12. Mexican GDP per Capita, by State, 1970, 1975, and 1980   230

I Comparative Analysis

1 Introduction

From 1929 to the early 1980s Brazil and Mexico were among the world's fastest growing economies. Some of the benefits of growth filtered down, and absolute poverty was mitigated as evidenced by figures on life expectancy and infant mortality. But both countries had inherited a pattern of inequality in social relations and gross inequalities of income and education that were not substantially modified either by considered acts of policy or by the spontaneous processes unleashed by economic growth. In the 1980s, the record was disastrous, in large part because of earlier recklessness in pursuit of growth and neglect of other problems and goals.

The political economy story underlying this combination of outcomes is told in chapters 2 and 5 of our parallel case histories (for Brazil and Mexico, respectively), the growth outcomes are analyzed in chapters 3 and 6, and the equity-poverty analysis is in chapters 4 and 7. Here in chapter 1 we make a more explicit confrontation of performance in the two countries than in the subsequent chapters, which are necessarily more disaggregated and detailed.

There are two main types of political economy. That of Malthus, Ricardo, and Marx, which looked at conflicts of major social classes, came to gloomy conclusions about the ultimate possibilities for raising income in a capitalist framework. The new political economy of Buchanan, Tulloch, Olson, and Krueger sees conflict in more fragmented terms, between different interest groups, each of which tries to use the state and its institutions to create rents for themselves to the detriment of the public interest and of economic efficiency. These contemporary political economists tend to be particularly gloomy about countries where the state has played a major role.

Neither set of views is confirmed by this study. Until the 1980s the outcomes in terms of growth for both Brazil and Mexico were bountiful by any standard and there was little loss caused by factionalist clashes of interest. There were glaring examples of inefficiency that resulted from the use of *dirigiste* commands, rather than market incentives, but when efficiency is measured by total factor productivity, the aggregate outcome for both economies was quite respectable. The political economy of class and vested interest certainly plays a role in explaining the outcomes in terms of equity and poverty, but in both Mexico and Brazil, over lengthy periods, there was a strong consensus about the legitimacy of ambitiously expansionist economic policy as long as it brought growth. In neither country did the political system favor clear articulation of alternative policy by opposition groups. However, there were few domestic voices urging greater caution to avoid inflation and indebtedness.

The catastrophic slowdown in both economies in the 1980s did not derive from a factionalist clash of interest groups, or from the micro inefficiency of *dirigisme*. It was the result of major errors in macroeconomic policy—attempting to push growth too fast and ignoring the canons of fiscal responsibility and sound money.

Comparing Growth Outcomes and Policy in Brazil and Mexico

There are several striking similarities between Brazil and Mexico, when they are viewed in comparative perspective. Both are very large countries, ranking tenth and twelfth among the world's two hundred economies in terms of real gross domestic product (GDP). Size has obvious implications for the dimensions of the internal market, economies of scale, and the degree to which their division of labor is international. It also affects national perceptions about policy and national destiny. Both are middle-income countries, poorer in per capita terms than the advanced capitalist countries, but much better off than most African and Asian economies (table 1-1). This position in the world income hierarchy seems to be favorable for exploiting opportunities to catch up with the world leaders, if it is properly used. Both countries have been independent and unified nation-states for nearly seventeen decades. This is a good reason for taking their story back before the 1950s, which was the starting point for autonomous national policy in most of the developing countries of Asia and Africa.

Until the 1980s, both Brazil and Mexico had considerable success with economic growth (table 1-2). In 1929–50, when most of the world was plagued by depression and war, Brazil and Mexico probably surpassed most countries in terms of GDP and per capita GDP growth. It was this experience that gave legitimacy to the inward-looking and dirigiste policies they adopted in this period and continued to deploy in a postwar world that was much more strongly oriented toward neoliberalism. In 1950–80, GDP grew faster in Brazil than in many developing countries; and though Brazil's growth was less rapid than that of Hong Kong and Singapore, the size and growth of those ministates were more than

Table 1-1. Comparative Levels of GDP per Capita in Ten Economies, 1950, 1980, and 1987
(1980 international dollars)

Area and country	1950	1980	1987
Latin America			
Argentina	2,324	3,843	3,302
Brazil	1,073	3,349	3,326
Chile	2,350	3,650	3,393
Colombia	1,395	2,838	3,027
Mexico	1,169	2,946	2,711
Peru	1,349	2,508	2,380
Asia			
India	359	570	662
Japan	1,116	7,954	9,756
Korea, Rep. of	564	2,583	4,143
Taiwan, China	526	3,185	4,744

Source: Appendixes A, B; Maddison (1989).

matched by the city of São Paulo. Mexico's growth was a little slower, but Mexico was also a top performer in the international growth league. Since 1980, the experience of both countries has been disastrous. Hence in an international context, the most appropriate periods for examining their economies are 1929–50, 1950–80, and 1980–87, though in the individual national contexts some variation is required.

In common with much of Latin America, Brazil in the past six decades has had a cavalier attitude to canons of sound money and fiscal rectitude. The government regarded inflation as a useful way of collecting revenue by printing money. Mexico moved in this direction in the 1970s. This attitude led both countries in the 1970s to accumulate large debt so that they could continue to grow rapidly in a period when the world economy was faltering. This tradition in public finance proved disastrous in the 1980s when they and Latin America as a whole found it almost impossible to break their inflationary mind-set.

Like many countries in Latin America, both Brazil and Mexico are rich in natural resources. One short-hand expression of this is the ratio of land to population. In this respect and in mineral resources they are very well endowed. For instance, Brazil had a twentyfold advantage over India in 1950 in terms of per capita land area, and an even greater advantage over the Republic of Korea. This natural resource endowment has affected policy. It caused Brazil in the first half of this century to overestimate the degree to which it could rely on coffee and it caused Mexico in the 1970s to exaggerate the degree to which it could depend

Table 1-2. Annual Average Compound Growth Rates of Ten Economies, 1929–87
(percent)

Area and country	1929–50	1950–80	1980–87	1950–87	1929–87
GDP					
Latin America					
Argentina	2.5	3.4	−0.6	2.6	2.6
Brazil	4.6	6.8	2.4	5.9	5.4
Chile	2.6	3.5	0.6	3.0	2.9
Colombia	3.6	5.2	2.8	4.7	4.3
Mexico	4.0	6.4	1.0	5.3	4.8
Peru	1.8	4.9	1.9	4.3	3.4
Asia					
India	0.7	3.7	4.4	3.8	2.7
Japan	1.1	8.0	3.7	7.1	4.9
Rep. of Korea	0.7	7.4	8.7	7.6	5.1
Taiwan, China	1.8	9.1	7.4	8.8	6.2
GDP per capita					
Latin America					
Argentina	0.6	1.7	−2.1	1.0	0.8
Brazil	2.4	3.9	−0.1	3.1	2.9
Chile	0.9	1.5	−1.0	1.0	1.0
Colombia	1.7	2.4	0.9	2.1	2.0
Mexico	1.6	3.1	−1.2	2.3	2.1
Peru	2.0	2.1	−0.7	1.5	2.0
Asia					
India	−0.5	1.6	2.2	1.7	0.9
Japan	−0.2	6.8	3.0	6.0	3.7
Rep. of Korea	−1.4	5.2	7.0	5.5	3.0
Taiwan, China	−0.9	6.2	5.9	6.1	3.5

Source: Appendixes A, B; Maddison (1989).

on oil.

Both Brazil and Mexico have had subsidies, price controls, and a good deal of dirigisme in allocation of domestic resources and in control over foreign trade, which have had adverse effects on efficiency. The overall impact of these factors is difficult to quantify and one of the few ways of assessing the impact is by analyzing productivity performance. In fact, both countries had respectable growth in total factor productivity in 1950–80, Brazil 2.2 percent a year and Mexico 2.3 percent. After that, however, factor productivity in each country turned negative.

In terms of partial indicators, there is evidence that distortions increased in Mexico between 1950 and 1980. In those decades the real exchange rate appreciated (table B-10), individual import items subject to quantitative controls rose from zero to 1,866 (table 6-12), effective tariff protection increased (table 6-29), the price scissors tightened against agriculture (table 6-23), subsidies to domestic oil consumption reached egregious proportions (table 6-14), and interest rate differentials widened (table 6-9).

In terms of the same sort of evidence, the degree of distortion may well have declined in Brazil from 1950 to 1980. In this respect the important institutional reforms of 1964–67 provided a basic organizational shake-up and were important in making the system more responsive to market forces. The complicated system of multiple exchange rates was abandoned in favor of a realistically floating peg, and tariffs were reduced (but raised again after the OPEC shocks). Quantitative controls on imports were smaller than in Mexico.

Brazil's terms of trade for domestic agriculture moved negatively in the 1950s but recovered sharply in the 1970s (table 3-12), consumer subsidies were smaller than in Mexico, and the pricing policy of public enterprises was probably not as extreme as in Mexico. However, differentials in the cost of credit to different kinds of borrowers were bigger in Brazil than in Mexico.

The Crisis of the 1980s

In the 1980s, economic performance worsened sharply in both countries. Mexico's GDP per capita fell by more than 10 percent, average income was further hit by worsened terms of trade and high debt service, and real wages fell by around a third. In Brazil GDP per capita stagnated rather than falling, and there too, wage and salary earners were hardest hit. In both countries inflation accelerated to unprecedented heights, and policy stumbled from one expedient to another. There were excess demand problems after the first OPEC oil shock but the real crisis arose with the second rise in oil prices in 1979–80 and came to a peak with the abrupt reversal of external financial flows in 1982.

The causes of Brazil's 1980s problem are relatively straightforward. Because Brazil is a large oil importer, its import costs rose sharply in 1979–80, as they had done in 1973–74, and it again tried to keep domestic activity at very high levels by restricting imports and borrowing abroad. Continuation of such policies was considered dangerous by the finance minister, Mario Simonsen, who resigned in 1979. His more expansionist successor, Antonio Delphim Netto, soon ran into major problems of accelerating inflation. His manipulation of the indexing

Table 1-3. Rates of Inflation and Importance of External Finance, Brazil and Mexico, Selected Periods, 1950–88
(percent)

Factor and period	Brazil	Mexico
Average annual rate of inflation		
1950–73	28.4	5.6
1973–80	48.8	21.8
1980–88	199.0	73.3
External finance as a share of GDP		
1950–73	1.32	1.90
1974–81	4.65	4.30
1982–86	−3.45	−6.64

Source: Inflation (consumer price index) from IMF, *International Financial Statistics;* external finance from World Bank, *World Tables* (1983, 1988).

apparatus damaged business confidence and in 1981 he was forced into a substantial adjustment program, whose effectiveness was destroyed by the 1982 debt crisis.

Since 1982, Brazil has made major transfers (3.5 percent of GDP—see table 1-3) to service foreign debt in spite of significant delinquency in interest payments. It has been unable to break the spiral of inflation in spite of trying both orthodox restraint and a heterodox combination of price and wage controls in its unsuccessful 1986 attempt to tackle inertial inflation painlessly. Political weakness has prevented firm measures to strengthen public finance and the situation has shown little sign of improvement in spite of the improved terms of trade when oil prices fell in 1986.

Mexico's position was much more favorable than Brazil's on the eve of the second oil shock. Mexico had a price windfall as world oil prices soared, and new oil reserves had permitted a quadrupling of its petroleum production between 1973 and 1980 (much bigger than that in Indonesia or Nigeria—see table 1-4).

The subsequent changes in Mexico's price and trade structure were a normal consequence of this windfall. The terms of trade improved sharply, and the real exchange rate was allowed to appreciate substantially to 1982 (table 1-5). Non-oil exports fell as their competitiveness sagged, imports boomed as the price of importable goods fell, and import licensing was relaxed (see table 6-12).

These problems of relative price and sectoral equilibrium were inevitable in the Mexican situation. But a much bigger problem arose because of the impact that this double windfall had on the government's conception of permissible levels of demand. In this respect it made

Table 1-4. Crude Petroleum Production in Seven Countries, 1973, 1980, and 1986

(thousands of metric tons)

Country	1973	1980	1986
Brazil	8,276	9,084	28,788
India	7,198	9,396	31,152
Indonesia	66,952	77,628	71,016
Mexico	23,257	99,936	126,228
Nigeria	101,765	102,204	72,804
United Kingdom	88	78,912	121,164
United States	454,190	400,200	428,210

Source: For 1973, United Nations (1977); for 1980 and 1986, United Nations, *Monthly Bulletin of Statistics.*

several mistakes: in assuming that the price windfall was permanent and even likely to grow substantially (whereas, in fact, the whole of the second OPEC price windfall had gone by 1986); in ignoring the fact that the apparent quantitative windfall involved very large investment costs; in giving huge subsidies (5.6 percent of GDP; see table 6-14) to domestic energy consumption; and in running up a huge budget deficit, which was financed by domestic money creation and foreign borrowing. Such was the extremity of Mexico's demand expansion that its external debt rose by $53 billion from 1978 to 1982, more in fact than Brazil's debt rose.

The pace of the Mexican boom, the blatancy of government macro and micro mismanagement, and the sharp rise in real interest rates on floating interest debt after 1981 (from an average of minus 8.7 percent in 1977–80 to a positive 14.6 percent average in 1981–84) created a crisis of confidence, capital flight, and the debt crisis of 1982. The conversion

Table 1-5. Relative Price Movements, Brazil and Mexico, 1978, 1981, and 1986

(1978 = 100)

	Terms of trade		Real exchange rate	
Year	Brazil	Mexico	Brazil	Mexico
1978	100.0	100.0	100.0	100.0
1981	64.2	151.4	83.7	130.6
1986	88.0	94.6	76.7	78.9

Source: For terms of trade, for Brazil, IMF *International Financial Statistics;* for Mexico, estimates kindly supplied by CEPAL. Real exchange rates, appendixes A, B.

of domestically held dollar accounts and the nationalization of banks in 1982 added another shattering blow to the government's domestic creditworthiness.

After 1982, oil production became static, oil prices declined, and Mexican terms of trade worsened sharply. Even more important was the change in the availability of foreign capital. In 1974–81 foreign capital provided a supplement to domestic resources equal to 4.3 percent of GDP on average. In 1982–86 this ceased, and external finance was negative to the extent of 6.6 percent of GDP because of the high cost of servicing foreign debt at high interest rates. This required a complete reversal of policies, with a very large depreciation in the real exchange rate, resurgence of non-oil exports, cuts in government expenditure and private consumption, and maintenance of a large trade surplus.

Its oil endowment gave Mexico substantial advantages (which it squandered), but there is a strong family likeness between the situations in Brazil and Mexico. Both countries indulged in excess demand and discarded "old-fashioned fiscal religion" to a degree that destroyed public creditworthiness and weakened effective taxable capacity. Both were left struggling with situations close to hyperinflation with huge foreign debt liabilities.

A Comparative View of Distribution and Redistribution

Both Brazil and Mexico have high levels of income inequality. In neither case is there evidence that this originated in the postwar period. In the colonial economy, rents from abundant natural resources were cornered by the state and by large landlords from Portugal and Spain. There was very little peasant agriculture in the European, Asian, or African sense. The labor force were slaves in Brazil and peons in Mexico, with official policy designed to keep labor cheap and brutish. After the abolition of slavery, landholding conditions changed in the south of Brazil as immigrants from Europe and Japan came into the country as sharecroppers and became small- or medium-scale cultivators; but there was no land reform, and access to new land on the frontier was almost entirely limited to propertied interests. Official policy continued to keep labor cheap and uneducated (with the illiterate also being disfranchised). In Mexico, the Revolution brought land reform, which only gained momentum in the 1930s. Peonage was replaced by a system that provides *ejidatarios* with the rights to farm collectively owned plots but not to own that land.

Mexico's education record since the Revolution is better than Brazil's, but the level of education is low for a country with Mexico's level of income. Although land is now only a small part of total assets in both countries, and most income is nonagricultural, the original gross inequality in land ownership has created a persistent culture of poverty in rural areas. Inequality of income is regional as well as personal. The interstate range of income in Brazil (table 4-1) is more than 8 to 1, and 3 to 1 among major regions. In Mexico, regional inequality is not much smaller, at 6 to 1 between states (table B-12). This contrasts with interstate ranges of 2 to 1 in countries like India and the United States. As with the personal distribution, regional inequality did not originate in the postwar period but has deep historical roots.

As in most developing countries there is now a marked dualism between productivity levels in different sectors of the economy. Brazilian manufacturing productivity is about a third of that in the United States, but agricultural productivity is one-tenth of the U.S. level. In Mexico, manufacturing productivity is about 30 percent of that in the United States, agricultural productivity 7 percent.

In neither country is there reliable information on the distribution of income between laborers, landowners, and proprietors of other reproducible assets. In any case, some of these forms of income are mixed, and important property assets are owned by the state. We have, therefore, concentrated on the distribution of income between persons rather than factors of production.[1]

Table 1-6. Inequality of Before-Tax Income of Households in Eleven Countries, Various Years, 1961–73

Country	Year	Gini coefficient	Top decile per capita income as multiple of that in bottom two deciles
Developing			
Argentina	1961	0.425	11.2
Brazil	1970	0.550[a]	20.0
Chile	1968	0.503	21.3
India	1964–65	0.428	12.4
Korea, Republic of	1970	0.351	7.6
Mexico	1969	0.567	25.5
Developed			
France	1970	0.416	14.4
Germany, Federal Republic of	1973	0.396	10.5
Japan	1969	0.335	7.5
United Kingdom	1973	0.344	9.1
United States	1972	0.404	13.5

a. Figure supplied by Christian Morrisson, of the OECD Development Centre.

Source: For developing countries, Lecaillon and others (1984), pp. 26–27. For developed countries, Sawyer and Wasserman (1976), p. 14.

When measured by the summary Gini coefficient shown in table 1-6, Brazil and Mexico are obviously alike, with extreme inequality of income by international standards. However, given the imperfection of the surveys the measures are based on and the fact that for both countries they include a fair amount of imputed undeclared income, these overall measures do little to differentiate the situation in the two countries. Judging by the various pieces of evidence examined in chapters 4 and 7, it seems likely that inequality is somewhat smaller in Mexico than in Brazil.

In the first place, land ownership in Mexico is more equal than in Brazil (table 1-7). One of the major pillars of the Mexican "revolutionary" system has been land reform. This has been a long-drawn-out process. Many peasants (*ejidatarios* and *comuneros*) do not have a freehold title, but big estates are much rarer in Mexico than in Brazil, and the proportion of land in small holdings is much larger. Even though the land that the Mexican government has distributed to *ejidos* is of poorer quality than that in private ownership, and the benefits of government irrigation work, credit, extension, and seed development have gone disproportionately to private landowners, land redistribution has been a major element in the legitimacy of the Mexican political system. The influence over allocation of land in Mexico, which is in the hands of local politicians, is a major instrument of social control.

Brazil has never implemented any serious program of land reform or redistribution, and the huge expansion of the agricultural area on the frontier has not done anything to equalize distribution.

The stock of education is somewhat better and the distribution between persons and regions less uneven in Mexico than in Brazil (table

Table 1-7. Distribution of Arable Land Ownership, Mexico in 1970 and Brazil in 1980

Size of holding (hectares)	Percentage of all holdings	Percentage of area held	Average size of holding (hectares)
Mexico 1970[a]			
Less than 10	87.9	42.1	3.6
10–100	11.5	36.9	24.1
Over 100	0.6	21.0	247.5
Brazil 1980			
Less than 10	50.3	2.5	3.5
10–100	39.1	17.7	32.0
Over 100	10.6	79.8	543.2

a. Arable land excluding communal *ejidos*.
Source: Tables 6-21, 4-10.

Table 1-8. Educational Standards in Brazil and Mexico, 1980

Category	Brazil	Mexico
Population 15 years old and older		
Percentage that is literate	74.0	83.0
Average years of primary and secondary education	3.9	4.9
Percentage with no education	27.4	16.1
Percentage with 1–4 years of education	49.9	24.1
Percentage with more than 4 years of education	22.7	59.8[a]
Percentage of children not attending primary school	27.0[b]	21.7[c]

a. Includes 21.7 percent who have completed the full six-year primary cycle and 30.1 percent with more than six years.
b. Children aged 7–9.
c. Children aged 6–8.
Source: For Brazil, IBGE (1983), pp. 14, 16. Enrollment from demographic census *Tabulacoes Avancadas: Resultados Preliminares*, p. 16, education levels from *Mao de Obra*, p. 14. Mexico from *X Censo General de Poblacion y Vivienda, 1980, Resumen General Abreviado*, Mexico, INEGI (1984a), pp. 51, 61.

1-8). Income differentials by level of education in Mexico are quite wide, but less so than in Brazil (table 1-9). This tends to mitigate inequality of income and opportunity in Mexico (by the extreme Brazilian standard). However, one of the major reasons for inequality in both countries is the fact that education is unevenly distributed, an inequality in human capital that has a powerful effect on earning power. By comparison with Japan or the fast-growing countries of Asia, the failure to focus on development of human capital is blatant in Mexico as well as in Brazil, but particularly so in Mexico because of the strong rhetorical commitment to education since the 1920s. People from poor families tend to get the worst education, and most families with a decent income level in Brazil and Mexico send their children to private schools; the education system therefore tends to reinforce the cycle of poverty and does little to promote social mobility.

Though both countries have a high degree of regional inequality, it is greater in Brazil. Brazilian interstate variance in per capita income in 1980 ranged from a high of 211,000 cruzeiros a year in the Federal District to lows of 24,500 cruzeiros in Piaui and 28,000 cruzeiros in Maranhão (table 4-1). In Mexico, the interstate range was also extreme, but smaller (table B-12).

The Mexican unemployed have the option of temporary migration to work in the United States. This escape valve mitigates the poverty problem in a way that does not show up in the national statistics,

Table 1-9. Income Differentials by Level of Education, in Brazil, Mexico, and the United States, in the 1970s
(university graduates = 100.0)

Level of education	Brazil (1970)	Mexico (1977)	United States (1971–75)
Illiterate	6.5	16.0	a
Primary education	14.1	(29.4)	44.8
Secondary education	28.3	(44.4)	59.3
Junior college	40.4	(53.5)	76.0
University	100.0	(100.0)	100.0

a. Illiterate included with those in primary education.
Source: For Mexico, Diez-Canedo and Vera (1982), p. 480; Brazil, Langoni (1974), p. 69; United States, Denison (1985), p. 118.

but it is important—it probably adds something like 10 percent to job opportunity at wages that are a good deal higher than the Mexican average.

Finally, it would appear that the Mexican tax-transfer system is the more progressive of the two in its impact. Comparison is of course difficult, but Mexican taxes are probably progressive in their impact, while those of Brazil are regressive. In both countries social transfers are mildly progressive.

Both countries have complex social security systems (neither of which includes unemployment benefits or family allowances). These have grown steadily since the 1940s, and in both cases they have a substantial clientele. The schemes are large and complicated enough to involve major administrative problems and some elements of "moral hazard" (with a rapid growth in the number of people claiming sickness benefits and handicapped status). In Brazil, there were 25 million contributors in 1983 and 9.8 million recipients of benefits. In Mexico contributors in 1980 numbered 24 million, and recipients about 6 million. The dominant feature of the cash transfer programs is their insurance character—they redistribute income over the life cycle of contributors but are only marginally redistributive among different kinds of persons. There are welfare elements in the benefit structure, which are small but growing in importance.

As a fraction of GDP, the social security systems proper are about comparable in the two countries. Brazil, however, has a very important provident fund system for all workers that requires a payroll deduction of the equivalent of a month's salary which is cumulated and protected against inflation. Funds can only be withdrawn to finance the purchase of housing or when the worker is unemployed or retires. Both social security systems comprise payment of cash benefits and provision of services in kind. Brazilian cash benefits are around two-thirds of total disbursements, Mexican only one-quarter.

Both countries provide basic preventive health facilities, such as water and disease control, on a more or less universal basis, as well as the curative treatment provided under social security arrangements. Expenditure on curative services is bigger than on preventive measures in both countries, but in real terms the public health services are much bigger in Mexico, with about 3.5 times more manpower than in Brazil. In both countries there is substantial private expenditure on health, and this is proportionately bigger in Brazil. In both countries, the health of the population has improved noticeably since 1950 as measured by infant mortality and life expectancy, developments that can probably be attributed in larger part to the impact of preventive health services, new drugs, and better sanitation and nutrition than to public expenditure on health. Both countries now provide family planning services, but this is rather recent.

There are quite clear differences in the level of health service supplied to different groups of the population. The level of provision for public employees in Mexico is much higher in terms of doctors and hospital beds than it is in basic hospital facilities provided by the social security system for the bulk of the population. In 1983 per capita government expenditure on health for state employees was eighteen times higher than for the bulk of the population (table 7-14).

In both countries, housing is mainly financed and constructed privately and the proportion of owner occupation is very high (68 percent in Mexico, 62 percent in Brazil). The bulk of housing is of poor quality and a large part of it consists of rough dwellings constructed by the owners, often on land to which they have no clear title. Government building or ownership of housing is relatively small, but in both countries government plays a significant role in housing finance. In Brazil government participation represented 64 percent of outstanding real estate lending in 1984, and it is probably bigger proportionately than in Mexico, as it is financed largely through the compulsory provident fund scheme. Brazilian government lending for housing goes to that part of the population that can mobilize a fair amount of capital to buy modern housing in the urban sector, definitely not to the lower-income groups. This is also true of housing finance supplied by the Mexican government. In Mexico, the allocation of housing funds seems to have a greater subsidy element and involves a greater element of patronage granted to special groups. In both countries governments have attempted at times to intervene in the private sector by controlling rents, with an erratic impact on income distribution.

In both countries, subsidies have been a large item of expenditure. In 1982 they were 6.1 percent of GDP in Brazil and 14.1 percent in Mexico.

Some subsidies have a distributive or compensatory income objective—for example, those to Brazilian agriculture, or those that provide food through Mexico's CONASUPO (Compañía Nacional de Subsisténcias Populares). Others are intended to cover deficits of public corporations or to steer resources in directions thought to be desirable for purposes of development. In most cases these subsidies have no distributive goals and are fuzzily or poorly targeted, so that their distributive impact is erratic. They involve wasteful use of resources and create strong lobbying pressures from the client groups that hope to benefit from them; there seems little doubt that these problems are more pronounced in Mexico than in Brazil.

Regulatory activity of government in the field of prices, import control, and investment allocation has generally been conceived in terms of development or in conjunction with other policy objectives; it also has had erratic distributive consequences. Regulation has been more pervasive in Mexico, particularly in import controls, and less strong in foreign exchange controls or allocation of capital at low or negative rates of interest.

In labor market policy, both countries have minimum wage legislation and various laws to protect labor that have little effect in the informal sector but some signaling function in the formal economy in triggering adjustments to inflation. Otherwise Brazilian policy has generally operated to reduce labor's bargaining power by repressing unionization, whereas the Mexican political system includes a powerful labor wing which protects the income and privileges of its clientele.

Note

1. For Brazil, the only information in the national accounts on factor shares is for 1970, 1975, and 1980 when compensation of employees represented 40.7 percent, 38.4 percent, and 37.9 percent, respectively, of GDP at factor cost. The rest was the gross operating surplus, representing property income gross of depreciation, rents, profits, and mixed income from enterprise and labor (de Gusmão Veloso 1987). For Mexico, the national accounts show employment compensation to have been 29 percent of GDP at factor cost in 1950, 32.5 percent in 1960, 37 percent in 1970, 40.5 percent in 1975, 39 percent in 1980, and 31 percent in 1986. In the United States, as in other developed countries, the share of employment compensation is much bigger than in Brazil and Mexico—65.3 percent in 1985 (OECD, *National Accounts*). However, the United States, with other advanced countries, has a much larger share of wage and salary earners in total employment—91.9 percent in 1985 including the armed forces (OECD, *Labour Force Statistics*). In Mexico, Altimir (1974) has calculated the proportions of the employed who were wage and salary earners in 1950, 1960, and 1970 were, respectively, 46.8 percent, 60.4 percent, and 62.2 percent. Table 6-3 gives a rough estimate of total labor income in Mexico (including imputed labor income of family workers and the self-employed), but no comparative information is available for Brazil.

II *Brazil*

2 Interests, Ideology, and the Exercise of Power

In the colonial period, Portuguese authority in Brazil was not strong. The control of the crown and clergy was decentralized and probably weaker than that of local oligarchs. Large landowners, sugar entrepreneurs, and commercial interests controlled the local militias and had a strong influence over judicial proceedings that were related to their security and property rights. They were the main economic beneficiaries of colonialism, and fiscal tribute to Lisbon was relatively small. The economy was primitive in terms of productivity and technical sophistication. A surplus was extracted by using brute labor in a land of abundant natural resources. Half the population were slaves, with no economic or civil rights, not even the right to a normal family life. The life expectancy of slaves was very short, and per capita income extremely low.

During the period (1822–89) that Brazil was an independent state ruled by an emperor, the central power was strengthened at the expense of the provinces. A national army and bureaucracy were created, slavery was gradually superseded by wage labor, and the country began to import rather than export capital. The basic function of the state continued to be the preservation of law and order to protect propertied interests and to keep labor cheap. A strong central government also served effectively to preserve the territorial integrity of the nation.

The first republic (1889–1930) was a decentralized oligarchy. Machine politicians at the state level used patronage in public appointments to satisfy a limited clientele of voters and frequently miscounted votes to stay in power. Local authority was in the hands of the dominant landlords, "colonels," who used mercenaries, *cangaceiros*, to guarantee their privileged access to the land and the docility of a population of former slaves. At the center of politics, the presidency alternated between the São Paulo coffee interests and the ranchers of Minas Gerais. These states were the two largest economically and had the biggest local militias to guarantee their autonomy. The Northeast was a backwater fiefdom of the "colonels."

Suffrage was limited to property owners, and the number of these was relatively low. As late as the 1920s, the electorate was proportionately only about a tenth of that in the United States. The three Brazilian presidents elected in the 1920s had the vote of only 1.6 percent of the population, compared with 15.6 percent for U.S. presidents (table 2-1).

The central government dispensed job patronage and fiscal and tariff favors to a cozy, opportunistically shifting coalition of propertied interests. There were few major clashes of economic interest within the ruling group, and no strong ideological splits. Warren Dean (1969) describes the symbiotic coexistence of agricultural and industrial interests in São Paulo in this period. The scope for conflict of interest was substantially cushioned by regional autonomy. The state of São Paulo ran an expensive coffee stabilization program with its own funds and foreign borrowing, which was backed by the central government. In the search for cheap labor to replace slaves, it also ran its own scheme for many years to promote immigration from southern Europe.

In trying to satisfy different parties, the central government was (by today's standards) mildly inflationary, running budget deficits, borrow-

Table 2-1. Presidents of Brazil and Percentage of the Population That Voted for Them, 1919–90

Term	President	Vote (percent)
1919–22	Epitacio da Silva Pessoa	1.1
1922–26	Arthur da Silva Bernades	1.6
1926–30	Washington Luis Pereira de Souza	2.2
1930–45	Getúlio Dornelles Vargas	0.0
1946–51	Eurico Gaspar Dutra	6.9
1951–54	Getúlio Dornelles Vargas	7.2
1954–55	João Café Filho	0.0[a]
1956–61	Juscelino Kubitschek de Oliveira	5.0
1961	Janio da Silva Quadros	7.9[b]
1961–64	João Belchior Marques Goulart	0.0[c]
1964–67	Humberto de Alencar Castelo Branco	0.0
1967–69	Arthur da Costa e Silva	0.0
1969–74	Emilio Garrastazu Medici	0.0
1974–79	Ernesto Geisel	0.0
1979–85	João Baptista de Oliveira Figueiredo	0.0
1985–90	José Sarney	0.0

a. Received 4.7 percent as vice-president.
b. In the "popular" election in 1961, Brazilian registered voters were 22.3 percent of the population, and 18.0 percent of the population voted. In the U.S. presidential election of 1960 the comparable figures were 59.3 percent and 37.9 percent.
c. Received 6.3 percent as vice-president.
Source: IBGE, Anuário estatístico (1984), p. 374.

ing abroad, letting the exchange rate float, with no central bank or sustained commitment to the gold standard. Tariffs were fixed on an ad hoc basis and representatives of new industries, mainly in São Paulo, could usually lobby successfully for protection when they started to manufacture a new product. There were also taxes on interstate movement of goods that were subject to ad hoc manipulation. Foreign mercantile and banking interests were important but were usually subordinate in conflicts with Brazilian interests.

Growth was concentrated in the south of the country. The per capita income of the northeast stagnated or declined. The mass of the population had no social security and little access to education or to land. Popular revolts, such as that in the backlands of the Northeast (Canudos) in 1897, were put down ruthlessly by the national army.

The Brazilian polity entered a fourth stage in 1930. Under the strain of a world recession and the power politics of presidential succession, there was a successful military rebellion led by the governor of Rio Grande do Sul, Getúlio Dornelles Vargas. Vargas, a wealthy rancher and member of the old oligarchic elite, was a Machiavellian manipulator who exploited the military and the economic stresses of the period to build a new kind of state apparatus with himself as dictator.

Vargas strengthened the central government at the expense of the states, burning their flags and removing their right to levy taxes on interstate commerce. He increased the central government's role in the economy, set up government enterprises and new mechanisms of control and licensing, and inflated the size and power of the central ministerial bureaucracy and the many new agencies of government. He created the Departamento Administrativo do Serviço Público (DASP, the Administrative Department of Public Service) to institute a merit system of selecting civil servants by examination, but in fact substantial parts of public employment continued to be dominated by patronage and the spoils system.

Vargas continued to hand out favors to the old oligarchic interest groups—maintaining coffee stabilization and augmenting tariff protection for industry by quantitative restrictions and exchange controls—but he widened support for his government by creating a national social security system for urban workers and making membership in government unions compulsory. This new part of the political system was run by the Ministry of Labor, and patronage jobs in the social security institutes were given to interest groups lower down the social scale than the more respectable hangers-on of the old oligarchy.

Vargas sought populist support from labor groups loyal to the government and created the Brazilian Labor party as his own vehicle. He made it virtually impossible to form free trade unions but created official unions to maintain work discipline. In return, the 1934 constitution established a minimum wage, the eight-hour day, holidays with pay, job security for industrial workers, and a national social security system for urban workers. The populist political measures of Vargas did not include universal suffrage, but the franchise was extended from property holders to literates. The exclusion of illiterates may explain why policy did little for those who were really poor.

Vargas pursued a more consciously nationalist policy than the old republic, stopping payment on foreign debts and reducing the role of foreign enterprise in public utilities and banking. In political terms, he borrowed from Mediterranean fascism. In 1937 he set up a corporatist system, abolished political parties, and established censorship. This *estado novo* was inspired by the Portuguese dictator, Antonio de Oliveira Salazar. Roberto Simonsen, the spokesman of São Paulo industrial interests, made a weak attempt to develop a corporatist philosophy for state guidance of industrial development, but in fact the regime had no clearly articulated ideology.

Following the defeat of the Axis powers, Vargas was gently deposed by the military. The fascist trimmings of government were dismantled and political freedom (with limited suffrage) was restored. Most of the other institutional changes of Vargas—the state capitalist framework and the inward-looking emphasis of policy—remained, as did his labor legislation.

After a conservative interlude under President Eurico Gaspar Dutra from 1946 to 1951, Vargas returned as an elected president in 1951 with a more explicitly development-oriented philosophy. In 1954, he committed suicide in order to forestall another military deposition, and after a brief interlude was succeeded by the arch-developmentalist, Juscelino Kubitschek, who increased emphasis on state enterprise for leading sectors of industry and governmental planning of resource allocation.

Within this framework, power was heavily concentrated on the presidency without the constraint of powerful political parties or any real budgetary control by congress. Agricultural and industrial interests continued to be favored clients of the state, but they did not set the economic agenda. Kubitschek welcomed foreign private investment but stressed nationalist objectives by reducing the role of foreign trade, refusing to borrow from the International Monetary Fund (IMF), and building a new national capital in Brasilia.

Labor interests were a weaker element of Kubitschek's policy than of Vargas's but were not completely ignored. Kubitschek extended the scope of labor legislation by creating an obligation for employers in the formal sector to pay workers a thirteenth monthly wage. Under João Belchior Marques Goulart, who had been Vargas's minister of labor and vice-president under Kubitschek and Janio da Silva Quadros, labor found greater favor. Goulart succeeded to the presidency in 1961 after the quixotic resignation of Quadros. Under challenge from the military, Goulart tried to win popular support by advocating large increases in the minimum wage, promoting unionism in the armed services, working for land reform, and extending public ownership to petroleum production.

Most of these measures were in direct conflict with the views of the military, who used the messy state of the economy and the acceleration of inflation as an excuse to oust Goulart in 1964. They restricted political freedom, abolished the old political parties, removed the civil rights of former politicians, and imposed their own succession of indirectly selected military presidents from 1964 to 1985.

The officer class of the military is drawn largely from an urban bourgeois background. Stepan (1971) reports that only 9 percent of the 1,176 cadets who entered the military academy in 1962–66 were from worker or peasant families, and even fewer were from wealthy backgrounds; 35 percent were from military families and 13 percent were sons of bureaucrats. None of them had illiterate parents (at a time when half the population was illiterate). Forty-two percent were born in Guanabara (Rio de Janeiro) and 14 percent in Rio Grande do Sul, areas around the capital city and the southern borders where the army was traditionally concentrated. Only 8 percent came from São Paulo, where sons of prosperous families preferred business to military careers. Most of the officers entered the services as cadets rather than by promotion from below. Ordinary soldiers generally were conscripts who served only nine months.

The officer class had participated in World War II. In postwar years, many officers attended training courses in the United States and were influenced by American ideas. They thought of themselves as a modernizing elite and used the military club of Rio de Janeiro as a forum for continuous discussion and analysis of political developments.

The intervention against the Goulart government was led by General Humberto de Alencar Castelo Branco, a military intellectual with relatively moderate views. He was president in 1964–67 when most of the institutional innovations of the military regime were enacted. During 1967–74 the hardliners who served as president pursued politically more repressive policies. Thereafter the regime became more liberal. Curiously enough, the military did not increase their claims on the national budget during their period of power. In relative terms, Brazil has the second smallest military budget (after Mexico) among the bigger countries of Latin America.

The military did not propound a coherent ideology as a backdrop for their policy, but their regime strengthened the state's economic role and delegated considerable power to a bureaucratic elite of technocrats. They increased the size and scope of nationalized industries, reinforced the role of the state as a supplier of credit and credit subsidies, multiplied fiscal leverage by new kinds of incentives and privileges, and maintained a broad range of controls over foreign trade. Public employment, both in the bureaucracy and in nationalized industries, continued to have a large element of patronage. The most powerful minister during the military period was usually the minister of planning.

The nationalist element in policy was less pronounced under the military, with foreign enterprise being given a warm welcome. The labor policies of the Vargas-Goulart period disappeared as the military disbanded trade unions, reduced the minimum wage in real terms, and restored the employer's power to hire and fire. The development philosophy of the military after 1967 was to maximize growth and rely almost entirely on trickle-down effects to increase social welfare.

Castelo Branco's ministerial team included Octavio Gouveia de Bulhões as minister of finance. Bulhões was an old-fashioned liberal, very much against state intervention in the economy. The minister of planning, Roberto de Oliveira Campos, had had a more pragmatic career as a planner under Kubitschek and as an ambassador under Goulart, but like Bulhões he was closely associated with the ideas of Eugenio Gudin, Brazil's leading free trade liberal who had been the major opponent of Roberto Simonsen's etatist views. In many respects, the basic ideas of Mario Simonsen, who was finance minister for President Ernesto Geisel for five years and briefly minister of planning for President João B. Figueiredo, were similar to those of Bulhões and Campos (see Simonsen and Campos 1974). Antonio Delfim Netto (1986), who was for seven years finance minister and for five years planning minister under the military, has also proclaimed his belief in liberal market economies. It is quite clear therefore that some of the top policymakers in the military era were out of sympathy with the basic etatist sanctions of the system they were running.

The long-run Brazilian experience has been one of nonconflictual accommodation of the interests of various propertied groups. However, the leverage of state economic power has grown more or less inexorably since the time of Vargas and has been administered by a technocratic elite who have taken steps to mitigate distortions in resource allocation by using quasi-market mechanisms such as exchange auctions and capital market indexation for inflation. The underground economy and the entrepreneurial hidden hand helped to offset some of the potential snags of bureaucracy. In terms of comparative growth performance, the system worked rather well until 1980.

There is no other country like Brazil in Latin America. Brazil has avoided the protracted factionalist conflicts and extremes of ideology that have damaged economic performance in Argentina, Chile, and Uruguay, and it has adapted flexibly to many more changes in regime than has Mexico, whose economic performance has been closest to Brazil's. However, Brazil has yet to test its capacity to survive without factionalist conflict in conditions of universal suffrage.

The Political Element in Macroeconomic Policy, 1929–87

For economic policy in the twentieth century, 1929 was a decisive turning point. World War I had given a stimulus to manufacturing as a substitute for imports, but this was reversed when foreign goods again became available. The poor quality and high prices of import substitutes and the fact that the coffee interests had greater political strength than manufacturers decided the matter.

Government policy in the 1920s centered on promotion of coffee production. The golden years, 1924–29, saw high foreign earnings and booming coffee prices (Villela and Suzigan 1975).

In 1929 the world crisis brought a collapse of export earnings that made it necessary to cut imports by three-quarters by 1932; even by 1938 they were still 30 percent below the 1929 peak. The new defensive policies of exchange control, increased tariffs, and debt default gave strong support to import substitution. It became clear that Brazil's destiny was changing, and there was massive destruction of coffee stocks. There was also a move toward a new populist political regime. The power of the rural oligarchy faded, and the domestic market became the dynamic core of the economy for the first time. Nevertheless, coffee interests had a persistent influence on exchange rate policy until the mid-1960s. Those interests won an overvalued exchange rate for long periods, assuring their earnings in a market they viewed as inelastic.

World Crisis and World War

Getúlio Vargas came to power in 1930 leading a revolution that overthrew the oligarchic republic. After four years at the head of the so-called provisional government he was elected president by the Constituent Assembly in 1934, and in November 1937 made himself president under a new constitution, clearly inspired by corporatist ideals and setting up an avowedly totalitarian *estado novo*.

Vargas came from a family of *estancieiros* (owners of large ranches) prominent in the state politics of Rio Grande do Sul. He served in the National Congress from 1922 to 1926, then became finance minister under President Washington Luiz, and in 1928 was elected governor of Rio Grande do Sul.

The domination of government by rural landholders and the preponderance of revenues from the external sector were features of the system that Vargas terminated in 1930. Taxes on intrastate commerce were ended and the power of the central government was greatly strengthened. The tax structure was revised, with greater reliance put on taxes levied by the central government; the electorate was quadrupled and the secret ballot created; women were given the right to vote; social security laws were enacted; labor was unionized under government control; a minimum wage was created and other labor benefits instituted, and the economy, chiefly industry, was actively stimulated. Vargas did not encroach on the private enterprise system nor extend his social reforms to rural areas.

Through the Conselho Federal de Comércio Exterior (the Council of Foreign Trade), many new industrial ventures were planned, such as the production of pulp and paper, steel, heavy chemicals, and cement.[1] They received loans from the Carteira Industrial (Industrial Department) of the Banco do Brasil, the first source of long-term industrial financing, established in 1937.

Government purchase of coffee, which sustained prices during the early 1920s, was phased out as production in competitor countries grew and the world market weakened. The fall of coffee prices was inevitable because of the structural imbalance between supply and demand for the product. The change in policy emphasis toward new interest groups thus aroused less conflict than it would have done in a different world setting. In any case, there were financial links between the coffee interests and industrialists, who were both heavily concentrated in the state of São Paulo.

Industrial expansion was impressive—10 percent annual average growth from 1930 to 1939—in view of the insignificant expansion of capacity. Though there were some imports of secondhand equipment at depressed prices, they were not sufficient to stimulate large-scale modernization of the industrial sector. In fact, in 1931–32 imports of capital goods fell to one-fifth the 1929 level and in most years in the 1930s they did not reach 50 percent of the pre-crisis level. Domestic productive capacity was, of course, not equipped to replace imports of capital goods, and apparent consumption of products like rolled steel (used here as a proxy for capital goods) generally did not recover to the 1929 level before 1937. All this indicates that there was an intensification of use of existing productive capacity.

The outbreak of World War II brought an increase in export volume and improved terms of trade (coffee prices doubled) but made it impossible to import capital goods. The wartime surpluses on trade account fueled inflation and reinforced the effect of budget deficits. In 1944, the government created *certificados de equipamento* (licenses for deferred import of capital goods), conceived to temporarily sterilize part of the foreign exchange derived from increased exports.

The structural balance between agriculture and manufacturing was gradually altered by the relative insulation of the economy, strong industrial growth, and stagnation of agriculture. The structure of government fiscal revenue reflects this phenomenon. Taxes on imports, which accounted for 55 percent of fiscal revenue in 1929, decreased to 12 percent in 1945. But income taxes rose from 9 percent in 1939 to 27 percent in 1945, and excise taxes represented 34 percent of revenue by 1945.

A Conservative Interlude, 1946–51

The war was followed by a transitional period—1946–51—reflecting, to a large extent, the conservative background of the new president, Eurico Gaspar Dutra, an army general who had served as minister of the army under Vargas. As the first democratically elected president since 1930, he pursued a middle-of-the-road position in both politics and economics.

Foreign exchange reserves had risen from $71 million in 1939 to $708 million by 1945. The government therefore felt able to introduce a liberal trade policy when the war ended. The currency was overvalued, however, and within a year the reserves were depleted. A current account surplus of $565 million in 1946 turned to a deficit of $150 million in 1947 and new exchange controls were introduced. Balance of payments management became the central focus of economic policy.

Populism and the Commitment to Rapid Development, 1951–64

In 1951 Vargas, the former dictator, returned to power as a democratically elected president. His administration, ended abruptly in 1954 by his suicide, was characterized by its strongly nationalistic posture. In this period the government created or conceived Petróleo Brasileiro S.A. (PETROBRAS, Brazilian Oil Company), the government oil monopoly (a clearly negative response to the advocates of foreign participation in the petroleum sector); the Banco Nacional de Desenvolvimento Econômico (BNDE, National Bank for Economic Development); Banco do Nordeste, the regional development bank for the Northeast; and Centrais Elétricas Brasileiras (ELETROBRAS, Brazilian Electric Power Company), the holding company for government enterprises generating and distributing electricity.

From 1947 to 1953 the government maintained a constant exchange rate against the U.S. dollar. From the beginning the rate was overvalued, and it became more so as internal prices rose. Quantitative restrictions were put on imports, with foreign exchange being readily available for essential imports like fertilizer, fuel, and machinery but with superfluous items put on a long waiting list.

It was a policy that depended on heavy bureaucratic controls with their inevitable and inherent inefficiencies and irregularities. Clearly, devaluation or a downward float would have reduced the need for controls, but coffee interests argued that devaluation would reduce earnings from coffee, which provided 60 percent of export earnings.

The BNDE was created in 1952 on the recommendation of the Joint

Brazil–United States Mission. Its creation was a condition for receiving Export-Import Bank and World Bank credits of $500 million—the foreign exchange component of an investment program (mainly in government projects) to prevent infrastructural bottlenecks from slowing economic growth.

In 1953 a short-term foreign debt crisis forced the government to introduce some changes in the mechanisms regulating foreign trade. Quantitative control of imports was replaced by an exchange auction system, which distinguished five categories of imports, depending on how essential they were. As to exports, the Banco do Brasil was granted a monopoly for acquiring foreign exchange. The exchange rate remained chronically overvalued, thus discouraging exports.

The auction system gave the government additional revenue from imports and thus generated resources to develop infrastructure and invest in basic industries. Its discriminatory structure acted like a tariff against imports deemed nonessential and thus stimulated the domestic production of these goods. From an administrative point of view the new system had the advantage of being flexible. This flexibility permitted alteration in the categories and in the operation of the system that made it progressively more complex until it was finally abolished in 1957.

In 1955 the Superintendency of Money and Credit (SUMOC) issued Instruction 113, which was designed to meet the need for imports of capital goods by the industrial sector and at the same time to alleviate the pressure on the balance of payments.[2] It permitted foreign companies to import secondhand machinery without spending foreign exchange, in projects approved by the federal government, and to enter the value in their books as a direct investment of their parent companies overseas. In fact, Instruction 113 was a strong incentive, for it enabled foreign investors to circumvent the problem posed by the differential between import and export exchange rates and to extend the useful life of capital goods already technologically outmoded in leading industrial centers. Clearly, by 1955 government priority was given to industrial development.

The administration of Juscelino Kubitschek, inaugurated in 1956, loudly proclaimed a pro-development ideology with emphasis on industrialization through import substitution. A histrionic man of humble origin, Kubitschek had climbed all the steps of the political ladder—from member of the city council of Belo Horizonte, capital of Minas Gerais, which was the second most important state of the federation, to state governor. He had the ability to distribute favors to satisfy political pressure at the same time that he surrounded himself with technocrats, who elaborated his Plano de Metas (Plan of Targets) for the period 1956–60.

This plan (prepared in the BNDE) assessed the investment requirements for attaining production goals in such strategic sectors as energy, transport, heavy chemicals, pulp and paper, steel, the automotive industry, shipbuilding, and consumer durables. To the targets for these industries was added construction of the new capital—Brasilia—in the Center-West region. This gigantic investment, for which there were no clearly budgeted funds, jeopardized the financial viability of the entire plan. It was one of the main causes of the high rates of inflation by the end of President Kubitschek's administration, whose popular motto was "50 anos em 5" (to accomplish in five years what required fifty).

Three instruments were of great importance in putting the plan into operation: creation of special groups (*grupos executivos*) in charge of sectoral plans, a protectionist tariff policy for import substitution, and public investment.

The special groups, which operated within the BNDE, were composed of *tecnicos*, professionals drawn from various branches of the bureaucracy. These *grupos executivos* designed policies for investment and production of specific sectors, facilitating the import of equipment, guaranteeing protection from foreign competitors, setting guidelines for size and structure of domestic production and the progressive nationalization of inputs. These groups allowed quick decisionmaking and execution, avoiding the traditional bureaucracy, which was recognized as heavy, inefficient, and often corrupt.

A clearly protectionist policy toward imports was followed, using existing mechanisms and creating new ones. The so-called Law of Similars, which had existed since the beginning of the century, became a fundamental tool in the import-substitution process in the 1950s. It allowed domestic manufacturers to obtain protection for their products by proving their capacity to produce import substitutes. This law stimulated foreign investment because foreign manufacturers would rather establish their plants in the country than be totally excluded from the market.

All of the exchange regimes applied after 1953 offered protection against imports. Nevertheless, in 1957 the auction system of foreign exchange control, which emphasized equilibrium of the balance of payments, was replaced by the Law of Tariffs. The new law was explicitly aimed at protecting industry and fostering the import-substitution process. It established value-added tariffs ranging from zero to 150 percent, and all imports were classified as either essential or nonessential. For the nonessential category, the exchange rate was two to three times higher than the rate set for essential imports. Some equipment and raw materials imports benefited from especially advantageous exchange rates. The new exchange system of 1957 was a deliberate instrument of industrial policy.

The government derived revenue from the differential between import and export rates and the program for controlling coffee supply. It also received compulsory loans in the form of the advance deposits of cruzeiros by importers.

Most new investment was concentrated in the Center-South, especially in São Paulo. The North and Northeast were penalized by the protectionist character of industrial policy. As producers of primary goods and users of manufactured goods, they had worsened terms of trade with the Center-South.

The Superintendência para o Desenvolvimento do Nordeste (SUDENE, Superintendency for the Northeastern Region Development) was created as a federal agency to coordinate federal and local development efforts in the Northeast. It administered the resources derived from fiscal incentives offered by law to industrial enterprises in the Center-South. These enterprises could invest 50 percent of their income tax liabilities in the Northeast. The impact of SUDENE was not significant in relation to the nature of the problem it was supposed to tackle.

The import substitution drive of the late 1950s emphasized steel, shipbuilding, automobiles, and chemicals, neglecting traditional industries like textiles, clothing, and food production, whose productive capacity had become obsolete. Agriculture also received little attention. Altogether, this led to serious imbalances and bottlenecks in the early 1960s.

Deep changes in the economy had occurred during the years 1951–64. Industrial production grew 3.5 times and import substitution was especially dramatic in cement, iron and steel, motor vehicles, chemicals, and electrical equipment. Traditional industries like textiles and food production, which had accounted for 40 percent of manufacturing output in 1949, had fallen to 26 percent in 1963. Agriculture's share of GDP declined from 28 percent in 1947 to 22 percent in 1964, while industry's share rose from 21 percent to 26 percent.

By 1964 inflation was accelerating to rates that made it very disruptive of market mechanisms; the GDP deflator rose 35 percent in 1961, 50 percent in 1962, 78 percent in 1963, and 90 percent in 1964. The foreign sector was in crisis. With the decline of the import coefficient (ratio of imports to total supply) to 6.8 percent in 1962 (from 11.1 percent in 1955), there was no longer much room for import substitution. There had been no stimulus to growth and diversification of exports, and coffee still accounted for more than half of the value of exports in 1960–62. Rapid growth had accentuated sectoral, regional, and social disparities, which led to political turmoil and rising instability at the beginning of the 1960s. The administration of President Janio Quadros, inaugurated in 1961, tried to enforce some corrective measures that would have worked to reduce some of these disequilibria. The more important measures were replacement of the multiple exchange system by a simpler one that implied a relative liberalization of imports and stimulated exports through substantial devaluation; an austere budgetary policy aimed at reducing the government deficit; and credit and wage controls.

Quadros's combination of relatively orthodox economics and left-wing foreign policy was not popular, and he resigned unexpectedly after less than a year in office. He was succeeded by Vice-President Goulart, whose leftist and populist proclivities led to pressure by the military to name a prime minister (Tancredo Neves) as a way of constraining his power. Goulart tried to win popular support by large increases in the minimum wage, constraints on remittance of profits abroad, extension of public ownership of petroleum, land reform, and, as a final provocation to the military, promotion of unionism in the armed forces.

The Military Regime, 1964–85

The political importance of the military coup d'état unequivocally makes 1964 a watershed. It was followed by a period of adjustment and sweeping institutional reform in 1964–67; a period of rapid growth from 1967 to 1979 when the first oil shock's impact was successfully cushioned by foreign borrowing; and a period from 1979 to 1985 when the regime, with its legitimacy and political power fading, had to live with the second oil shock and the debt crisis.

ADJUSTMENT AND INSTITUTIONAL CHANGE, 1964–67. The first president of the military regime, Humberto Castelo Branco, put at the helm of the country's economic management two well-known economists, Octávio Gouveia de Bulhões and Roberto Campos. They became finance minister and planning minister, respectively (table 2-2). Campos built a strong core of technocrats who helped shape the numerous institutional changes originating from the *fuor legiferandi* that prevailed in the years 1964–67.

The stabilization policies involved classic measures—budgetary and credit austerity and wage squeeze—but care was taken not to push deflation too far. Rather than killing off inflationary expectations, the goal was to bring inflation down to a Brazilian "norm."

Several measures were designed to reduce the budgetary deficit and its inflationary impact. Government expenditures were curtailed, especially current ones. Government investment in strategic sectors like hydroelectric generation of power was maintained. Government interference in the price system was severely curbed, with subsidies on imports and public utilities rates reduced or eliminated. The immediate impact was inflationary, but the government's action helped to restore a price system that reflected relative scarcities and reduced the federal deficit. On the revenue side, mechanisms for collecting taxes were improved, which increased the ratio of taxes to GDP. These measures were

Table 2-2. Finance Ministers, Planning Ministers, and Governors of the Central Bank, 1964–90

President and term	Finance minister	Planning minister	Governor of Central Bank
Humberto Castelo Branco (April 1964–March 1967)	Octávio Gouveia de Bulhões	Roberto de Oliveira Campos	Denio C. Noqueira
Arthur da Costa e Silva (March 1967–August 1969)	Antonio Delfim Netto	Hèlio Beltrão	Ruy A. Leme; Ernani Galveias
Military junta, (September–October 1969)	Antonio Delfim Netto	Hèlio Beltrão	Ernani Galveias
Emilio G. Medici (October 1960–March 1974)	Antonio Delfim Netto	João Paulo dos Reis Velloso	Ernani Galveias
Ernesto Geisel (March 1974–March 1979)	Mario H. Simonsen	João Paulo dos Reis Velloso	Paulo H. Pereira Lyra
João B. Figueiredo (March 1979–March 1985)	Carlos Richbieter; Ernani Galveias	Mario H. Simonsen; Antonio Delfim Netto	Carlos Brandão; Ernani Galveias; Carlos G. Langoni; Affonso C. Pastore
José Sarney (March 1985–March 1990)	Francisco N. Dornelles; Dilson Funaro; Luis Carlos Bresser Pereira; Mailson Ferreira da Nobrèga	João Sayad; Anibal Teixeira; João Batista Abreu	Antonio C. B. Lengruber; Fernão Bracher; Francisco Gros; Fernando Milliet; Elmo Camoës

Source: Annibal Villela.

highly successful in reducing the federal deficit, which declined from 4.3 percent of GDP in 1962 and 1963 to 0.6 percent in 1969.

The government also undertook major institutional reforms, which were intended to create a more flexible, market-oriented economy. The tax system was reformed, with fiscal responsibility redistributed among the three levels of government—federal, state, and municipal—and the sales tax, the main source of revenue of the states, was replaced by a value added tax. The foreign exchange system was simplified by the elimination of subsidies and multiple exchange rates. The exchange rate became more realistic and was kept so by the introduction of a crawling peg in 1968. The system of rigid job security was replaced by the Fundó de Garantia por Tempo de Serviço (FGTS), intended to provide both a cushion of liquidity to people who lost their jobs and a new source of savings, which was to be managed by the newly created Banco Nacional de Habitação (National Housing Bank). Public utility rates were readjusted to a more realistic base.

The government also took a number of measures to improve the operation of the financial system and the mechanisms for collecting and allocating savings. These measures were probably the most far-reaching attempt any government has made anywhere to "cohabit" with inflation. "Monetary correction" worked remarkably well in the next decade, when inflation remained within the Brazilian norm of 20 to 30 percent a year. In a key measure to modernize the financial markets, the federal government began to issue indexed treasury bonds, *Obrigacoes readjustaveis do Tesouro Nacional* (ORTN), whose value was readjusted in accordance with the rate of inflation. They represented a new means of financing the deficit with a reduced inflationary impact.

Diffusion of the use of monetary correction to readjust debts and revenues was a powerful instrument to stimulate saving and reorganize markets that depended on long-term financing. The creation of the National Housing Bank in 1964, to provide long-term housing finance, was only possible after the introduction of the monetary correction mechanism.

In 1967 a new tariff law substantially reduced protection to domestic manufacturing industry. Average protection declined from 58 percent to 30 percent. This reform exposed domestic manufacturing to foreign competition, stimulated efficiency, and helped restore the role of market prices.

Finally, a whole set of incentives to exports began to be established, reinforcing the positive effects of the new exchange rate policy. Provisions for the use of drawbacks and exemptions from income and value added taxes were incorporated in the last quarter of 1967.

Between 1964 and 1967, export earnings grew substantially—at an average annual rate of 12.5 percent—with the share of manufactures increasing from 9.3 percent of total exports in 1964 to 14.7 percent in 1968. This growth of exports resulted essentially from sluggish domestic demand and led to a higher level of utilization of productive capacity. The stagnation of economic activity caused a decline of imports, which fell continuously from 1962 to 1965, representing in the last year only 3.9 percent of total supply (11.1 percent in 1962). The combined trends of increasing exports and decreasing imports generated trade surpluses by the mid-1960s; the surpluses were not sufficient, however, to compensate the negative balance on services and the low level of private loans and direct investment.

Very substantial value added tax credits were given to manufactured exports from 1969 onward, reinforcing the stimulus represented by previously existing mechanisms. Thus, by the end of the 1960s a whole set of incentives to exports, particularly manufactured exports, had been established, which led to a continuing expansion of foreign sales.

THE "MIRACLE" YEARS, 1967–79. By 1968, there were clear indications that the economy was moving to a new phase of fast and reasonably healthy growth. The austerity policy had been successful in correcting some bottlenecks, and government investment in energy, transportation, and heavy industry—especially steel and petrochemicals—had begun to pay off. Inflation had been reduced to a stable pace, 20–30 percent annually, which was maintained until 1974. Moreover, the introduction of indexation made it easier to manage an economy chronically affected by inflation. The price signaling system was restored, which led to higher economic efficiency. Finally, the stability of the regime attracted a renewed flow of both domestic and foreign investment.

Castelo Branco's successor, General Arthur da Costa e Silva, died after less than two years in office (1967–69) and was succeeded by General Emilio Garrastazu Medici (1969–74). The finance minister, and economic overlord, in both of these administrations was Antonio Delfim Netto (formerly professor of economics at the University of São Paulo). He proved to be a politician as well as a technocrat, and being a paulista (born in São Paulo, the richest state of the federation), though of humble origin, he not only got the support of São Paulo's powerful business community but also courted it, and thus managed to steer the country's economy safely through the years of the so-called *milagre brasileiro* (Brazilian miracle).

The spurt of growth stimulated foreign trade. Imports went up to 14 percent of GDP in 1974. Exports also increased, but at a slower pace. Deficits in the balance of trade and the chronic deficit in services were met by foreign loans. Consequently, net foreign debt (foreign debt minus foreign exchange reserves) increased from $3.75 billion in 1969 to $11.70 billion in 1974.

The government had an active part in this process of intense growth. The creation in the middle and late 1960s of retirement and insurance funds like the FGTS, Programa de Integração Social (PIS), and Programa de Formacão do Patrimonio do Servidor Público (PASEP) and the indexation system had a positive role in stimulating savings, which rose to 25 percent of GDP in 1973.

Monetary policy was also used to stimulate the economy. In 1967, the government had relaxed credit controls and the money supply expanded at an annual rate of 43 percent, well above the 28 percent rise of the general price index.

Finally, government affected the growth pattern strongly by its investments. In 1969, general government and state enterprises accounted for 60 percent of total investment. Substantial capital formation was concentrated in steel making and petrochemicals, sectors in which government enterprises were leaders. By 1974, government enterprises were conspicuous among the fifty largest Brazilian firms.

The oil price hike late in 1973 created serious problems since oil imports represented about 81 percent of total energy supply. The value of imports went up from $4.2 billion in 1972 to $12.6 billion in 1974. Since exports did not expand at the same rate and there was still a chronic deficit in the balance of services, net foreign debt quickly rose to $22.5 billion in 1976.

Geisel's administration started in March 1974. He retained João Paulo dos Reis Velloso (a professor of economics at the Fundação Getúlio Vargas, the Vargas Foundation) as planning minister from the Medici administration and transformed the ministry into the Secretariat for Planning of the Presidency of the Republic. Mario Simonsen (also a professor at the Vargas Foundation) replaced Delfim Netto as finance minister.

Geisel's strong personality and keen interest in economic matters led him to an almost day-to-day involvement in economic policymaking. He created and was the chairman of the Conselho de Desenvolvimento Econômico, which included the planning minister (its executive secretary), the finance minister, and the sectoral ministers. This council made the most important economic decisions.

Reportedly Velloso, taking advantage of the physical location of his office at the president's palace, was able to influence President Geisel's decisions by successfully countering Simonsen's pressure for stabilization measures. This concern of the president to avoid or postpone a recession was directly linked to his political strategy of gradual return to a democratic order.

The government's decision to sustain growth through foreign borrowing aggravated the balance of payments deficit. The Second National Development Plan, for 1975–79, envisaged high rates of growth and a continuous flow of investment in heavy industries, mining, and infrastructure. In fact, economic growth was considered a political requirement to lessen political repression and slacken wage controls, which could lead to an improved distribution of income.

Economic policy was successful in maintaining high rates of growth until 1980, though at a lower level than during the years of the economic miracle. The average annual growth rate fell to 7 percent between 1974 and 1980 (from 11 percent in 1968–73), which was still a considerable achievement. This growth was based on an ambitious investment program aimed at promoting a new round of import substitution intended to reduce further the scale of imports, by lessening dependence on capital imports and intermediate products. The investment program was intended also to promote an increase of exports, by expanding foreign sales of manufactured goods.

The government responded to the first oil shock by establishing substantially higher import tariffs, creating a system of compulsory deposits for imports, and completely banning imports of consumer goods. As a result, the value of imports stabilized from 1974 to 1977 at about $12 billion annually, despite continuous and relatively strong economic growth. Except for oil, imports actually fell in dollar value in this period.

Special emphasis was given to replacement of imported oil, both to reduce the pressure on the balance of payments and to lessen the risk of economic chaos that a sudden interruption of supply would create. In 1975, Programa Nacional de Alcool (National Alcohol Program, or PROALCOOL) was created to stimulate production of alcohol from sugarcane to replace gasoline as fuel for automobiles. The government also embarked on an ambitious nuclear program, directly financed by public funds.

Both programs from the beginning had many opponents. Investment in PROALCOOL required huge expenditure and a myriad of subsidies by the government, with negative effects on both public finance and the use or resources. The nuclear program was contested on technological, economic, and political grounds, and NUCLEBRAS (Empresas Nucleares Brasileiras), and other government enterprises created for the execution of the program were continuously subjected to criticism.

However, public investment in some industries was of key importance in promoting a second round of import substitution. The growth and diversification of the chemical industry was achieved by the creation of joint ventures between PETROBRAS—the state-owned oil enterprise—and private firms. The PETROBRAS system, which includes a large number of enterprises downstream from the oil industry, has been successful in adopting highly sophisticated technology and in developing import substitutes. The government investment program in steel making expanded capacity from 7.5 million tons in 1974 to 15.3 million tons in 1980 and led to an increase of exports. One clearly new approach in economic policy was the group of projects specially conceived to supply the foreign market. The Tubarão steel plant, for example, was an export-oriented initiative, undertaken to explore advantages in the quality of iron ore and in location to produce steel plate for the foreign market.

Policy Development after the Second Oil Shock, 1979–85

In March 1979 Figueiredo succeeded Geisel as president. Simonsen, who in the previous administration had been minister of finance, became minister of planning, but after a few months in office, he resigned, unhappy over his inability to control the level of spending. His replacement, Delfim Netto, acted throughout 1979–83 as a superminister, concentrating the reins of economic power. This time he had a much rougher ride than in his previous experience as economic overlord in 1967–74.

The already overheated economy was subjected to a major external shock from oil in 1979. At a time of poor harvests, an acceleration of inflation brought on by domestic factors, and growing labor unrest, Delphim Netto proclaimed a policy of fighting inflation by raising production. The government responded to labor pressure by changing the system of wage indexation to allow for current rather than forecast inflation; it gave higher adjustments for lower-paid workers and switched to six-monthly rather than annual wage adjustments. The economy did not have the supply potential to repeat the old miracle. The result was a new wave of inflation and balance of payments crisis. (See E. L. Bacha in Williamson 1983 and Diaz-Alejandro 1983 for an analysis of this period.)

The new challenges were met by a proliferation of devious ad hoc measures that damaged the arrangements for living with inflation that had been set up after the coup d'état in 1964. Government began to accept or promote relaxation of the established rules, alleviating the burden of indexation on certain groups, increasing the rate of subsidy for selected goods and services, accelerating the rate of minidevaluations, and so forth. The outcome was the creation of a new set of disequilibria in foreign trade and a growing federal deficit.

On the foreign front, the cost of oil imports went up from $4.2 billion in 1978 to $9.9 billion in 1980. The crunch on the balance of payments was especially severe at such high levels of activity, and payments for interest and amortization were on the rise both because of the foreign debt and because of the increase in interest rates, which practically doubled between 1978 and 1980.

Very shortly the government was obliged to engage in a stabilization exercise (but was unwilling to allow any role for the IMF). The intention was to curb inflationary expectations and to reverse the rising trend of prices. Monetary correction was arbitrarily set at 45 percent for the year. The government carried out a special 30 percent devaluation of the cruzeiro relative to the dollar, intending to correct the disequilibrium in the exchange rate that had accumulated since the creation of the crawling peg system in 1968.

From the beginning there was public skepticism about the announced measures. In fact, the government measures did not have the psychological effect hoped for, mainly because they lacked credibility. The goal of a 50 percent limit on credit expansion was not taken seriously, since by midyear many banks had attained that limit. Actually, credit increased 71 percent for the entire year of 1980. Moreover, there were no concrete signals that the government would act to reduce its huge deficit (8.1 percent of GDP in 1979). Finally, the general level of demand was too high to permit deceleration of inflation.

Faced with an arbitrarily fixed rate of monetary correction, investors moved away from financial assets, increased consumption, and bought real assets to a growing degree. There was increased demand for durable consumer goods, capital goods for investment, and all types of intermediate goods for speculative formation of inventories. At the same time, there was a boom in real estate and land.

Preference for real assets and lax credit controls, compounded by the rise of oil prices, led to inflation rates that reached 92 percent in 1980 and 103 percent in 1981.

The failure of the 1980 economic measures led the government to return to a policy of monetary correction in 1981 in line with the real trend of price rises. At the same time, monetary policy became the main tool to reduce aggregate demand. The result was a rise of real interest rates and a decline of investment and consumption. It was in the midst of this tardy adjustment exercise that the next major external blow hit Brazil. In August 1982 Mexico's debt deliquency brought the flow of foreign capital to a sudden halt and ruined any prospects for the adjustment exercise.

Between 1981 and 1983 the economy went through the most severe crisis of its postwar history. Gross domestic product actually declined in 1981 and 1983. The reduction of demand affecting sectors like machinery and transport equipment reverberated through the entire industrial sector. And the 20 percent fall in industrial employment from 1980 to 1984 had a further recessive impact on demand.

As a consequence of lower economic activity, imports fell continuously from their high 1980 level of $22.9 billion to $13.9 billion in 1984. Fiscal incentives on goods manufactured for export—which accounted for 15 percent of their f.o.b. value—stimulated their growth and partially compensated for the reduction of the value of primary exports, which were hit by falling prices. Because of the reduction of imports and the expansion of exports, there were small trade surpluses in 1981 and 1982. From 1983 on, these surpluses became substantial, alleviating the burden of servicing the enormous foreign debt, which had grown continuously for fifteen years and had reached $100 billion in 1985.

High rates of interest fueled financial speculation. Instead of investing in their principal activities, many enterprises held financial assets. These assets guaranteed a positive return because of interest plus monetary correction, which was generally higher than the return obtainable on productive activities that involved considerable economic risk. It was thus common to observe balance sheet gains on financial assets that were larger than the income derived from the main activity of the enterprise.

Higher interest rates also meant higher costs for servicing the domestic public debt. Public debt had been increasing with the mounting pressure to spend (current expenditure, government investment, subsidies, and the like) coupled with difficulties—political and other—in raising revenue. Moreover, the surplus in the balance of trade created new needs for financing the cruzeiros corresponding to the excess of exports over imports. In February 1983, there was another maxi devaluation of 30 percent, which helped promote exports but increased the public debt burden because many government bonds were insured against fluctuation of the exchange rate. These government bonds indexed to the foreign exchange rate (ORTN *com clausula cambial*) had been created when the minister of planning tried to outsmart the financial market. By mid-1982, strong expectations of a new large devaluation of the cruzeiro brought sales of government bonds with monetary correction to a standstill. Delfim Netto created bonds indexed to the exchange rate as a substitute but subsequently taxed the gains that bondholders derived from the devaluation, an action the market deeply resented.

Another critical area that was disastrously administered was the public deficit. In fact, effective control was impossible because of certain mechanisms that allowed for increases in public expenditure without the provision of funds to pay for them. This was possible because only the fiscal budget was under effective control. Expenditures in the budgets of government enterprises and in the so-called monetary budget were nonplanned burdens that could lead to the issue of money or an increase in public debt. As a result, both the public deficit and monetary policy frequently departed from established goals or commitments to international agencies. For instance, the 60 percent limit on credit expansion for the year 1983 was abandoned by midyear, when new measures that increased compulsory deposits in the Central Bank were enforced.

The failure to reduce inflation to desired and preannounced levels led to some tampering with the inflation indexes used for monetary correction. In 1983 inflation indexes were declared reduced from 211 percent to 175 percent through the use of gimmicks—the argument was that the index should not be affected by accidents (atypical events like floods and droughts that affected the prices of certain products) or by "corrective inflation." The effects were a redistribution of income that benefited government and other debtors and a severe blow to the credibility of savings banks and to government itself.

Instability and lack of government credibility reinforced the effect of high rates of inflation and interest on economic activity. As a result of recession, unemployment rose until mid-1984 in all metropolitan areas. Nevertheless, the expansion of informal activities represented a decompression valve for social unrest.

Between 1979 and 1984, the rules for wage readjustments were often changed. In 1983 alone, six different readjustment procedures were successively adopted. At the end of 1984, 100 percent indexation for inflation was established, and this had a positive effect in boosting demand.

The economy started to recover in 1984. After three years of recession the private sector had reorganized itself by reducing its debt and increasing its productive efficiency. Export-led growth was fostered by the increased competitiveness of Brazilian goods abroad, and a stable policy of exchange rate devaluation (exchange rate devaluation was 220 percent and inflation 194 percent) began to permeate the economy in 1984. Industry grew by 6.7 percent, industrial employment went up to 6.4 percent, and industrial wages grew by 9.3 percent.

The trends initiated in 1984 were reinforced in 1985. The efforts to increase the fiscal base and reduce the deficit, which began in 1984, when there was a substantial increase of income tax receipts, were continued in 1985. A minor fiscal reform, the consolidation of the federal budget (fiscal budget, monetary budget, and government enterprises budget), and the consequent amelioration of monetary control, together worked in a positive direction.

The Return to Civilian Government in 1985

On political grounds the new civilian administration that took over in March 1985, after more than twenty years of military rule, gained a vote of confidence from the public and from the international community. This approval coupled with the comfortable trade balance (the trade surplus was $13 million in 1984 and $12.4 billion in 1985) constituted a solid basis for the negotiations with foreign creditors by the end of 1985.

In the first year of civilian rule there were no major changes in economic policy. GDP grew 8.3 percent, and the policy of keeping the exchange rate competitive ensured continuance of a large trade surplus, sufficient to cover interest payments on the foreign debt and healthy enough for Brazil to resist pressure of foreign bankers for more deflationary policies (table 2-3). In August 1985, Francisco N. Dornelles, the cautious minister of finance, was replaced by Dilson Funaro. The booming economy did, however, lead to a rising pressure on resources, which led to accelerating inflation.

On February 28, 1986, the government tried to handle the situation with its cruzado plan, a heterodox policy intended to break inflationary expectations by abolishing indexation and establishing an overall freeze on prices, wages, and the foreign exchange rate. A new currency unit, the cruzado (equal to 1,000 cruzeiros) was also created.

These measures had considerable psychological effect for several months, but the government did not reduce its own claim on resources, and private demand expanded rapidly because of wage increases that

Table 2-3. Economic Indicators, Selected Years, 1929–85

Indicator	1929	1950	1964	1973	1979	1985
Production						
Raw steel (thousands of tons)	27	789	2,939	7,150	13,866	20,356
Electric power (millions of kilowatt hours)	—	7,500	29,094	63,319	124,345	176,763[a]
Cement (thousands of tons)	96	1,386	5,206	13,398	24,871	20,612
Motor vehicles (thousands)	n.a.	n.a.	184	750	1,128	968
Paper (thousands of tons)	—	248	650	1,567	2,979	3,742[a]
Alcohol (millions of liters)	33	135	376	653	3,450	11,783
Petroleum (thousands of tons)	n.a.	46	5,296	9,876	9,609	31,724
Foreign trade						
Coffee (percentage of exports)	71	64	53	20	13	9
Manufactures (percentage of exports)	0.4	1.2	14	31	56	66
Soybeans (percentage of exports)	n.a.	n.a.	n.a.	15	11	10
Imports of capital goods (percentage of value of imports)	17	42	28	33	20	19
Oil (percentage of imports)	2	5	18	14	35	43
Oil imports (thousands of tons)	794	4,195	10,803	35,521	49,969	28,040
Foreign debt (billions of dollars)	0.3	0.6	3.1	12.6	49.9	100.5
Debt service (percentage of exports)	18.2	6.3	19.0	24.0	42.0	24.0

n.a. Not appicable.
— Not available.
a. For 1984.

Source: FIBGE, *Anuário estatístico* (1951); CNF; IBC; IAA; Brasil, Ministério da Fazenda, Banco do Brasil (1950, 1951); BACEN; FUNCEX (1986); Baer (1985); Villela and Suzigan (1975).

had preceded the stabilization plan and, increasingly, because of anticipatory buying as expectations began to revert to normal. In 1986, GDP rose by more than 7 percent. The pressure of domestic demand plus the fixity of the exchange rate led to rapid erosion of the trade balance, so that the government had to run down exchange reserves to meet debt payments.

The government delayed corrective action until after the November elections in which the government party won a massive victory. A week later the government had to raise taxes to check some forms of demand; it permitted some price increases, but these "cruzado II" moves were ineffective, price controls had created the kind of erratic shortages common in Eastern Europe, and public faith in economic miracles was broken.

In February 1987, the government suspended payment of interest on its debt to foreign commercial banks, which held two-thirds of its total debt. This move did nothing to relieve the chaos in domestic resource allocation and pressure of demand. Nor did it produce the desired effect on the creditor banks who, in effect, started to write down the value of their claims on Brazil and ended the previous process of debt renegotiation and relending.

In May 1987 Funaro was replaced by Luiz Carlos Bresser Pereira, who was in turn replaced in December by Mailson Ferreira da Nobrèga, who adopted a more orthodox policy with some deflation of demand and the resumption of debt service. However, the problems of Brazil's economy were tremendously enlarged by the Funaro policies. The ingenious mechanisms for living with inflation, which mitigated its adverse effects on allocation of resources, were destroyed, as was Brazil's international creditworthiness; inflation was higher than it had ever been, and resource allocation was very messy.

Notes

1. This institution, founded in 1934 to handle problems in the area of foreign trade, became a center of economic studies, which not only proposed incentives for industries but also the creation of state enterprises such as Companhia Siderurgica Nacional, the first integrated steel plant in South America; Companhia Vale do Rio Doce, for exporting iron ore; and Companhia Nacional de Alcalis, for production of caustic soda.

2. A government agency, SUMOC exercised many of the functions of a central bank before such a bank existed. It was actually a department of the Banco do Brasil.

3 Brazilian Growth Performance since 1950

In the five decades before 1980, Brazil's economic growth was probably the fastest in the world. In real terms GDP grew by 5.9 percent a year, and per capita GDP by 3.3 percent (more than fivefold). This is significantly better than in Mexico, where the figures were 5.4 percent and 2.5 percent, respectively.

Overall Economic Performance

Until 1980, the growth story was one of gradual acceleration. The recession of the 1930s was moderate and brief, there was very respectable growth during the war and early postwar period, and very fast growth from 1950 to 1980. Since then the record has been poor. Between 1980 and 1988, GDP rose by 2 percent a year, and per capita GDP fell by 0.4 percent a year. The oil crisis of 1979 and the debt shock of 1982 threw the overheated economy out of kilter. In spite of experimentation over several years with a variety of orthodox and heterodox adjustment policies, there was no fundamental progress in reestablishing prospects for steady growth, and inflationary problems grew to unprecedented dimensions.

The Overall Growth Accounts

For more than five decades, Brazil was involved in a successful catch-up process, exploiting the "advantages of backwardness," pushing its growth potential very hard, and reducing the gap between itself and the advanced countries.

Its growth strategy resulted in a substantial increase in investment, from 12 percent of GDP in 1950 to 23 percent in 1980 (table 3-1). This reflected a significant increase in domestic saving as well as large inflows of foreign capital. Average levels of education in Brazil are low even by Latin American standards, but they did rise noticeably (table 3-2). And Brazil has been helped on the human capital side by its rich

Table 3-1. Main Expenditure Categories of GDP, Selected Years, 1950–87
(percent)

	Consumption		Gross capital	Foreign trade		
Year	Private	Public	formation	Exports	Imports	Balance
1950	74.7	11.4	12.3	9.2	7.6	1.6
1960	72.5	11.5	17.0	5.3	6.4	−1.1
1964	71.1	11.1	16.9	6.5	5.6	0.9
1970	68.6	11.3	20.5	7.0	7.4	−0.4
1980	69.8	9.2	23.3	9.0	11.3	−2.3
1987	62.3	12.3	22.2	9.2	6.0	3.2

Source: To 1964, de Gusmão Veloso (1987), table 1; thereafter, FIBGE.

mix of immigrants with skills, energy, education, and entrepreneurial ability—Lebanese bankers, Japanese horticulturists, Italian shoemakers, German engineers.

The large reserves of land were successfully exploited as part of the growth process (table 3-2). The cropped area increased by 30 million hectares from 1950 to 1980—Brazil is still a frontier country, as the United States was in the nineteenth century. For nearly five centuries, Brazil has had a large-scale export-oriented agricultural sector and its resource advantage has nearly always had a powerful influence on its growth strategy.

There have been few government inhibitions in borrowing foreign

Table 3-2. Basic Indicators of Growth Performance, Selected Years, 1940–80

Year	Index of net fixed reproducible stock (1950 = 100)	Cropped area (thosands of hectares)	Employment (thousands)	Average education level of labor force (years)
1940	70.7	18,835	14,002	1.17
1950	100.0	19,095	17,117	1.83
1960	157.0	28,712	22,750	2.09
1970	305.8	33,984	29,557	2.86
1980	738.6	49,185	43,236	3.94

Source: For capital stock, Goldsmith (1986), p. 154; cropped area, IBGE; employment, Merrick and Graham (1979), p. 158; education level in 1940–70, Langoni (1974), p. 67; in 1980 IBGE (1983), p. 14.

Table 3-3. Indexes of Basic Indicators of Growth Performance, Selected Years, 1940–80
(1950-100)

Year	Net fixed reproducible capital stock (weight = 25.0[a])	Land (weight = 10.0[a])	Employment (weight = 65.0[a])	Combined factor input (weight = 100.0)	GDP	Total factor productivity
1940	70.7	98.6	81.8	80.8	59.3	73.4
1950	100.0	100.0	100.0	100.0	100.0	100.0
1960	157.0	150.4	132.9	140.7	187.4	133.2
1970	305.8	178.0	172.7	206.6	327.4	158.5
1980	738.6	257.6	252.6	374.7	715.3	190.9

a. For Brazil, information on factor incomes is poor (for rough estimates, see Langoni [1974], table 60). Weights are those used for Mexico (see table 6-3).

Source: First three columns derived from table 3-2; the fourth is a weighted average of the first three. For GDP, de Gusmão Veloso (1987).

technology (though critics have complained about the scale of multinational operations, and the government in the 1980s restricted operations of foreign computer manufacturers). The main technique has been to encourage or cajole foreigners to make direct investment. This was true even in otherwise nationalist phases like the Kubitschek presidency. Most foreign investment has been concentrated on manufacturing where nearly a quarter of output in the formal sector is produced by firms with a majority foreign ownership. Brazilian industries have shown evidence of a capacity to adapt and develop this borrowed technology—for example, in the case of aircraft exports.

Total factor productivity growth was positive in all four decades from

Table 3-4. Sources of Growth by Decade, 1940–80
(annual average compound growth rates, percent)

Decade	Net fixed reproducible capital stock	Land	Employment	Combined factor input	Total factor productivity	Labor productivity	Capital productivity
1940–50	3.5	0.1	2.0	2.2	3.1	3.3	1.8
1950–60	4.6	4.2	2.9	3.5	2.9	3.5	1.8
1960–70	6.9	1.7	2.7	3.9	1.8	3.0	−1.1
1970–80	9.2	3.8	3.9	6.1	1.9	4.1	−1.0

Source: Derived from table 3-3.

1940 to 1980, though it was slower after 1960 than before (table 3-4). Capital productivity growth was substantial in the period 1940–60, which probably reflects high yields during a period of catch-up and easy import substitution, but it was negative in 1960–80, which may be an indication of efficiency problems arising from high capital accumulation in new and sophisticated sectors.

The record of inflation, over the long term, is paralleled only in the Southern Cone countries of Latin America (whose growth record in the past five decades has been pitiful compared with Brazil's). There is no doubt that inflation had efficiency costs through distortion of real interest rates, real exchange rates, and the terms of trade for various sectors of the economy, particularly in periods of suppressed inflation when controls were pervasive. The welfare costs are also obvious, the main one being the uncertainty and instability of real income flows.

However, the institutional mechanism that was constructed to deal with inflation mitigated its adverse allocative impact. There was less distortion in real exchange rates or terms of trade for agriculture after 1960 than in Mexico, and the record of productivity growth was better. The worst recorded period for growth of total factor productivity was the 1960s, when there were major problems of both macroeconomic adjustment and microeconomic distortion. It is likely that total factor productivity was negative in the 1980s (as it was in Mexico), judging from the limited indicators available.

Economic Structure

One striking feature of Brazil's economy is the wide regional variation in per capita income—greater than that of any other country for which figures are available. The Northeast, which is the poorest region, was the most prosperous in the seventeenth century; it gradually declined from its original concentration on sugar exports to a heavy dependence on subsistence agriculture. By the early nineteenth century the Southeast had become more prosperous than the Northeast, and the differential probably grew steadily at least to 1929, when there was almost no per capita economic growth outside the Southeast and South. Since 1950, there has been a slight reduction in regional income differentials, mainly because of migration from the Northeast to more prosperous areas. In the past century, the Northeast's share of total population fell from 47 percent to 29 percent, in spite of the generally higher fertility of its population (table 3-5).

Brazil, like most developing countries, has a relatively low rate of productivity in agriculture, probably only a third of the rate in other sectors of the economy. However, real product per person in agriculture seems to have risen at roughly the same rate as in the economy as a whole since 1950.

Table 3-5. Distribution of Population and Per Capita Income, by Region, Selected Years, 1819–1980
(percent)

Region	Population 1819[a]	1872	1920	1950	1980	Per capita income 1950	1980
North	4.0	3.4	4.7	3.5	4.9	55.6	70.2
Northeast	47.4	46.7	36.7	34.7	29.3	42.9	45.5
Southeast	40.4	40.4	44.6	43.4	43.5	153.4	151.8
South	5.5	7.3	11.5	15.1	16.0	109.6	116.8
Center West	2.8	2.2	2.5	3.3	6.3	54.7	94.9
Brazil	100.0	100.0	100.0	100.0	100.0	100.0	100.0

a. Excludes 800,000 tribal Indians.

Source: For population, in 1819, M. L. Marcilio, in Bethell (1984), vol. 2, p. 63; in 1872 and 1920, census figures from (FIBGE), *Anuário estatístico* (1984), p. 78, 1950 and 1980, figures supplied by FIBGE. For per capita income, figures supplied by FIBGE.

Since 1950, in spite of the emphasis on commodity output in government policy, Brazil has become a predominantly service economy. In 1950, services represented 25.9 percent of employment, and by 1980 their share had grown to 44.5 percent. Industry (manufacturing, mining, utilities, and construction) also grew rapidly from 14.2 percent of total employment in 1950 to 25.5 percent in 1980, but agriculture's share fell from 60 percent to 30 percent in those years (table 3-6).

Within manufacturing, there has been a big shift in the structure of output from traditional branches such as manufactured foodstuffs and textiles toward chemicals and machinery. This intrasectoral change is perhaps more striking than the increased role of the sector in the economy, because it reflects a major change in the technical sophistication of Brazil.

In interpreting structural change within manufacturing, heavy or exclusive emphasis is usually placed on government policy, which certainly plays a major role in bringing about change. However, the hidden hand also has a strong role. In economies where income is rising rapidly, the hierarchy of consumer tastes tends to move in a predictable direction no matter what the policy regime. And the direction of growth is affected by the changing array of technological options determined more or less exogenously by technical advances around the world—for example, in the development of plastics and other chemical products. The pattern and level of investment and exports also affect structure.

One striking structural feature of Brazil's economy is the changing

Table 3-6. Structure of Brazilian Employment and Gross Value Added, 1950, 1980, and 1985
(percent)

Sector	Employment 1950	Employment 1980	Share of GDP before deducting intermediate financial services 1950	1980	1985
Agriculture, forestry, and fishing	59.9	30.0	24.3	10.0	9.8
Manufacturing	9.4	16.4	18.7	29.2	24.8
Mining and utilities	1.4	1.6	1.4	2.3	3.7
Construction	3.4	7.5	4.1	6.6	5.9
Financial services	0.7	2.3	3.6	7.9	11.4
Trade	5.5	9.6	15.6	14.5	12.9
Transport and communication	3.7	4.3	3.4	4.4	4.5
Real estate and housing	0.0	0.0	11.5	6.7	8.3
Public administration and defense	3.0	4.1	6.6	6.3	6.6
Other services	13.0	24.2	10.8	12.1	12.1
Total	100.0	100.0	100.0	100.0	100.0
Intermediate financial services	—	—	−3.2	−7.4	−11.6

— Not available.

Source: For employment, FIBGE, *Censo Demográfico*, with 1950 adjusted to reflect 1980 classifications in IBGE, *Anuario estatístico* (1984), p. 16. For GDP, at current prices, de Gusmão Veloso (1987).

pattern of exports (tables 2-3 and 3-7). In spite of inflation, the exchange rate was generally kept competitive from the mid-1960s, and the export structure was transformed—in 1950 coffee represented 64 percent of total exports, but it represented only 9 percent of total exports in 1985. Manufactured exports rose from 1 percent to 66 percent of the total; moreover, they vary in character, including sophisticated products like military aircraft. Some important agricultural exports like orange juice and soybean products demonstrate that flexibility is a characteristic of agriculture as well as of industry. This responsiveness to new challenges is a source of great strength and reflects a "can do" mentality far removed from the defensive thinking of the once dominant coffee interests.

The enormous growth in financial services resulted in that sector having a bigger value added than agriculture by 1985. From 1950 to 1985 financial services grew from 3.6 percent to 11.4 percent of GDP (table 3-6) compared with a rise from 2.8 percent to 4.5 percent in the

Table 3-7. **Share of Leading Primary Commodities in Total Exports, Selected Periods, 1821–1983**
(percent)

Period	Cotton	Sugar	Coffee	Rubber	Cocoa
1821–23	25.8	23.1	18.7	0.0	—
1871–73	16.6	12.3	50.2	0.0	—
1901–03	2.6	2.4	44.7	22.5	2.5
1927–29	2.0	0.5	71.1	2.0	3.8
1949–51	10.0	0.3	60.5	0.2	4.8
1983	2.3	1.8	10.6	0.0	1.4

— Not available.

Source: For 1821–73 Leff (1982), vol. 2, p. 9; 1901–51, IBGE (1960); 1983, IBGE, *Anuário estatístico* (1984).

United States. This growth undoubtedly was due in large part to the rapidity of inflation and the elaborate institutional arrangements that savers and investors made to protect themselves against real loss. As a result, the degree of financial intermediation is much higher than it would otherwise be. It would seem therefore that the swollen financial system is one measure of the real cost of living with inflation.

The degree of government intervention in the financial system is very large—in regulating and steering resource allocation between different uses, in creating possibilities for new types of institutions and instruments, and in the direct supply and demand for credit. But private market forces have a dynamic effect on the growth and sophistication of the financial system. After all, the private role in this sector is the predominant one. This is certainly true in insurance and real estate. Even in banking and finance in the narrow sense, there is less state control in Brazil than in Mexico (and that was true before the Mexican bank nationalizations of 1982). There is also a significant element of foreign private banking. Furthermore, the historical record of Brazilian banking is more successful than that in the United States and some European countries, because the system has never been in serious threat of collapse in times of crisis.

The Investment Effort

One of the major messages of development economics in the 1950s was the importance of investment in the growth process. There were some second thoughts about this when human capital became the leading fad in the 1960s, and third thoughts by the new political economists of the

1980s who put greatest stress on efficiency of resource allocation. Over time, even those who retain the emphasis of the 1950s have come to lay more stress on the growth of capital stock than on the investment rate, and neoclassic analysts give capital inputs a weight proportionate to the share of capital income in GDP.

Investment is a shaky area statistically for Brazil. Production statistics on construction activity are weak, with economic censuses only for 1949 and 1975; there is an especially large discrepancy between employment reported in these activities in the demographic census of 1980 and in the special construction inquiries for 1980. Direct estimates of savings from disposable income and of expenditure on investment are poor.

The latest official estimates show the share of GDP devoted to fixed investment rising from 15.1 percent in the 1950s to 16.2 percent in the 1960s, and to 21.6 percent in the 1970s, then falling off sharply in the 1980s.

It appears that there was a respectable and fairly steady rise in investment that peaked in the 1970s. In the military period, the investment effort was helped by the compulsory savings of 8 percent levied on payrolls in the formal sector, by the protection of real savings provided by indexation, and by large-scale foreign borrowing, which financed a much larger proportion of investment from 1973 to 1982 than in earlier years and then suddenly dropped off. From 1970 to 1984 gross investment averaged 20.9 percent of GDP, and net foreign borrowing 3.2 percent, so the savings rate was 17.7 percent.

There have been two significant efforts to measure the growth of capital stock, by Langoni (1974) and Goldsmith (1986). Langoni used the 1973 Vargas Foundation estimates of capital formation from 1948 to 1966 to measure increments to his own (unexplained) benchmark estimate of the 1948 net stock. He used the Vargas Foundation's unpublished deflators for investment goods and its estimates of depreciation.

Langoni used the capital stock estimates in a growth accounting exercise for 1948–66, where he broke down labor inputs by age, sex, and level of education; he combined these in an index of total factor productivity, using the net stock of physical capital and land as the other inputs. He massaged the national accounts information to get capital and labor shares. This gave rather high weights for physical capital and educated labor, with small shares for crude labor and land. The role of human and reproducible physical capital looms large in Langoni's "explanation" of growth.

Goldsmith (1986, p. 154) used the same 1948 benchmark as Langoni for his capital stock and cast it back to 1913, using his own rough investment indicators (consumption of steel and cement, imports of capital goods, growth of railway mileage, and so forth); he carried his estimates forward from 1948 using the Vargas Foundation's revised (1977) estimates of the investment rate. Over the long term, for the period 1928–80, Goldsmith's estimate of capital stock grows more or less parallel with GDP; his estimates are used here in our calculation of total factor productivity (table 3-3).

Labor Inputs and Their Quality

In overall terms the demographic census must be used for rough estimates of labor input. These refer to the economically active population, and, for earlier years, one cannot separate out the unemployed. Use of this source for estimates of labor input by sector is a rather shaky procedure given the difficulties in reconciling the economic and demographic censuses. The virtual absence of figures on working hours is a further constraint on productivity analysis.

Between 1950 and 1980 the ratio of labor force to total population rose from 33.4 percent to 36.3 percent. There was a small increase in the proportion in the population of working age, a marked rise in female activity and a fall in the male activity rate due to a slight extent to increased school attendance but mostly to a greater incidence of retirement among older males. As there is no evidence that the rate of unemployment rose from 1950 to 1980, labor input probably increased a bit more rapidly than population growth

By comparison with developed countries, the proportion of the population that works in Brazil is low—the 36 percent ratio compares with 48 percent in the United States. One reason for this is the low activity rate for females. The other is the high proportion of children in the population—38 percent of the population was less than fifteen years old in 1980 compared with 23 percent in the United States.

During the past decade, the birth rate fell substantially. As a consequence, the structure of the population is changing in ways that should tend to raise labor force activity—the ratio of young dependents should fall, and the proportion of working age rise. The fall in the proportion of children should facilitate a continued growth in female activity.

There is no doubt that Brazil lies within the range of countries where the quality of labor input has been adversely affected by poor health and nutrition. Since the 1950s health indicators have clearly improved, and so has the calorie intake. In overall terms, nutrition levels are well below those in Argentina and the United States, but in both of those countries people probably eat and drink too much for their work efficiency. More pertinent is the fact that nutrition levels were still about 10 percent below those in Japan according to statistics for 1975 (table 3-8). Brazil has not therefore crossed the threshold where nutrition ceases to be a problem affecting labor quality, particularly in poor regions like the Northeast or among migrants from that region who work in more prosperous areas. However, nutritional levels are well above those in the poorer parts of Asia and Africa, where deprivation

Table 3-8. Per Capita Food Supply in Six Countries, 1975–77
(calories per day)

Country	Total	Cereals	Fruits and vegetables	Meat	Fish	Milk	Oils and fats	Sugar	Alcohol
Argentina	3,419	971	174	715	8	255	422	425	221
Brazil	2,491	869	133	181	15	130	196	449	44
India	1,779	1,153	59	6	5	55	115	173	10
Japan	2,776	1,286	131	155	175	79	272	247	139
Mexico	2,686	1,319	116	142	9	132	205	444	69
United States	3,441	611	183	711	19	368	544	541	167

Source: FAO (1980).

of this type may cause both physical lethargy and brain damage on an important scale.

There has been a distinct improvement in the educational quality of the labor force—between 1950 and 1980 the average years of education of an employed person increased from 1.8 to 3.9 years. However, the level of education is poor even by Latin American standards. Generally, the government has given low priority to spending on education. The quality of public education below the university level is poor and the drop-out rate among pupils before they are functionally literate is large and wasteful. There are two partial offsets to this weakness in public formal education. One is the excellent system of apprenticeship training; the other is private expenditure on formal education, with its benefits concentrated on children whose families can afford it.

Although the relation between educational quality of the labor force and economic performance is not as clear cut as human capital pundits have sometimes claimed, the backwardness of Brazilian public education is so marked that it is hard to avoid the conclusion that this is the weakest link in Brazil's strategy for eliminating the productivity gap between itself and the advanced capitalist countries.

Have Natural Resources Favored Growth?

The popular impression that some countries are "born rich"—that growth is greatly facilitated by abundant natural resources—is certainly influential in Brazil. This idea accounts in part for the notion that "God is Brazilian."

In resource terms, Brazil is certainly well endowed. With a land area of 8.5 million square kilometers spread over tropical, subtropical, and temperate zones, with plenty of sun and rainfall, it can grow practically any agricultural product. Its mineral resources are impressive and its forestry resources enormous. In comparison with the ancient and well-established Asian countries, Brazil's population density is relatively low.

Brazil is therefore in the same natural resource category as countries like Argentina, Australia, and the United States. Its endowment contrasts starkly with that of Japan, which has been the most successful country in catching up economically with the advanced capitalist countries. It is therefore worth asking whether Brazil's resource advantage has been a trap.

Brazil has had several product cycles in its development that were based on its natural resources. It was a highly export-oriented economy that had a sugar boom, a gold and diamond boom, a coffee boom, and a rubber boom. From very early days until 1889, Brazil exploited these possibilities by using the most primitive kind of human capital—slave labor. The heavy reliance on one primary crop for the bulk of export earnings persisted until the early 1960s. For the first five decades of the twentieth century, economic policy was locked in an expensive, defensive commitment to protecting this rent element in its foreign earnings.

Brazil's very respectable agricultural performance from 1950 onward was certainly helped by its frontier status. The area of cropland grew from 19 million to 49 million hectares from 1950 to 1980. This is a growth rate of 3.2 percent a year compared with 1.9 percent in Mexico and virtual stability in the United States and Argentina. Furthermore, Brazil, unlike Mexico, has had little need to expand irrigation.

Brazil's natural resource advantage was also a major feature in the expansion of mineral production, where iron ore output grew very rapidly.

Official policy since the mid-1960s has not been locked into wasteful concentration on coffee, and a new flexibility has been demonstrated by rapid diversification into new product lines like soybean products and orange juice. Thus it would be difficult to argue that Brazil's natural resources have not been used to foster growth. However, even if natural resources now play a more sensible part in growth strategy, it is not a dominant role. Value added in the whole primary sector in 1985 was only 13 percent of GDP, so growth now depends most heavily on inputs from other sectors and the efficiency with which they are used.

Access to the International Stock of Technical Knowledge

One of the advantages of economic backwardness for countries of low standing in the international productivity league is that they are in a position to buy, borrow, and adapt foreign technology. Their costs are much lower than those of countries operating at the technological frontier where research and development costs are high and attempts to grow rapidly tend to be difficult and costly in terms of investment.

Brazil's government has concentrated heavily on use of foreign direct investment for borrowing technological know-how. This has been done with few nationalist inhibitions or restricted areas of the economy from which foreign enterprise was excluded. It has not been much affected by changes in political regime.

The borrowing has been greatest in industrial sectors, where import restrictions and tariffs have induced foreign firms to set up plants, in the same way that the common tariff of the European Community has induced U.S. investment in Europe. In 1977 about a quarter of manufacturing output appears to have been produced in foreign-owned firms, and their role has been biggest in technologically sophisticated sectors like motor vehicles, machinery, equipment, and chemicals. As Brazil is a significant exporter of manufactured products (which now account for two-thirds of its exports), this borrowing of industrial technology seems to have been successful.

In 1983, 74 percent of foreign equity capital was invested in manufacturing, with very little in agriculture or in public utilities. For about forty years before 1929, the main foreign investment was in public utilities, but once foreign know-how had been absorbed, investors in this sector were squeezed out by the government. About 20 percent of foreign equity capital in Brazil is now invested in services. It is doubtful whether there is much transfer of know-how in this type of foreign investment, but because Brazil borrows heavily from foreign banks, it helps ease the flow of loans if those banks are given a toe-hold in the country.

One striking feature of foreign direct investment is its highly cosmopolitan character, with just under a third from the United States, about the same from the large European countries, and 9 percent from Japan in 1983 (table 3-9). Thus a variety of competing technologies has been introduced, with no heavy dependence on a single source

In some areas where outside technology was not relevant, there has been a significant domestic research effort. In a few cases, the policies that have fostered research seem to be wasteful. One such program is the development of sugar-based alcohol as a source of energy and of automobile engines to use this costly fuel. Another is the development of nuclear energy and a third is the encouragement, through heavy protection, of a domestic computer industry, which had to replicate technologies that could have been imported more cheaply. However, these are aberrations from a policy that has been more sensible than that of other large developing countries such as India and China, which have been much more reluctant to borrow technology.

Japanese strategy for borrowing foreign technology has involved little direct investment and large payments for patents and licenses. Because Brazil does not have a labor force with anything like Japanese

Table 3-9. Foreign Equity Capital in Brazil, by Country of Origin, 1930, 1975, and 1983
(millions of dollars)

Country	1930	1975	1983
Canada	100	411	1,016
France	198	300	705
Germany, Fed. Rep. of		871	2,646
Japan		841	2,037
Switzerland		736	1,938
United Kingdom	575	430	1,133
United States	210	2,295	7,198
Other	251[a]	1,420	5,427
Total	1,235	7,304	22,302[b]

a. Includes "other European countries" (16.2 percent) and Argentina (4.0 percent).
b. Of the total, 73.5 percent was in manufacturing and 20.7 percent in services, with a minor share in agriculture, mining, and utilities.

Source: Braga (n.d.), p. 17.

levels of education, such a strategy is effectively ruled out. Brazil's strategy has probably been somewhat more market oriented in giving foreign firms broad leeway in choosing the technologies they imported.

Use of External Finance

Before independence in 1822, Brazil was generally a net capital exporter as the main economic objective of the colonial power was to extract a surplus. After independence, Brazil became a net capital importer, as a variety of foreign interests (particularly British) began to invest and lend to the government. When the Empire gave way to the Republic in 1889, the accumulated external government debt was already about 15 percent of GDP. By 1914 this kind of government debt had risen to 44 percent of GDP and private direct investment was even bigger, so that total gross foreign assets were equal to 116 percent of GDP (which was the historic peak). Government borrowing was useful in covering government budget deficits, in financing investment, in tiding over periods of payments difficulty, and in financing buffer stocks of coffee, which were part of the price stabilization schemes.

In spite of the need for refunding the debt in 1898 and 1914 because of temporary difficulty in meeting payments schedules, Brazil was able to continue modest borrowing abroad through the 1920s, though a period of deflationary policy was required to bolster external cred-

Table 3-10. Brazilian External Debt and Foreign Direct Investment Assets, Selected Years 1889–1984

Item	1889	1914	1930	1945	1975	1984
Brazilian GDP						
Millions of current national units	1,778	5,630	27,260	133,800	887,424	353,857,117
Millions of current dollars	951	1,671	2,913	8,109	109,154	191,481
Brazilian public external debt (millions of dollars)	151	737	1,229	682	13,923	66,502
Foreign direct investment in Brazil (millions of dollars)	—	—	—	—	7,303	22,234[b]
Brazilian private external debt (millions of dollars)	—	1,195[a]	1,178[a]	669[a]	9,593	33,263
Ratio of Brazilian government external debt to GDP (percent)	15.9	44.0	42.2	8.4	12.8	34.7
Ratio of total foreign assets to Brazilian GDP (percent)	—	115.6	82.6	16.7	28.2	63.7

— Not available.
a. Foreign direct investment included in private external debt except in 1975 and 1984.
b. For 1983.

Source: For GDP in 1889–1945 (milreis = old cruzeiros), Goldsmith (1986), 1975 and 1984 (new cruzeiros = 1,000 old cruzeiros), IBGE. For public debt in 1889, Villela and Suzigan (1977), p. 451; public and private debt in 1914, 1930, and 1945, Abreu (1977); disbursed public debt and private foreign debt in 1984, IDB (1986); private debt in 1975, IDB (1982).

itworthiness in the 1920s. As a result of the world crisis of 1929–32, collapse of export earnings, evaporation of foreign willingness and ability to lend, and the rise in the real burden of debt service caused by falling price levels, Brazil eased its payments burden considerably in the 1930s by debt delinquency. In September 1931 it suspended amortization payments on all except the funding loans (issued to consolidate earlier delinquencies in 1898 and 1914) and shortly thereafter suspended interest payments as well. There was also delinquency in remitting dividends and meeting trade debts, and in 1937 all debt service was suspended for three years by government decree. The main creditors, the United Kingdom and the United States, imposed no commercial or financial sanctions, and in the end the foreign debts were written down to less than a quarter of their nominal value in the 1943 agreements with the United Kingdom and the United States. By 1945, gross foreign assets in Brazil were less than 17 percent of GDP (table 3-10).

In the early postwar years the foreign capital flow recovered rather slowly because potential foreign lenders had other priorities and remembered the delinquencies of the 1930s. In the 1960s, however, the flow began to be important again and made a modest but welcome contribution to Brazilian investment funds and foreign exchange. Foreign direct investment never regained the relative importance it had before 1930, but it became clear that the government, public corporations, and even private borrowers could raise significant sums in foreign capital markets. After the first oil price shock, foreign borrowing assumed a bigger role as a supplement to domestic saving and it helped to cover the large payments deficit that arose through the continuance of expansionary domestic policies in face of worsened terms of trade. The borrowing option looked all the more attractive because of the rapid rise in world price levels and relatively modest rates of interest. Over the four-year period 1977–80, the average real interest rate on developing countries' external debt (based on floating rates) was –8.7 percent a year, so there was little reason for hesitation in borrowing.

However, the situation changed abruptly in 1981, when world prices stopped rising and a tight monetary policy in the United States raised nominal interest rates. In the four years 1981–84, the real interest rate on developing countries' floating-rate debt averaged 14.6 percent, so that the real burden of debt service suddenly became horrific. Furthermore, in 1982, after Mexico's debt moratorium, the flow of new voluntary lending ceased for all Latin American borrowers. There were some already committed, nondisbursed loans that could be drawn on, but this cushion had vanished by 1984.

The debt problem of the 1980s occurred in a different environment from the 1930s. In the first place, there was no collapse in world trade, but rather a buoyancy, which permitted a substantial rise in export earnings. Second, there was no collapse of the international capital market; the IMF operated as a system preserver, nudging reluctant lenders to fund big amortization rollovers and keeping alive some hope of reestablishing creditworthiness. Third, there was the expectation that real interest levels would fall back nearer to historic norms. Fourth, there was a decline in petroleum prices and the international value of the dollar (the unit in which most debt is measured). In spite of this, Brazil seems to have reverted to the debt delinquency option of the 1930s. But the consequences of delinquency might not be as benign as in the 1930s. The creditors now are well-organized international banking syndicates with cross-default clauses interlocked with the IMF and the World Bank. In the 1930s, the creditors were largely private bondholders without such solidarity.

Given the role that debt service burdens had in inducing deflationary policy, and in reducing investment and economic growth in the 1980s, one may well question the wisdom of borrowing heavily to finance economic growth in 1973–81, but it is still too early to make a final judgment, if the consequences of delinquency turn out to be mild.

What does seem clear is that in Brazil borrowing in the 1970s contributed more to augment domestic capital formation than was the case in other big Latin American borrowers, like Mexico or the Southern-Cone countries. Mexico is a smaller economy, its debt is about the same size as Brazil's and has risen more quickly since the early 1970s, but the net contribution of foreign investment in 1974–84 in Mexico averaged only 1.8 percent of GDP compared with 4.1 percent in Brazil. This means that a much larger part of Mexico's borrowing must have gone to finance capital flight from the country than was the case in Brazil.

On the whole, therefore, with due reservation about the ultimate balance of experience in the 1970s and 1980s, it appears that in Brazil growth was facilitated by access to foreign finance and that the opportunities were intelligently used, without major interference by foreign creditors in domestic affairs. However, the role of foreign capital has been more modest over the long run than in Argentina, Australia, and Canada, nor has it had as much importance in the postwar period as in other fast-growing economies like Israel, Korea, and Singapore.

International Migration

Brazil differs from Mexico in that it has had relatively large immigration flows from the outside world since the 1880s. The inflow has generally helped to promote economic growth as the immigrants have almost always had, on average, better educational qualifications and skills than the native-born population. Immigrants have also had energy and ambition, which have contributed to building the work ethic and entrepreneurial drive, and they have probably helped to attract capital from their countries of origin. The broad ethnic variety of the immigrants has also helped to make Brazil a cosmopolitan country open to outside ideas and not defensively nationalistic.

Brazil is unlike Mexico in having little out-migration. Although there is a significant temporary outflow of educated Brazilians, they generally come back home with enhanced skills.

International Trade

Trade relations with the outside world have gone through several phases. In the colonial period Brazil was a primary product exporter constrained by mercantilist restrictions on domestic production of manufactured goods and with its ports closed to all but Portuguese and British ships. After independence in 1822, these restrictions disappeared, but until 1844 tariffs were limited to a maximum of 15 percent by a treaty with the United Kingdom. Thereafter Brazil built up one of the highest tariff levels in the world. The intent was mainly to provide tax revenue, but the incidental protection was important. The 1900 tariff systematized the structure. The characteristic rate on consumer goods was 50 percent but the rate went as high as 80 percent on some items. At the same time, the tariff on capital goods and industrial materials was very low and items such as machinery, dyestuffs, and chemical products for industrial use entered duty free.

Behind the tariff barrier, Brazil became a major producer of textiles, particularly in Rio de Janeiro, São Paulo, and Minas Gerais, and to some extent in Bahia. Cotton cloth production rose from 21 million meters in 1885 to 548 million in 1917 (Stein 1957, p. 100), and Brazil had the most highly developed textile industry in Latin America. In 1920 manufactured imports of all kinds represented only 36 percent of total domestic supply, and self-sufficiency in textiles was much higher.

There does not seem to have been the same sort of domestic political problem with tariffs as there was in the United States in the nineteenth century when Southern cotton planters wanted free trade and Northern industrialists wanted protection. In Brazil the money for industrialization came from coffee-producing interests in São Paulo who protected their coffee interests by a valorization scheme, which involved stockpiling and withholding coffee from the market to keep prices high, and protected their industrial products with tariffs.

Thus on the eve of the 1929 world crisis Brazil was certainly not a free-trade country and it had an industrial base larger than most developing countries, including the beginnings of a steel industry (the Belgo-Mineira, started in 1921).

It was external shocks that pushed Brazil further into import substitution. World War I cut off foreign supplies temporarily, and the collapse of the world economy in the 1930s caused a collapse in export earnings and provoked import controls in the form of foreign exchange

Table 3-11. **Brazilian Foreign Trade Indicators, Selected Years, 1929–87**
(percentage GDP in current prices)

Year	Commodity imports	Commodity exports	Coffee exports	Noncoffee exports	Terms of trade[a]	Import volume[a]	Export volume[a]
1929	10.8	11.9	8.4	3.5	101.3	79.9	74.4
1950	8.2	10.0	6.4	3.6	100.0	100.0	100.0
1964	5.2	6.9	3.7	3.2	73.7	97.9	123.4
1973	7.8	7.8	1.6	6.2	81.4	337.2	309.9
1980	10.5	8.4	1.0	7.4	56.1	443.3	528.5
1984	6.6	12.9	1.2	11.7	49.1	282.8	813.4
1985	6.3	11.3	1.0	10.3	48.0	279.1	828.9
1986	5.8	8.3	0.8	7.5	54.8	321.3	678.0
1987	—	—	—	—	52.5	330.0	780.4

— Not available.
a. Index (1950 = 100).
Source: For export and import volumes and terms of trade, in 1929–64, CEPAL (1976); in 1964–87, IMF, *International Financial Statistics*. For export current values, 1950–86, IMF, *International Financial Statistics*. For imports and exports in 1929, IBGE (1960). For GDP in 1929, Goldsmith (1986); in 1950–87, table A-2.

rationing. As there was a large home market and a dynamic class of industrial entrepreneurs, this phase of import substitution was relatively easy. It did not raise major technical problems or require large investment. Nor did such problems arise during World War II, when the government's response was to create the first five important state companies to build a steelworks, to develop iron ore, to maintain and repair vehicles, to generate electricity, and to make chemicals.

At the end of World War II, during which substantial exchange reserves were accumulated, there was one year of liberalization, 1946–47, when imports were free. As the exchange rate was overvalued, the surge in imports quickly exhausted the reserves and there was a reversion to old policies of exchange rationing until 1950.

In 1950–64, policy action to promote import substitution became much more intense under governments committed more strongly to nationalist policies of development. Imports continued to be controlled by rationing foreign exchange, and currency overvaluation reached grotesque proportions.

Imports of manufactured goods were reduced from 14 percent of domestic consumption in 1949 to 6 percent in 1964 (World Bank 1983), and during this period the government had specific goals for the type of industrial structure it wanted. Apart from exchange rationing, government objectives were implemented by channeling credit through the BNDE (the national development bank, created in 1952), by creating many more state enterprises, and by encouraging foreign investment in preferred sectors. In this period both exports and imports dropped sharply in relation to GDP, heavy reliance was still placed on coffee for export earnings, and the country had to live with chronic foreign exchange constraints (table 3-11).

When the military regime took over in 1964, there were a number of changes in the orientation of policy. However, the new liberalism was constrained by tradition and was by no means as radical as the later experiments with Chicago-style liberalism in Argentina, Chile, and Uruguay.

The complex system of multiple exchange rates was scrapped in favor of a crawling peg intended to maintain a competitive exchange rate. The tariff structure was rationalized with an average effective rate in 1967 of 66 percent (Bergsman 1970), and there was a clear intention to allow a much wider range of foreign participation, with higher levels of imports and exports and much less emphasis on coffee.

However, the emphasis on government targets and on planning remained. The government had objectives for specific industries, the role of state enterprise was increased, and there was a continued effort to entice and steer foreign direct investment into new fields. Direct fiscal subsidies, tax exemptions, and credit subsidies became important in encouraging new exports, and wide discretion was allowed in the day-to-day administration of policy.

It was therefore a highly dirigiste system in which major industrial interests, both domestic and foreign, had to maintain close liaison with the government and its agencies. In the new industrial sectors, production was highly concentrated. It is obvious that there was a substantial "rent" element in the profits of industry.

In the two decades after 1964, substantial progress was made in raising and diversifying exports, both agricultural and industrial. Generous subsidies were provided for the exports of infant industries. For 1980 the World Bank estimated that the average export subsidy was 20.8 percent. Between 1964 and 1973, there was also some reversal in the policy of import substitution, and imports of manufactured goods rose from 6 percent of domestic supply in 1964 to 12 percent in 1974. The tariff structure was modified so that the incidence of effective protection was more even by type of product.

The two oil price shocks worsened the terms of trade substantially. Competitiveness was bolstered by large devaluations, and the government stepped up its foreign borrowing. But it also reverted to a new round of import substitution, including rapid expansion of the sugar-based fuel and nuclear power programs and exploitation of Brazil's poor-quality petroleum resources.

It is difficult to make clear-cut judgments on foreign trade policy. To a considerable extent it has been induced by external shocks—two world wars, the world depression of the 1930s, the two oil price shocks, and the debt crisis of the 1980s. The worst period clearly was 1950–64, when world market conditions favored a more liberal regime than the government followed and when the complexity of intervention resulted in a high degree of inefficiency. Throughout the period we are examining, the degree of protection was high enough to create arbitrary rent elements in the income of industrial entrepreneurs. How high these have been is difficult to judge, because the economy is large enough to have a fair degree of competition and most observers have concluded that a substantial part of the protection was redundant. Bergsman (1978) suggested that these rent elements could have amounted to 9 percent of GDP in the 1960s and the inefficiency element to only 1 percent of GDP; the basis for his estimate was, however, rather weak.

Generally, foreign analysts have taken a benign view of the dynamic impact of this dirigiste protectionist system. Bergsman (1970), Fishlow (1972b), and the World Bank (1983) have pointed to the successful transformation from a relatively simple manufacturing structure in 1929 and high concentration on one agricultural export crop to a much more sophisticated economy in the 1980s, with great flexibility in producing new export products. Within a highly cosseted sector like automobiles, there has obviously been change and competition, with some firms dropping out of the market (including the government's own enterprise) and concentration of output on Ford, General Motors, and Volkswagen. In 1984, exports were almost twice as high in relation to GDP as they had been in 1964 and were higher than in 1929. However, the volume of exports and the trade balance deteriorated subsequently, particularly in 1986 as a consequence of the ill-fated cruzado experiment.

When Brazil is compared with Italy and India—two economies of similar size in real terms—its exports are only about 40 percent of those in Italy and more than two and a half times as large as India's. Clearly the adverse effect on resource allocation of Brazilian dirigisme has not had the dimensions characteristic of India, and Brazil did not have the market opportunities that Italy has enjoyed from membership in and propinquity to the European Community. In terms of trade ratios, the U.S. economy in real terms is just over seven times as large as Brazil's, and its exports are about eight times as large in dollar terms. By the standards of the U.S. market economy, Brazil still has some way to go in expanding the ratio of trade to GDP.

Agricultural Policies

By comparison with many countries, Brazil's agricultural performance has been fairly successful (tables 3-12 and 3-13). The rapid growth in agricultural output has been faster than that in most countries. Agriculture's successful structural adjustment to changing demand and market opportunities has led to dramatic changes in the role of particular products and to diversification of exports. Its substantial progress in productivity per person engaged may have been faster than in industry. But agricultural growth has depended heavily on a huge extension in cropped area that would be impossible in other countries. The opening up of new land should have made it easier than in most countries to establish a more egalitarian distribution of land ownership, but extreme inequality has persisted. And government financial subsidies have also been disequalizing.

Evolution of Government Policy

The concentration of wealth is not surprising, since there was never a deliberate policy to tackle the problems of land ownership and social inequality in rural areas. Government action toward agriculture for many years was aimed at defending and preserving the coffee sector. After 1929, both the federal and the São Paulo state government changed their policies, refusing to continue financial aid that had led to an expansion of coffee production far above the level of demand. Policy in the 1930s was still clearly centered on coffee but its objective was to

Table 3-12. Key Indicators for Brazilian Agriculture, Forestry, and Fishing, Selected Years, 1950–80

Indicator	1950	1960	1970	1980	Annual average growth, 1950–80 (percent)
Gross value added (millions of 1970 cruzeiros)	8,535	13,248	20,157	32,024	4.5
Employment (thousands)	10,253	12,279	13,088	12,661	0.7
Output per person employed (1970 cruzeiros)	832	1,069	1,540	2,529	3.8
Crop area (thousands of hectares)	19,095	28,712	33,984	49,185	3.2
Output per hectare (1970 cruzeiros)	447	461	593	651	1.3
Tractor stock	8,372	61,324	165,870	530,691	14.8
Crop area per person employed (hectares)	1.9	2.3	2.6	3.9	2.4
Sectoral terms of trade (1950 = 100)	100.0	70.2	71.2	136.8	n.a.

n.a. Not applicable.

Source: FIBGE. For sectoral terms of trade (sectoral deflator divided by GDP deflator), which for 1950–66 is for São Paulo only, *Conjuntura*, January 1962 and June 1972; linked for 1966–80 to index for Brazil, supplied by Vargas Foundation. Employment (persons engaged) from population census.

Table 3-13. Index of Output per Person Engaged in Agriculture, Forestry, and Fishing, in Ten Countries, 1975
(United States = 100.0)

Country	Index
Argentina	47.2
Brazil	10.3
France	45.0
Germany, Fed. Rep. of	32.6
India	1.9
Japan	11.6
Korea, Rep. of	4.0
Mexico	7.0
Netherlands	91.6
United Kingdom	57.6

Source: van Oostroom and Maddison (1984) with revisions.

adjust production to demand without causing bankruptcy of coffee growers and banking institutions. By the end of 1937 the policy toward coffee changed. Coffee stocks were destroyed and a further fall of prices was permitted to help in restoring equilibrium between demand and supply.

Expansion of cotton production, while not specifically supported by federal policies, reduced the impact of the coffee crisis on the value of exports. Between 1935 and 1939 cotton represented 47 percent of Brazil's exports; coffee represented only 19 percent, down from 72 percent between 1925 and 1929, when cotton exports were only 2 percent (Villela and Suzigan 1977, pp. 186–87). Production of cotton permitted a smooth transition to profitable use of the land, manpower, and physical infrastructure previously linked to coffee production. By the end of World War II, cotton had emerged as Brazil's main crop, accounting for about a fifth of the value of agricultural production.

Between 1945 and 1965, the government's main direct measures of aid changed, but cotton and coffee continued to receive the greatest attention (W. H. Nicholls in Roett 1972, pp. 147–84). A technical assistance network, inspired by a privately sponsored initiative in Minas Gerais, was created in 1948. Subsidies were introduced to encourage imports of fertilizers and tractors. In 1951, the government established a new minimum-price program; government purchases consisted mostly of coffee and, eventually, cotton. Crop production credit was expanded, though most of the resources were directed toward coffee (40 percent of the value of credit between 1957 and 1959).

None of these measures seems to have had a significant effect on agricultural production during the 1950s. Only a few crops concentrated in São Paulo showed gains in physical yields that indicated benefits from federal policies, particularly from subsidized imports of inputs and machinery. However, agricultural performance was strongly affected by transport improvements. The rapid expansion of the highway network permitted a fantastic increase in cropland, of 3.2 percent a year, from 19.1 million hectares in 1950 to 49.2 million in 1980. Better transport facilitated migration, which occurred independently of government policy. Movement of workers served to alleviate economic and social pressures in the Northeast and supplied the much needed manpower on the moving frontier (Paraná, Mato Grosso, Goiás, and Maranhão).

Land Reform

Unequal distribution of land has its origins in the colonial period. Land was allocated in very large holdings (*capitanias hereditarias*). The "sugar cane cycle," in which large holdings of land were worked by slave labor, reinforced the pattern of accumulation in the Northeast, concentrating economic and political power in the hands of landowners. This was critical in molding social values and in determining legislation that preserved land rights. Until 1963 the Constitution guaranteed land rights, and expropriation by the government required prior and fair cash payment. Thus the practical limit on the stock of land for reform purposes was state-owned lands with poor soil or difficult access to markets. No serious program of land reform could depend on these resources.

The government has had only a marginal role in direct promotion of the occupation of the frontier through colonization. The landless migrants who have opened up the frontier were usually families who farmed on a small scale and who occupied land without legal sanction; the result often was conflict and eventual expulsion. Large holdings of land have been opened up to exploit fiscal incentives that allow owners to invest profits free of income tax.

The occupation of new land and the progressive break up of holdings in long-occupied areas contributed to an increase in agricultural holdings from 1,904,589 in 1940 to 5,159,851 in 1980. There was a noteworthy increase in the number of squatters and a smaller increase in the proportion of tenants. Squatters occupied 5.7 percent of holdings in 1940 and 16.5 percent in 1980. Tenant occupancies rose from 11.6 percent to 17.2 percent. Squatters were especially active at the frontier—in the Northern region in 1980 the agricultural census showed that 44 percent of producers were squatters.

Widespread debate and popular interest in social and economic conditions in rural areas and their impact on other sectors led the government to take some important legal steps. In 1963 the Estatuto do Trabalhador Rural introduced the basis for extending to rural workers the benefits of labor legislation that protected urban workers. All kinds of difficulties arose, however. The protective measures eliminated the traditional relationship between landless peasant and the landowner, with the peasant losing the right to have a house and grow crops or livestock for himself on a small plot on the employer's land. The result was a rapid process of proletarization. As rural workers progressively lost their traditional informal access to their employer's marginal land, many migrated to cities. Others became seasonal or day laborers, thus aggravating social conditions in the countryside. The government did not take advantage of the road construction program to promote a more egalitarian occupation of new land. In fact, holdings of 10,000 hectares or more in the Center-West region increased from 26 percent of the total area in 1960 to 30 percent in 1970.

Results of the 1964 Land Reform Law were modest. The Instituto Brasileiro de Reforma Agrária (Institute for Agrarian Reform, or IBRA), created to carry out resettlement on public lands, had limited success—only five thousand families were resettled in the first six years. The successor of IBRA, the Instituto Nacional de Colonização e Reforma Agrária (Institute for Colonization and Land Reform, or INCRA), distributed land titles and created settlements, mainly along the Trans-Amazon highway, but the results were mediocre. The financial resources appropriated to execute the 1985 National Plan for Land Reform suggest that implementation will be slow and probably well below target.

Research and Extension

Agricultural research has been scattered in a few institutions. The Instituto Agronômico de Campinas became famous in the period 1923–39 for developing improved seeds of long-staple cotton, which radically transformed the quality of Brazilian cotton. The agronomic stations in Rio Grande do Sul developed wheat seeds of excellent quality, which were exported to Argentina, where ecological conditions for growing this cereal are among the best in the world.

In 1973 Brazil launched a bold program to reorganize investment in agricultural technology. It created the Brazilian Agricultural Research Enterprise (EMBRAPA) and the Brazilian Enterprise for Technical Assistance and Rural Extension (EMBRATER), both under the supervision of the Ministry of Agriculture. The former agency is well known for its continuing policy of developing human resources through agreements with both national and foreign universities. Substantial resources raised largely out of taxes on growers fund specialized institutions such as the Sugar and Alcohol Institute (IAA), the Brazilian Coffee Institute (IBC), and the Executive Commission for the Planning of Cocoa Cultivation (CEPLAC), which supply research and extension services in their sectors. In the 1980s public research expenditure was equivalent to around 1.0 percent of agricultural value added, a much higher proportion than is spent by other Latin American countries (World Bank 1982, p. 68).

Extension programs have expanded a good deal, but they are still insufficient in relation to needs, given the backwardness of agricultural activity. They reach only a fraction of rural producers, and principally those in the most developed areas.

Agricultural Credit

Although financing for farmers had been available since 1937 through the Banco do Brasil (Carteira de Crédito Agricola e Industrial, CREAI), the creation of the new National System of Rural Credit (SNCR) in 1965 made financing the main policy instrument for agriculture. The value of credit as a percentage of agricultural income rocketed upward from 27.4 percent in 1965 to 65.3 percent in 1970 (Rabello de Castro, in Villela and Baer 1980, p. 256).

Table 3-14. Production of Main Crops, Selected Years, 1950–85
(thousands of tons)

Crop	1950	1960	1970	1980	1985
Black beans	1,248	1,730	2,211	1,968	2,547
Cocoa	453	163	197	319	419
Coffee	1,071	4,169	1,509	2,122	3,753
Corn	6,023	8,671	14,216	20,372	22,017
Cotton.	774	1,609	1,955	1,676	2,836
Manioc	12,532	17,613	29,464	23,465	23,072
Rice	3,217	4,794	7,553	9,775	9,019
Soybeans	77[a]	206	1,508	15,155	18,278
Sugarcane	32,670	56,926	79,752	148,650	245,904
Wheat	532	713	1,844	2,702	4,247

a. For 1952.
Source: FIBGE, Anuário estatístico.

There was a strong decline in coffee's share of these resources. In 1957–59 around 40 percent of rural credit went to coffee; this declined to 10 percent in 1966–68. By the latter period most of the credit was used to finance rice, corn, and cotton crops (respectively, 27 percent, 19 percent, and 13 percent), evidencing a clear trend toward diversification. As inflation rose, the fixed interest rates for agricultural loans became negative in real terms. The Banco do Brasil remained the main lending agent but commercial banks were required to apply at least 10 percent of the value of their short-term deposits to rural credit. Credit became the principal governmental incentive for agricultural production.

The policy of frequent devaluation introduced at the end of the 1960s improved the profitability of agricultural exports and established a better relationship between costs and prices for some crops. Differences in profitability among crops led to a substantial change in the structure of production during the 1970s. Soybeans became a major crop and a substantial foreign exchange earner. After 1975 the oil substitution program led to a substantial increase in the production of sugarcane (79.7 million tons in 1970 and 245.9 million in 1985) for use in the production of alcohol. Both trends had the effect of displacing food crops for the domestic market. Thus production of beans, rice, and manioc grew only modestly during the decade (table 3-14).

A system of rural insurance—PROAGRO—was created in 1975 closely linked to rural credit. The insurance applied only to the part of production financed through the SNCR. Since a system that would cover the risks of all producers was not considered financially viable by private enterprise (too costly for the producer or a sure loss for the insurer), the PROAGRO implied a net transfer to borrowers whenever a loss occurred.

One aspect of the credit system was the technical assistance it provided. Farmers seeking loans were required to describe how their projects would be carried out and defend their agronomic soundness. Though small producers criticized this barrier to access to rural credit (and it was abandoned in the early 1980s), this provision promoted technical improvements among those who received rural credit. And whether they used rural credit or not, producers in regular contact with technical assistance programs became more quickly and more easily informed of agronomic research findings. The creation of EMBRAPA in 1973 and the installation of specialized research centers, as well as efforts to increase the number of high-level researchers, generated substantial progress in agronomic knowledge.

Despite the surge in rural credit in the 1970s, the perverse distribution of credit left certain important crops lagging behind. Moreover, sudden government intervention in the retail market through price fixing, imports, and sale of stocks had a further disorganizing effect on production.

After 1980 resources for rural credit—the most important incentive for agriculture—were reduced because of the need to control monetary

Table 3-15. Evolution of Rural Credit, 1969–84
(millions of 1969 cruzeiros)

Year	Value of loans
1969	6,489
1970	7,720
1971	8,921
1972	11,063
1973	15,614
1974	19,309
1975	28,188
1976	28,872
1977	25,764
1978	26,206
1979	32,649
1980	31,220
1981	27,077
1982	26,223
1983	19,793
1984	12,090

Source: Supplied by Banco Central do Brasil, Departamento de Crédito Rural.

expansion (table 3-15).
The Minimum Price Program

The most important change in government action toward agriculture in the first half of the 1980s was the increased governmental role in the acquisition and sale of primary products. Minimum prices had been set at levels that led to heavy government acquisitions. The consequent side effects—pressure on monetary aggregates and the cost of administering much larger stocks than necessary to regulate the market—demonstrated the need to reexamine minimum price policy.

Price support for agricultural products dates back to 1943 with the creation of the Comissão de Financiamento da Produção (CFP), which in the early 1980s was transformed into a public enterprise and renamed Companhia de Financiamento da Produção.

The minimum price program now covers some forty-two commodities. However, it excludes sugarcane, coffee, wheat, and cocoa, which account for about 25 percent of the value of total crop production.

The Política de Garantia de Precos Mínimos (PGPM, Minimum Price Support Policy) aims at giving the rural producer a guarantee against sharp declines in prices that would adversely affect his income (see Mollo 1983). The two basic instruments of the PGPM are the Empréstimos do Governo Federal (EGF, Federal Government Loan Program) and the Aquisicaes do Governo Federal (AGF, Federal Government Acquisition Program).

The EGF offers two loan programs, one with and the other without a sale option for the government. The first one requires an official classification of the product and its storage in an approved warehouse; the owner of the crop is eligible for a 100 percent loan (based on the minimum price). If the government buys the product, it absorbs the costs of storage, classification, and so forth. The second program requires storage on the farm, with the loan covering 80 percent of the value of the crop. The EGF is not a policy instrument that lends itself to use by small farmers; it reaches only those whose production is for market. The loans are available to producers and cooperatives, as well as to processors, industrialists, and exporters.

It has been the availability of subsidized credit rather than the minimum price that accounts for any benefits the program may have provided through price stabilization and production incentive. The minimum price program could not alleviate long-standing intercrop and interregional disparities in infrastructure, technology, or education.

Food Subsidies

The most important food subsidy is for wheat. The wheat subsidy policy was aimed at self-sufficiency, suppression of inflation, and a relative lowering of food prices for the urban population. The policy was easy to implement as the government was the only buyer for both the domestic product and imports. Normally an above-market price was paid to farmers, with government selling below cost to millers. The government also set the retail price. The producer subsidy did not change much during the 1970s (despite a substantial increase in domestic production), but the consumer subsidy increased enormously. The total subsidy reached $1 billion in 1979, but the government subsequently began to cut back, aiming to bring the subsidy program to an end.

Milk prices are fixed at the retail level, and milk distributors are paid a subsidy equivalent to 10 percent of the retail price. One consequence of this policy was the diversion from liquid milk toward production of powdered milk, cheese, butter, and other products whose prices were not controlled.

Maximum prices for beef are set at the retail level, and a program to store frozen beef for off-season release was established in 1975 so as to avoid seasonal price variations.

Alcohol Plan

In 1975 the government launched PROALCOOL, the National Alcohol Program, for the purpose of partially replacing gasoline. New distilleries, production incentives, and low world sugar prices helped to raise alcohol production sixfold between 1975 and 1979.

In 1980, in the second phase of PROALCOOL, the production target for 1985 was set at 10.7 billion liters, of which 9.2 billion would substitute for gasoline and 1.5 billion would be used as chemical feedstock. The overall figure for 1985 was exceeded—production reached 11.8 billion liters—and during the period a new technology for 100 percent alcohol-powered automobiles was developed. Today, more than 80 percent of passenger cars produced in the country are fueled by alcohol!

The result of PROALCOOL in terms of energy substitution was a saving of about 120,000 barrels a day of imported petroleum. However, the program has been criticized for its financial cost, opportunity cost in terms of food production, and ecological cost. For the period 1978–82 as a whole it is estimated that credit subsidies amounted to $1.9 billion (Borges and others 1985, p. 115a).

Policies toward Industry and Services

Brazilian economic policy, which has favored industrialization since the

Table 3-16. Levels of Manufacturing Productivity in Five Countries Compared with the United States, 1975

(based on value added per hour worked; United States = 100.0)

Country	1975
Argentina	22.5
Brazil	37.6
India[a]	5.5
Korea, Rep. of	9.5
Mexico	31.6

a. Excludes small firms and household activity.

Source: The estimates are derived from detailed binary comparisons with the United States, using data from censuses of manufacturing. See Maddison and van Ark (1989) for a description of the method.

1930s, has created a manufacturing sector with the highest productivity in the developing world (table 3-16). With the possible exception of China, Brazil's manufacturing sector is also the largest in the developing world. Labor costs have been kept low by an official policy of suppressing trade union activity, so that the country was able to develop a large range of manufactured exports quickly when government exchange rate policy permitted. In this respect Brazil had an advantage over Mexico, where labor productivity was lower and manufacturing wages higher because of strong government support of trade unions.

Until the 1950s, the state had few entrepreneurial activities, but from 1950 to 1985 the number of state enterprises rose from 35 to 646. In 1985 there were more than a million employees in such enterprises. This growth was not attributable to a socialist ideology but to the etatist ambition of an increasingly centralized state and a powerful technocratic bureaucracy that saw state enterprise as a major vehicle for modernization, and particularly for industrialization. Nevertheless, the government consistently favored foreign investment in industry (with a brief xenophobic exception in 1962–64). As a result, foreign firms control about a quarter of manufacturing output, being particularly important in modern heavy industry.

Partly for national security reasons and because of supply problems, the government created a number of companies during World War II—an integrated steel mill; an iron ore processing plant; a plant for maintenance and repair of airplane engines that later added manufacture of tractors, trucks, automobiles, and other items; a plant for processing soda ash and caustic soda; and an electricity generation plant.

In the 1950s, the number of government enterprises in basic industries and infrastructure increased rapidly. The most important addition was PETROBRAS, the government-owned oil and petrochemical monopoly. Two firms were set up in the electric energy sector, Centrais Elétricas de Minas Gerais (CEMIG) and Furnas Centrais Elétricas S.A., in 1951 and 1957, respectively. The BNDE supplied long-term credit to strengthen the position of state enterprise during the 1950s and 1960s. Control of public utility rates encouraged a gradual expansion of public enterprise in areas such as electricity generation and distribution, public transportation, and telecommunications as private enterprise found such activity unprofitable.

In the 1960s and the 1970s state conglomerate holding companies like PETROBRAS were set up for specific areas of production—ELETROBRAS in 1962 for electricity generation and distribution, TELEBRAS (Telecomunicações Brasileiras S.A.) in 1972 for telecommunications, and SIDERBRAS (Siderúrgica Brasileira S.A.) in 1973 for steel.

These conglomerates not only gathered different government companies belonging to the same sector under central control but also engaged in vertical expansion, creating or taking over several enterprises up- or downstream. Twenty-two companies were added to the PETROBRAS parent holding company, eleven of them in petrochemicals and fertilizers, one in mining, two in the distribution of gasoline and other oil derivatives, and three in oil exploration and drilling abroad (which along with oil refining are carried out in Brazilian territory by the holding company itself); five are trading companies.

In 1967, an administrative reform gave state enterprises substantial organizational and administrative advantages. They were to benefit from the same conditions and autonomy as private firms (F. Rezende in Abranches and others 1980, p. 45). The possibility of bypassing restrictive rules regarding personnel recruitment, wage policy, and other organizational procedures led federal, state, and municipal administrators to create, or transform public services into, state enterprises. However, the pricing policy of state enterprises is subject to government control, and that has created major financial problems for them and for budgetary equilibrium.

Causes of Creation and Expansion of State Enterprises

The motives for establishment of state enterprise have been mixed. The railway system was progressively nationalized because of the government's stop on payment of interest guaranteed to foreign capital. The consequent discouragement of the railroads and the unwillingness of domestic capital to undertake the expansion of the network were the chief reasons for governmental (both federal and state) takeover.

Companhia Siderúrgica Nacional (CSN), the government's steel mill, was created after several attempts to attract foreign capital or to encourage domestic groups to establish an integrated steel mill. Further expansion of state activity in the sector was a natural consequence of the successful government administration of CSN in its first years (Baer 1969).

Nationalistic motivation was important in establishing two major public enterprises, Companhia Vale do Rio Doce (CVRD) and PETROBRAS. The former was created after a long series of granting and canceling charters to domestic and foreign groups to exploit the rich deposits of iron ore in Minas Gerais. Encouragement of popular nationalistic feelings was an easy way for the Vargas administration to get around interest groups linked to foreign oil companies in creating PETROBRAS.

In Brazilian conditions of continuously high inflation, large long-term investments always seemed risky, particularly in industries where there was a risk of government constraint on pricing policy. So inflation itself was a powerful force behind the etatist nature of industrial development.

Balance of Emphasis between Private and Public Sector

The policies adopted in the 1950s for diversifying industrial structure and attracting foreign investment offered protection through quantitative restrictions up to 1957, and thereafter through the new tariff system that lasted until 1967. During this time importers of industrial machinery enjoyed special favors under the system of multiple exchange rates; favored industries like motor vehicles and ships were exempted from payment of customs duties and received subsidized loans from the BNDE; and from 1955 to 1963 foreign firms were permitted to import second-hand capital goods without foreign exchange coverage.

There was a substantial growth of foreign ownership, especially in industries with foreign dominance. Thus, while the average annual growth rate of manufacturing as a whole was 8.3 percent in 1955–64, electrical machinery and equipment reached 22.7 percent a year, and transport equipment 25.1 percent. Growth in industries where domestic private capital dominated was substantially lower—in textiles 3.5 percent a year, in apparel and shoes 1.4 percent.

The inability of the domestic private sector to contribute the technology, management, and financial resources necessary for the development of some of the industries considered crucial by policymakers made its relative weakening unavoidable. However, the domestic private sector benefited in absolute terms (as, for instance, in the mushroom growth of firms supplying assembly industries like motor vehicles, shipbuilding, and consumer durables).

Nevertheless, the perceived weakness of the domestic private sector and its relative decline aroused some anxiety, particularly in the 1960s.

The growing importance of the foreign private sector placed domestic private enterprises in a difficult position whenever the government adopted stabilization policies. Since foreign firms were stronger and had better access to credit, there was a tendency toward the takeover of domestic enterprises. The so-called denationalization of the pharmaceutical industry illustrates this situation. It was partially caused by takeover and partially by the stronger capacity in research and development of the parent companies of foreign firms. The denationalization process was gradual throughout the 1950s and became stronger in the years 1957–74, when the estimated share of local firms in total sales declined from 20 percent to 17 percent and the number of local firms among the top thirty-five (in terms of sales) fell from eleven in 1957 to one in 1974.

After 1964, public policy measures included expansion of resources of the official development bank (BNDE) through the creation of affiliated agencies for financing the sales of capital goods, strengthening private domestic firms, financing the training of scientists and engineers, and supporting research and development. Measures offering generous fiscal and credit incentives were adopted not only to help less developed regions, but also to encourage sectors that enjoyed governmental priority—such as the export of manufactured goods, tourism, reforestation, and development of the capital market.

Public enterprises, mainly through administrative reforms, became more efficient and were stimulated to diversify into other areas. This led to the formation of conglomerate enterprises like PETROBRAS and CVRD. At the municipal and state levels many public enterprises were created in such areas as water supply, transportation, gas, and sewerage. And public enterprises in steelmaking, electricity, and telecommunications were consolidated in the holding companies SIDERBRAS, ELETROBRAS, and TELEBRAS.

In the mid-1970s a debate over etatism broke out. In fact, the debate was about the posture of the military administrations since 1964 whose rhetoric had continuously favored private initiative. The results of their policies had been, once more, to increase the relative size of the foreign and public sectors. In the years 1967–73, the zenith of industrial growth, with an overall average of 14 percent, the branches dominated by the domestic private sector (textiles, apparel, food, paper, furniture) increased at an average rate of only 8 percent.

Measures Used to Influence Private Sector Investment

During the intensive phase of import substitution, policy ranged from outright bans on imports of certain products to special exchange rates during the period of multiple exchange rates. Thereafter, the measures used to promote investment in private industry were the new tariff law of 1957 plus the action of the *grupos executivos* in industries like motor vehicles and shipbuilding and more vigorous application of the Law of Similars (which dates from the nineteenth century; in 1911 a Register of Similar Products was created). The law, which prohibited imports of products when similar goods were produced locally, encouraged vertical integration; it brought in many foreign firms, which moved from importing to assembly or full-fledged manufacturing (Gordon and Grommers 1962, pp. 23–24).

Fiscal incentives were widely used, both to help less-developed regions and to encourage industrial development. Generally speaking, they were aimed at lowering the cost of capital or had that result, even when one of their targets was to increase the level of employment, as for instance with Law Number 4,239 of June 1963, whose major objective was the development of industrial activities in the Northeast. The chief incentive granted by the law was deduction (up to 50 percent) of corporate income tax liability on condition that the tax-free element was applied to investments approved by the Superintendency for the Northeastern Region Development (SUDENE). It is common knowledge that industrial projects established in the Northeast to a large extent replicated the industrial basis of the Center-South, and that, contrary to expectations, they were capital intensive. The law also granted reduction or exemption from customs duties on imports of components, parts, or capital goods, and reduction of or exemption from the federal tax on industrial products for projects approved by SUDENE).

After the founding of the BNDE in 1952 the domestic industrial sector gained access to credit for investment on a substantial scale. Until the mid-1960s such credit was granted at highly negative real interest rates. And even when it charged positive interest rates, the BNDE pursued a policy of extending loans at preferential rates, thus subsidizing some sectors at the expense of higher interest rates for others.

Favors to Particular Industries

At different times, different manufacturing industries have received special attention from the government. In the 1950s the motor vehicle and shipbuilding industries were favored, in the 1960s chemicals and petrochemicals, and in the early 1970s capital goods in general and made-to-order capital goods in particular. More recently special favors have gone to the manufacture of micro- and minicomputers.

The special incentives granted to these industries were mainly subsidized credit offered through the BNDE and reduction or exemption from customs duties. In the case of custom built capital goods, the government directed that public enterprises should channel their purchases to national firms.

Aid for Exports of Manufactured Goods

In 1965 the BNDE created a subsidiary, the Agencia Especial de Financimento Industrial (Special Agency for Industrial Financing, or FINAME), which became the most important source of financing for capital goods. Its role was crucial after 1973 when the country embarked on a policy of import substitution of capital goods. Its guidelines called for progressive increments in domestic content, and the interest rates, maturities, and the size of FINAME's financial participation were dependent on the level of domestic content.

After 1964, exports of manufactured goods enjoyed subsidized credits and fiscal incentives. After 1965 firms engaged in export were exempted from the corporate income tax on profits derived from sales abroad, and by the end of 1966 companies in the export business could use the drawback regime. The creation in 1967 of a value added tax (collected by the states) gave the government an occasion to increase fiscal incentives.

In 1972 the Comissão para Concessão de Beneficios Fiscais a Programas Especiais de Exportação (Commission for Granting Fiscal Incentives to Special Exports Programs, or BEFIEX) was created to administer a special program for exports of manufactured products. This included full or substantial exemption from customs duties; product and value added taxes on imports of machinery; a reduction of 50 percent in customs duties and product taxes on imports of raw materials, parts, components, and inputs; and dispensation from the national similarity checks on imports of machinery, equipment, instruments, raw materials, and inputs. The only conditions were that the firm make a commitment to a certain foreign currency value of exports and if its target was not fulfilled within a given period, the firm was subject to severe penalties.

The BEFIEX program accounted for an important portion of exports of sophisticated goods such as computers, office machines, motor vehicles, and motors. In general, multinational firms took advantage of the program, as they could plan exports between their affiliates, using their own channels of marketing.

In 1977 the government began a policy of barring production of micro and minicomputers by foreign firms, either alone or in joint ventures. The government's initial unprecedented step was to refuse IBM, Burroughs, NCR, and other multinational corporations permission to manufacture minicomputers in Brazil.

A good indicator of the degree of competitiveness attained by Brazilian industry is the growth and diversification of the country's manufactured exports. Sophisticated industries like machinery, electric and electronic equipment, and transportation equipment accounted for 15.0

percent of Brazil's exports in 1985. There are growing exports of airplanes by Emprèsa Brasileira de Aeronáutica S.A. (Brazilian Aeronautical Corporation, or EMBRAER), a public enterprise—the United States is its main market for Bandeirantes and Brasilia, and the company recently won an international competition to supply training airplanes to Britain's Royal Air Force.

4 Brazilian Outcomes in Terms of Equity and Alleviation of Poverty

Brazil is a country with high income inequality, much higher than in advanced capitalist countries, and high by the standards of Latin America and the developing world. This is a characteristic it shares with Mexico. It is a country of extreme and long-standing regional inequality of income. The poorest region is the North east, which prospered in the sixteenth and seventeenth centuries because of sugar exports, but per capita income there may well be lower now than it was then. The most prosperous part of the country in every respect is the South and South east where the bulk of industry and the most productive farms are located (table 4-1). Income differentials are usually stated in terms of Brazil's five main economic regions, some of which are bigger than most countries. It is more pertinent, however, to look at the variance between the states and the federal district, which was 8.6 to 1 in 1980 (table 4-2). In the United States, by contrast, the 1985 range in income was 2 to 1 for the fifty states and the federal district, and the 1980 range in Mexico was 6.3 to 1 for the thirty-one states and the federal district.

Income inequality appears to have increased significantly in the 1960s (see Fishlow 1972a; Langoni 1973). In 1970–80, the trend was less obvious; if there was an increase in inequality, it was much milder than in the 1960s (see table 4-3; Denslow and Tyler 1983; Hoffmann 1984). The absolute real income and living standards of the poorest section of the population increased modestly in the 1960s (Fields 1977) and much more markedly in the 1970s (table 4-4; Pastore, Zylberstajn, and Pagotto 1983). In fact, the level of absolute poverty declined in 1970–80.

Income Distribution

There are major statistical problems in measuring the distribution of income in Brazil. Much of the literature on income distribution is devoted to interpretation, adjustment, and sensitivity analysis (or sometimes outright repudiation) of the sources. These include the decennial demographic censuses since 1960, surveys conducted by the Pesquisa

Table 4-1. Social and Economic Indicators for the Northeast and Southeast, 1960 and 1980
(percent)

	1960		1980	
Indicator	Northeast	Southeast	Northeast	Southeast
Share of total population	31.7	43.7	29.3	43.5
Share of industrial value added	6.9[a]	79.2[a]	8.1	72.6
Share of domestic income	14.4[a]	65.0[a]	11.6[b]	63.5[b]
Illiterate	65.7	36.7	52.9	21.5
Households with electricity	16.4	58.2	43.6	85.4
Share of population in rural areas	66.1	43.0	49.5	20.8
Share of households with sewerage or cesspool	6.1	40.4	18.2	63.5

a. Data for 1959.
b. Data for 1975.
Source: IBGE, *Anuário estatístico* (1960, 1980).

Nacional por Amostra de Domicilios (Household Sample Survey, or PNAD), various wage indexes, and, for regional analysis, the national accounts.

The decennial demographic censuses raise problems because the total income they have reported has been less than 60 percent of that recorded in the national accounts, and the missing parts are at the extreme ends of the distribution. Furthermore, the national accounts do not cover informal economic activity; thus they understate income by a significant amount.

The Brazilian discussion has been mainly concerned with inequality within the economically active population. This is greater than the inequality between households, the basic consumption unit. The variation in the two measures is affected by the proportion of people with jobs. In the period 1950–70, for a combination of demographic and social reasons, the ratio of employed persons to total population fell, but from 1970 to 1980 it rose from 31.9 percent to 36.3 percent (table 4-5). The rise largely reflected the increased participation in the labor force of women whose fertility and family obligations had fallen. The consequent increase in the number of wage earners per household was considered a major cause of the reduction of poverty at the household level in 1970–80 by Pastore, Zylberstajn, and Pagotto (1983). A continuing decline in fertility is likely to reinforce this tendency, which obviously has a long

Table 4-2. **Population and Income per Capita by Region, State, and Territory, 1950 and 1980**

Region and state or territory	Population (thousands) 1950	Population (thousands) 1980	Per capita income (current cruzeiros) 1950	Per capita income (current cruzeiros) 1980
Center West	1,731	7,498	2.45	95,539
Mato Grosso	521	1,363	2.80	89,339
Goiás	1,209	3,842	2.29	63,690
North	1,834	5,838	2.49	70,672
Rondônia[a]	37	484	n.a.	67,979
Acre	115	300	n.a.	53,731
Amazonas	508	1,421	3.33	101,007
Roraima[a]	18	78	n.a.	73,817
Pará	1,120	3,380	2.10	60,509
Amapá[a]	37	174	n.a.	55,582
Northeast	17,992	34,687	1.92	45,827
Maranhão	1,578	3,978	1.18	28,073
Piauí	1,047	2,130	0.97	24,461
Ceará	2,707	5,271	1.83	39,727
Rio Grande do Norte	970	1,892	2.19	42,849
Paraíba	1,717	2,763	2.03	31,511
Pernambuco	3,396	6,125	2.68	54,930
Alagoas	1,095	1,975	1.83	44,808
Sergipe	644	1,136	1.77	46,825
Bahia	4,838	9,418	1.84	60,546
South	7,835	18,984	4.91	117,578
Paraná	2,113	7,616	5.47	101,178
Santa Catarina	1,563	3,614	3.67	114,399
Rio Grande do Sul	4,160	7,753	5.10	135,170
Southeast	22,549	51,511	6.87	152,768
Minas Gerais	7,840	13,343	3.17	89,605
Espírito Santo	915	2,015	3.38	91,891
Rio de Janeiro	4,667	11,248	9.60	152,024
São Paulo	9,128	24,904	8.99	191,872
Federal District	0	1,165	n.a.	211,060
Brazil	51,942	118,518	4.48	100,657

n.a. Not applicable.
a. Territory.
Source: Supplied by national accounts divisions of the Vargas Foundation and IBGE.

Table 4-3. Personal Income Distribution by Decile, 1960, 1970, and 1980
(percent)

Decile	1960	1970	1980
Bottom	1.17	1.11	1.08
Second	2.32	2.05	2.15
Third	3.43	2.97	2.85
Fourth	4.65	3.88	3.70
Fifth	6.15	4.90	4.39
Sixth	7.66	5.91	5.49
Seventh	9.41	7.37	7.21
Eighth	10.85	9.57	9.92
Ninth	14.69	14.45	15.40
Top	39.66	47.79	47.81
Top 5 percent	27.69	34.86	—
Top 1 percent	12.11	14.57	—
Gini coefficient	0.499	0.562	0.581

— Not available.
Source: For 1960 and 1970, Langoni (1973); 1980, Camargo (1981). Both sources use the demographic censuses, which give information on income before taxes and transfers.

way to go, as female participation is still much lower than in advanced capitalist countries.

A problem that arises with macroeconomic measures of inequality is the variation in price levels between regions. Thomas (1982) found that the average cost of food and nonfood items was two-thirds higher in Rio de Janeiro than in the cheapest region in 1974–75. There are also problems in comparisons over time because the adjustment of various kinds of income to inflation moves at different rates. People in business, whether they keep shops or shine shoes, can generally adjust their prices upward as inflation rises. But the bulk of Brazil's wage and salary earners had annual adjustments until November 1979 and semiannual adjustments (in May and October) thereafter. Their real income therefore zigzagged in discontinuous jumps. In extreme inflationary conditions, such as in 1984 or 1985, a semiannual adjustment could well result in a 100 percent increase in wages. Between these two extremes, there were other situations involving more frequent adjustment, for example, by people changing jobs, but the indexation jumps were a very powerful element. Generally, the PNAD household surveys were taken in November after the wage adjustment, but in 1982 the survey was spread over three months and included periods before the adjustment in which incomes were low. The results were so different from the previous November surveys that they were not published.

The complexity of these statistical problems is so great that Pfeffermann and Webb (1979) were skeptical about most of the basic facts put forward in the Fishlow–Langoni debate.

The Controversy over the Causes of Inequality

The controversy over the distribution of income has essentially been about the causes of increased inequality and their policy implications. Fishlow (1972a), one of the main protagonists, stressed the predominant role of government policy after 1964 in squeezing real wages. Langoni (1973), the other principal protagonist, ignored the wage squeeze but stressed nonpolicy Kuznetsian forces inherent in a situation of fast growth with a shortage of skilled and educated labor. There is no necessary conflict in the two viewpoints, each of which may be regarded as a partial explanation. But the strong political overtones of the debate inhibited a synthesis of the views, even though both protagonists were highly sophisticated economists presenting their arguments in a scholarly framework. Fishlow's argument was a critique of government wage policy that was echoed and developed by opponents of the military regime. Langoni's book can be interpreted as a defense of government policy; its forward was written by Delfim Netto, the ministerial

Table 4-4. Average Personal Income by Decile, 1960, 1970, and 1980
(1970 cruzeiros per month)

Decile	1960	1970	1980	Growth (percent) 1960–70	1970–80
Bottom	25	32	47	28.0	46.9
Second	48	58	94	20.8	62.1
Third	71	84	125	18.3	48.8
Fourth	86	110	162	14.6	47.3
Fifth	127	139	193	9.5	38.9
Sixth	158	168	241	6.3	43.5
Seventh	195	210	316	7.7	50.5
Eighth	225	272	434	20.9	59.6
Ninth	305	411	674	34.8	64.0
Top	815	1,360	2,095	66.9	54.0
Total	206	282	438	37.9	55.3

Source: Same as for table 4-3.

Table 4-5. Miscellaneous Social Indicators for Brazil, Selected Years, 1950–80

Indicator	1950	1960	1970	1980
Crude birth rate (births per thousand population)	44.4	43.5	40.8	33.8
Crude death rate (deaths per thousand population)	20.9	20.1	12.6	8.9
Life expectancy at birth (years)	44.5	51.6	53.5	60.1
Infant mortality rate (deaths per thousand births)	146.4	121.1	113.8	87.9
Literates as a percentage of population 15 years old and older	49.3	60.5	65.9	73.9
Percentage of households with				
Piped water	15.6	24.3	33.3	55.1
Sewerage connection	—	23.8	26.6	43.2
Electricity	24.6	38.5	47.6	68.5
Refrigerator	—	11.6	26.1	50.4
Radio	—	35.4	58.9	76.2
Television set	—	—	24.1	56.1
Owner-occupied house	52.1	57.1	60.3	61.7
Labor force as a percentage of population	33.4	32.6	31.9	36.3
Passenger cars per thousand population[a]	3.7	6.6	18.4	67.2

— Not available.

a. Figures are for 1951, 1963, 1972, and 1981.

Source: Appendix A; Morley (1982), Hoffman (1984); FIBGE, *Indicadores Sociais* (1984), vol. 2, and demographic censuses.

overlord of economic policy, who flatly rejected the relevance of inequality as a measure of welfare.

Both sides in the controversy stressed earned income, neglecting property income and wealth distribution, on which there is much less hard information. This is unfortunate because the share of property income in total income appears to be much higher in Brazil than in advanced capitalist countries. According to Langoni (1974) the property share was over 40 percent in the 1960s compared with about 25 percent in the United States. The national accounts give no information on this breakdown, but the industrial census shows that labor costs were a particularly low share of manufacturing value added in Brazil (about 30 percent in 1975 as against 45 percent in Mexico and 51 percent in the United States). The distributive controversy also failed to assess the impact of the tax-transfer system (which we cover below).

The Wage Squeeze

Over the period 1964–80 real GDP per capita in Brazil rose by 5.2 percent a year, but the minimum wage in real terms actually fell by 1 percent a year. Comparison of the two figures certainly suggests a severe wage squeeze.

Furthermore, there is no doubt that the military government in its initial "corrective" phase from 1964 to 1967 was trying to squeeze wages severely. The previous labor-oriented government of Goulart was overturned precisely because it was attempting to squeeze property income and was exacerbating inflation by promoting high nominal rates of increase in wages.

The military government inherited the power to set a "minimum wage," which had existed since 1940, and it attempted to widen its influence over wages by converting an existing system of voluntary wage guidelines, which was limited in coverage, to an obligatory system covering the whole urban formal sector. In addition it imposed fairly draconian settlements on its own employees (Morley 1982) and suppressed trade union activities, jailing or exiling militants. The military government imposed a system of forced saving as part of the social security system so that the squeeze on wages was greater than the squeeze on labor compensation. However, it seems likely that the effective squeeze on wages from 1964 to 1967 was the result primarily of three years of economic austerity in which the rate of economic growth was reduced to allow some reallocation of resources and to shift income away from labor and into profits. Thus in a climate of slacker demand, the phenomenon of "wage drift" (wage settlements beyond the guidelines) was less likely to occur.

During the period of the "economic miracle" from 1967 to 1973, the demand situation in labor markets changed completely, but wage controls remained rather light, and the indexation arrangements for wages continued to be based on the government's usual underestimate of expected inflation. From 1974 to 1980, wage policy was more liberal as the military regime was politically weaker.

Although the reality of the wage squeeze cannot be challenged, it is difficult to determine how large it was and what quantitative role it played in exacerbating inequality. Interpretation of wage statistics is much more difficult than interpretation of the admittedly shaky information on income distribution contained in the census. This is true in all countries, but especially so in a highly dynamic and segmented labor market. The urban population in Brazil was growing about 6 percent a year in 1964–80, and the urban labor supply may have grown faster. The economy was undergoing major structural change with the switch from agriculture to industry and services, and, within industry, from traditional to modern sectors. Labor turnover was high as people moved from the rural sector to the informal urban sector, then moved on to the formal sector. There is also a wide range of part-time work situations between complete unemployment and full-time activity.

Because this fluid labor situation was combined with an inflation rate that averaged 38 percent a year from 1964 to 1980 and varied from 18 percent to 95 percent from one year to another, it is very difficult to construct wage or earnings indexes for particular categories of workers, and to say what percent of the labor force they cover. Furthermore, it is not legitimate to compare the "minimum wage," which is determined by government fiat, with wage indexes that reflect conditions in the labor market.

The so-called minimum wage is not an effective floor on earnings but represents a threshold of respectability. It indicates that a worker has entered the modern urban sector. It was introduced as part of the populist labor legislation of the *estado novo*, and it still serves this theoretical purpose. Many people still work for less than the minimum wage, and the proportion changes over time. In 1960, 58 percent of the labor force earned less than the minimum wage whereas in 1981 only 28 percent did (see table A-8).

The minimum wage helped to provide a crude yardstick for coping with inflation. It played an important role in the indexation apparatus and was a useful reference point (for want of something better) even for people earning several times the minimum wage. Thus, the minimum wage had wide influence, but this does not mean that it is a good guide in assessing general wage movements, because of the phenomena of wage drift, regrading, promotion, job change, and so on.

One way of assessing changes in actual earnings is to look at the average wage per employee, which can be derived from industrial censuses. For 1970–80, when the minimum wage rose from 2,501 cruzeiros, on an annual basis, to 53,996 cruzeiros, the average earnings of industrial employees rose from 4,681 cruzeiros to 151,183 cruzeiros—thirty-two-fold as compared with twenty-two-fold for the minimum wage. In real terms, using the deflator for the Rio de Janeiro area, the rise in real earnings in industry was 57.3 percent compared with a rise of 5.2 percent in the minimum wage, 77.8 percent in GDP per capita, and 55.3 percent in GDP per employee.

The Langoni View

Langoni based his explanation of inequality in the distribution of income on human capital theory and the dualistic character of the labor market. In an economy with generally low and unequal levels of education, he argued, pay differentials by level of education had widened in the period of high demand and tight labor market conditions for the highly educated and skilled. On the other hand, rapid population growth had resulted in an elastic supply of unskilled labor, so that wage increases at the bottom end of the market were smaller. He argued that increased inequality was an inevitable concomitant of rapid growth in a developing country, in line with Kuznets's (1955) hypothesis that there is a U curve of increasing then decreasing inequality in the course of economic modernization.

Thus, for Langoni, increased inequality was a byproduct of success in raising the growth rate and was inevitable because the military regime had inherited a socioinstitutional situation characterized by rapid population growth and poor and unequal access to education.

It is clear that educational inequality plays a substantial role in Brazilian inequality, and in the transmission of poverty from one generation to the next. Langoni did assemble reasonable evidence that suggests that earning differentials by level of formal education widened in the period he covered.

Levels of education are low in Brazil. The average worker had only 1.8 years of education in 1950 and 3.9 years in 1980. The 1950 level was less than one-quarter and the 1980 level about one-third of that in Japan. Brazilian levels are below those in some other Latin American countries with lower income levels, such as Peru. They are no higher than those of Japan in the 1890s.

Nominal literacy rates indicate that about one-half of the population was literate in 1950 and about three-quarters in 1980, but these rates are based on the flimsy evidence of answers to questions in the population census. Functional literacy is usually attained after four years of completed formal education and by 1980 only 41 percent of the population had achieved this.

Because of the unusually wide spread in income levels between states and the fact that public funds for education largely reflect local income levels, school attendance varies widely in Brazil—perhaps more so than anywhere else in Latin America. In the poorer areas of the country, many children drop out of school before completing the first four years. Thus in Piauí, the poorest state, only 18 percent of the population had achieved the level of schooling required for functional literacy in 1980, whereas in São Paulo, the most prosperous state, 54 percent had. In Piauí, the bottom 62 percent of the adult population had had no education or less than one year, and in São Paulo the bottom 22 percent were in this condition. Thus even in the most prosperous parts of Brazil there is a wide spread in levels of education, much greater than the spread in advanced capitalist countries (table 4-6).

This inequality in educational opportunity, at all levels of education, is closely correlated with parental income. Thus the Brazilian middle class generally sends its children to private secondary schools of higher quality than state schools. A significant fraction of the cost can be deducted from income tax liability. These privileged children later occupy most of the places in state universities, which are heavily subsidized and of better quality than private universities.

There have been some remedial measures to improve post-formal education, notably the Serviço Nacional de Aprendizagem Industrial (National Service of Industrial Apprenticeship, or SENAI) and the Serviço Nacional de Aprendizagem Comercial (National Service of Commercial Apprenticeship, or SENAC), which were started in the 1940s to meet shortages of skilled labor. These training programs are similar in quality to German apprentice training and have facilitated the rapid expansion of industry. However, such programs and the Movimento Brasileiro de Alfabetização (Brazilian Campaign to Abolish Adult Illiteracy, or MOBRAL) cannot do more than partially redress the gaps in formal education, which is obviously one of the major roots of inequality. There has been some progress and the degree of inequality is less for younger than older people, but even for young people the situation is unsatisfactory. In Piauí, 33 percent of twenty-to-twenty-four-year-olds had completed four years of education or more in 1980, compared with 13 percent of fifty-to-fifty-nine-year-olds; in São Paulo the comparable figures were 79 percent and 42 percent. It is likely to take several decades before this kind of inequality can be removed.

Another basic feature, which Langoni does not adequately discuss, is the high fertility rate, particularly in the poorest families and regions. This accentuates the cycle of inequality and increases the dependency rate (table 4-7). For anyone who accepts the basic Coale and Hoover (1958) arguments, it seems that per capita income could have grown faster, and inequality and dualism would have been mitigated, if there

Table 4-6. Variation in Levels of Education between Persons in Brazil and Six Other Countries

Country	Year of survey	Gini coefficient[a]
Brazil	1970	0.60
Brazil	1980	0.50
Rural Northeast	1980	0.84
Urban Southeast	1980	0.37
France	1968	0.18
Germany, Fed. Rep. of	1970	0.14
Italy	1961	0.31
Japan	1970	0.15
United Kingdom	1961	0.08
United States	1970	0.17

a. Derived from figures on years of completed education.

Source: For Brazil, Denslow and Tyler (1983), p. 44; other countries from OECD (1975), pp. 41–42.

Table 4-7. Dependency Ratios in Four Countries, Selected Years, 1950–80

(ratios of relevant age group to population aged 15–64)

Category	1950	1960	1970	1980
Young dependents (under 15)				
Brazil	74.7	78.2	76.6	66.1
Mexico	80.6	89.5	93.6	86.4
Japan	59.5	47.1	34.7	35.0
United States	41.5	52.0	45.6	34.0
Old dependents (over 64)				
Brazil	4.4	5.0	5.7	6.9
Mexico	6.3	6.6	7.0	6.9
Japan	8.8	9.5	10.2	13.4
United States	12.5	15.5	15.8	17.1
Total dependents				
Brazil	79.1	83.2	82.3	73.0
Mexico	86.9	96.1	100.6	99.8
Japan	68.3	56.6	44.9	48.4
United States	54.0	67.5	61.4	51.1

Source: For Brazil and Mexico, appendixes A, B. For Japan and the United States, in 1950 and 1960, OECD (1979); in 1970 and 1980, OECD, *Labour Force Statistics*.

had been a government policy to foster access to birth control. In fact, policy has generally favored high birth rates or been indifferent on this issue, and the most that can be said for the military regime was that after 1974 it took a somewhat more permissive attitude toward birth control.

Between 1970 and 1980 there was a sharp reduction in fertility, which was part of a general Latin American trend and not strongly influenced by policy. This can be seen in table 4-8. There are wide regional differences, with fertility being lowest in the southeast, where in 1980 the average woman would have 3.45 children between the ages of fifteen and forty-nine, whereas in the impoverished Northeast, the expectation was for 6.45 children. Here again the situation points to a perpetuation of inequality.

Wage Spreads

One characteristic feature of developing countries is the wide spread between wages and the salaries of professional personnel who operate in a capitalist world economy that allows highly educated people to move freely in response to job opportunities. Many professional Brazilians who are fluent in English or other languages have the option of working abroad. In fact, most of them do not exercise this option be-

Table 4-8. Total Fertility Rates, Selected Years, 1950–80

Region	1950	1960	1970	1980
Brazil	6.21	6.28	5.76	4.35
Center West	6.80	6.71	6.42	4.51
North	7.80	8.33	8.15	6.45
Northeast	7.60	7.46	7.53	6.13
South	5.90	6.01	5.42	3.63
Southeast	5.70	5.83	4.56	3.45

Note: The total fertility rate is the sum of age-specific fertility rates for women between the ages of 15 and 49 (multiplied by the number of years to which each age-specific rate refers).
Source: FIBGE, *Anuario estatístico* (1984), p. 154.

cause both the private sector and the government sector often pay salaries equal to what a professional could earn abroad minus the cost of expatriation. Thus the spread between the salaries of the managerial and professional class and the wages of unskilled workers is a good deal wider than it would be in the United States.

It is sometimes suggested that the military regime followed salary policies within the public sector that increased these differentials. Unfortunately, there is no evidence on this, only the impression that the phenomenon is less marked than in Mexico.

Another general feature of earned income distribution, which was noted by Pareto ninety years ago, is the unusual tail of high managerial incomes. As top managers have many of the powers of owners, they are usually paid quasi-proprietorial or quasi-entrepreneurial incomes, so that they will run the enterprise as carefully as if they owned it. If, as seems likely, the military regime engineered an increased share for profits, it is possible that the higher managerial group followed suit in terms of earned income. Here too, the evidence is flimsy.

Ethnicity

In general, little attention is given in Brazil to ethnicity as a source of inequality. That is somewhat surprising in view of the historic importance of slavery and the marked absence of blacks in the higher-paid occupations. There are two main schools of thought on the problem of ethnicity. One, put forward by Gilberto Freyre (1959), argues that Brazilians are more or less color blind and that Brazil is a social continuum from poor to rich with no sharp segmentation. In particular he held that Brazil was different from the United States, mainly because the Portuguese had a Muslim-Arabic and not a Protestant civilization. The other viewpoint is represented by Florestan Fernandes (1969) who took a much more critical view of a Brazilian society that practices *de facto* but generally discreet discrimination.

There was a brief ethnic political movement in São Paulo in the 1930s, the Frente Negra Brasileiro, with a newspaper, *Voz da raça*. The movement became a political party in 1936 and was suppressed by Vargas in 1937, along with all political parties. This experiment has not been repeated and the Brazilian government has never pursued policies of positive discrimination.

Most of the evidence adduced by Freyre or Fernandes about contemporary effects of ethnicity on socioeconomic performance are anecdotal, but a recent official study shows that earnings of blacks were only 35 percent those of whites in 1976. Part of this was the result of differences in education level, which affected the kind of jobs blacks could obtain. However, the data on professional earnings in table 4-9 suggest that there may also have been substantial pay discrimination. Within the professional employment sphere, where few blacks had penetrated, their earnings were only 37 percent of white professionals.

It should be noted that there are differences in vocabulary on this ethnic issue in different countries. In U.S. parlance, "blacks" refers to a much wider group than in Brazil, because Brazilians distinguish between mulattos and blacks. Table 4-9 suggests that there is also discrimination against mulattos, but not against orientals (mainly Japanese in origin), who have a fair share of top jobs and average incomes that differ from those of whites in the same ratio as their educational qualifications.

Inequality of Property

Inequality of property, as in all countries, is bigger than inequality of income. This is particularly true of landed property. In colonial times, large areas of land were owned by slaveholders, and unlike Mexico, Brazil had no substantial landholdings by indigenous Indians. After the abolition of slavery, the immigration of Europeans and Japanese into the South and Southeast led to some development of small and medium landholdings there, but in the Northeast the colonial pattern prevailed.

In fact, Brazil is still very much a frontier country, whose crop area increased from 19 million hectares to 49 million hectares from 1950 to 1980 (compared with a decline in the United States). However, the new land has been allocated to large farmers and companies, so these new distributions by the state have not mitigated inequality. Settlement schemes connected with development of new areas have achieved little and agrarian reform has been a dead letter. The Gini coefficient for family landownership was 0.86 in 1980, and when the measure includes families without any land whose head of household works in agri-

Table 4-9. Ethnic Characteristics and Income of Employed Persons, 1976

Category	White	Oriental	Mulatto	Black
Percentage of employed persons	57.1	2.5	30.9	9.3
Percentage of professional employment	81.4	2.7	14.0	1.7
Average years of education	4.8	3.9	2.8	2.1
Average earnings (cruzeiros)	2,542	2,038	1,146	891
Average professional earnings (cruzeiros)	10,230	9,733	5,070	3,777

Source: Garcia de Oliveira, Porcaro, and Araujo (1985).

culture, it was 0.90. It seems that the current distribution is much the same as it was in the 1920s (Hoffman 1984).

As the proportion of the population working in agriculture has not fallen to 30 percent and agricultural land in 1980 was only 12.8 percent of tangible assets (Goldsmith 1986), land distribution does not have the predominant significance it once had as a source of inequality (table 4-10).

According to Goldsmith, structures represented 31.2 percent of tangible wealth in 1980, and it seems reasonable to assume that the housing stock accounted for somewhat over half of this. Owner-occupiers in Brazil were 52 percent of households in 1950 and 63 percent in 1983. Brazil's compulsory provident fund scheme, started in the mid-1960s,

Table 4-10. Distribution of Agricultural Landownership, 1950 and 1980

Size of property (hectares)	Percentage of holdings 1950	Percentage of holdings 1980	Percentage of area 1950	Percentage of area 1980	Average size of holding (hectares) 1950	Average size of holding (hectares) 1980
Less than 10	34.0	50.3	1.3	2.5	4.3	3.5
10–100	50.9	39.1	15.3	17.7	33.8	32.0
100–1,000	12.9	9.5	32.5	34.7	281.6	259.6
1,000 and more	2.2	1.1	50.9	45.1	3,619.7	3,439.7
Total	100.0	100.0	100.0	100.0	112.5	70.8

Source: IBGE, *Anuário estatístico* (1985).

permits withdrawals to finance housing and helps to promote a wider distribution of ownership.

Goldsmith shows a growing share of consumer durable goods in tangible wealth, with a share of 7.8 percent in 1980. It seems quite likely that this form of wealth has become more widespread over time, though it has undoubtedly been partially offset by the growth of associated consumer debt.

Most other tangible assets are used in the production process in the nonagricultural sector and their ownership is probably highly concentrated, though a significant part of productive assets belongs to government.

The overall Gini coefficient for wealth distribution for Brazil is not known, but it may well be higher than the 0.84 that prevailed in the United Kingdom in 1971, which was probably the highest in the advanced capitalist countries (Maddison 1984).

The wealth picture is more equal if future pension rights are considered as capital. Few people consider nonnegotiable rights in state pensions (or other social benefits) as part of their wealth, but it is undeniable that expansion of such rights adds to personal security and accounts for the fact that a bigger proportion of old people in Brazil can now retire.

The Impact of Taxes, Transfers, and Government Spending

Although the income tax has a progressive structure, the total effect of Brazilian taxes is highly regressive. A person earning $481 a year in 1975 paid 36 percent in taxes, and one earning $40,810 a year paid 14 percent.

The social transfer system mainly affects horizontal distribution between people at different ages or between the sick and well. The vertically redistributive (welfare) elements are rather small. Government help to agriculture in the form of subsidized credits has been large and regressive in its impact. Educational expenditure is probably regressive in its impact. Health expenditure probably has a progressive impact as the more prosperous contribute to the health budget but, broadly speaking, use private facilities. Most other current spending is difficult to apportion and is probably distributively neutral. Overall, it would seem that the tax transfer system has a regressive impact.

Social Mobility

Measures of intergenerational mobility are fraught with difficulty. They are nearly always confined to father–son comparisons, are made in terms of a small number of occupational categories, and have to cope with the problem that occupational structure is changing over time and that the birth dates of the fathers of any randomly selected group of sons in 1980 could range from the 1860s to the 1960s.

Nevertheless, sociologists have developed crude measures of mobility and made comparisons between countries. Pastore (1979, p. 122) compared Brazil in the mid-1970s with nine other countries and found that in Brazil mobility was higher than in European countries for most age groups, and particularly for younger age groups, whereas in Argentina mobility levels were well below European levels. For younger age groups (less than fifty years old), mobility was higher in Brazil than in the United States. Within Brazil intergenerational mobility was greater in São Paulo than in the Northeast. For the elite group, social mobility seems to have been relatively low. The Brazilian index of father–son occupational association in elite jobs was 8.5—that is, 8.5 times greater than could be expected on a random basis—whereas Miller (1960) had lower figures for most European countries and association indexes of 3.3 for Japan and the United States.

In terms of geography there has certainly been mobility in Brazil, with a rise in the urban population from 36 percent of the total in 1950 to 68 percent in 1980, and big movements from low- to high-income states. In 1970–80, for example, net migration from the Northeast was 5.6 million persons. Migration to the Southeast was over 3 million, and the movement to the frontier in the Center-West was 1.9 million (FIBGE, *Indicadores Sociais*, 1984, p. 25).

Poverty

The problem of alleviating poverty has not been a high priority of Brazilian governments either during the military period or earlier. Their major priority over the past four decades has been to maximize the overall growth rate. As a result there has been no official poverty guideline to serve as a measuring rod. The minimum wage did not have this function, as it was never intended to provide an income floor.

There have been several attempts to define poverty in Brazil according to standardized international criteria, and these measures differ according to the criteria chosen. Ahluwalia, Carter, and Chenery (1979) measured poverty in a standardized way by a crude measure of real income. They had some kind of distributive measure for thirty-six countries, they had the official GNP per capita figures at official exchange rates, and the Kravis, Heston, and Summers (1982) proxy for purchasing power parity, which they multiplied together to get a standardized international comparison. They defined the poor as those who fell below the 46th percentile in India. By this method they found that 15 percent of Brazilians were poor and 14 percent of Mexicans compared with a 38 percent average in thirty-six developing countries in 1975.

In a later standardized estimate also published by the World Bank Altimir (1982) estimated that 49 percent of Brazilians were in poverty and 34 percent of Mexicans compared with a Latin American average of 40 percent in 1970. In the same year, another World Bank study (Thomas 1982) suggested that on his "middle" definition of poverty, 29 percent of Brazilians were poor in 1974–75. This study was based on the U.S. method (of Orshansky) of calculating the cost of a minimum food basket and doubling this amount to establish the poverty line. Account was taken of regional price differences, so that the lowest regional poverty line was 74 percent of that in the most expensive area. The incidence of poverty on the Thomas measure varied from 54 percent in the poorest region to 11 percent in the richest.

In 1983, another World Bank study, by Hicks and Vetter (1983), dealt with urban areas only. Its middle estimate for 1980 showed 34 percent in poverty, with a regional variance of 27–49 percent, much lower than Thomas's.

None of these four studies tried to estimate the change in the incidence of poverty over time. There has, in fact, been surprisingly little effort of this kind. Fields (1977), using the minimum wage in the Northeast as the poverty line for a family of 4.3 people as a criterion, estimated that 37 percent of the population was poor in 1960, with a small reduction to 35.5 percent in 1970.

Table 4-11 gives a rough indication of the proportion of families falling below a constant real poverty line from 1960 to 1980. It is based on a family income of 3.3 new cruzeiros at 1960 prices (about half of the highest regional minimum wage level of that time), using the GDP deflator for annual adjustments. On this basis it appears that the proportion of families in poverty hardly budged from 1960 to 1970 but fell appreciably from 1970 to 1980—from 38 percent to 22 percent of the population. These rough findings are in line with the generally accepted facts on Brazilian income distribution.

Table 4-11. Number of Families below the Poverty Line, 1960, 1970, and 1980

Measure	1960	1970	1980
Poverty line (current new cruzeiros)	3.30	150.00	4,153.50
Deflator	1.00	45.46	1,258.64
Poverty line in 1960 prices (new cruzeiros)	3.30	3.30	3.30
Number of families (millions)	5.27	7.04	5.83
Percentage of families below poverty line	38.90	37.90	21.70

Source: Unpublished estimates by A. V. Villela and Associates.

The Distributive Impact of Social Welfare Programs

The first initiative for creating a modern social security system came in 1923 with the Eloy Chaves Law that provided pension funds for railway employees. This system, which functioned at the company level, was administered jointly by employees and employers without governmental participation. During the 1920s and 1930s it was adopted by enterprises in other sectors, so that by 1937 there were 183 such funds in operation.

The Social Security System

The growing social and political influence of the urban working class prompted the creation of the Ministry of Labor in the 1930s. The structure of the social security system was fundamentally altered. Though some enterprises continued to maintain funds, the social security system began to be structured around institutes that provided assistance to workers by professional category. The new system, organized between 1933 and 1953, grouped funds into *institutos* at the national level under state supervision. Though this system guaranteed coverage for most urban workers in the formal sector, it was essentially nonredistributive. Benefits were based on previous earnings.

In 1966 the Instituto Nacional da Previdencia Social (National Institute of Social Security, or INPS) was created by consolidating the six existing *institutos*.[1] It broadened the insurance base to cover employers and self-employed workers, permitted a rationalization of services rendered, and reduced administrative costs. In 1971 rural employees were added, and in 1972 domestic employees. In 1974, rural employers and their dependents were included in the INPS system. In 1974 a minimum monthly income—half the minimum wage—was granted to persons seventy years old and older, as well as to the handicapped, who had previously been outside of the system.

In 1930 only 157,000 workers were covered by the system. In 1940, 2 million persons (14 percent of the labor force) were insured, and the number grew to 25 million (50 percent of the labor force) in 1984.

Insured persons are eligible for benefits while they are working since the system provides sickness pay and medical assistance for the worker and his dependents during his active life and after retirement (or death). The retired are divided into three categories: women at least sixty years old and men at least sixty-five years old who have contributed to the system for at least five years, and those over seventy years old who have not contributed but have no other source of income; any woman who has worked thirty years and any man who has worked thirty-five years; and the handicapped, both those who have contributed to the system and those outside the system who have no other source of income.

The current organization of the system is the result of two initiatives in the 1970s. In 1974, Social Security became an independent ministry, separated from the Ministry of Labor. In 1977 the Sistema Nacional de Presidencia e Assistencia (National System for Security and Social Assistance, or SINPAS) was created. Its functions are divided among five agencies.

The INPS is one of the SINPAS agencies. It is in charge of collecting contributions from the working population and distributing benefits; in each period receipts are used for the payment of benefits in the same period—that is, without capitalization of resources. Originally the social security system was conceived as a capitalization scheme, with contributions paid today capitalized for future benefits. The capitalization gradually evolved into a distributive system; no clear decision was made to do this nor was there a precise date for implementation of the change.

The Instituto Nacional de Assistencia Médica da Previdencia Social (National Institute of Medical Assistance, or INAMPS) guarantees medical assistance in urban and rural areas both directly and through contracted services from private institutions. The Legiao Brasileira de Assistencia (Brazilian Assistance Corps, or LBA) gives direct aid to the most deprived segments of the population, regardless of whether they contribute to the social security system. The Fundacão Nacional do Bem-Estar do Menor (National Foundation for the Welfare of Minors, or FUNABEM) protects deprived and abandoned youngsters. And the Instituto de Administração Financeira da Previdencia e Assistencia Social (Institute for Financial Administration, or LAPAS) is in charge of the financial management of the entire system.

The five agencies differ drastically in the funds they expend. Between 1971 and 1983 the INPS disbursed 67 percent of social security funds and INAMPS 27 percent. The LBA and the FUNABEM accounted for only 0.8 percent and 0.3 percent, respectively, of total expenditure.

Although expenditure by the latter two agencies, which are dedicated specifically to social assistance, is low by any standard, some of their activities are handled by INPS and INAMPS, which, respectively, make money transfers and provide medical assistance to especially needy groups (elderly and disabled). A substantial part of social assistance has traditionally been in private hands, outside the social security system. Religious institutions, especially the Catholic church, play an important role in collecting contributions—which are deductible for income tax purposes—for social assistance.

Some benefits that contribute to social welfare are paid by employers, such as the Fundo de Garantia por Tempo de Serviço (FGTS). The FGTS was created in 1966 to compensate employees for the abolition of the legal guarantee of job security. Employers credit monthly to each employee's account in the fund the equivalent of 8.0 percent of the wage paid. The individual accounts in the fund are in fact a forced saving mechanism; beneficiaries can only call on the capitalized value (which includes interest and monetary correction) in special cases, such as unemployment, permanent disability, purchase of housing, and marriage. The employee receives the capital sum in his account when he retires.

Social security has become a distributive system in which present contributions are supposed to cover present benefits. In fact, although receipts have represented by far the most important source of funds (88 percent on average between 1971 and 1983), the federal government has traditionally supplemented the system (an annual average of 7.6 percent in the same period) to compensate for unforeseen commitments. For example, federal government contributions were as low as 4.9 percent in 1979 but expanded to 9.5 percent in 1981 and 9.7 percent in 1982 to compensate for the large operations deficits in those years. The federal government's share in revenues is less than the tripartite model—government, employees, and employers—envisaged when the system was created.

Until 1982 employees and employers each contributed 8.0 percent, or a total of 16.0 percent, of urban wages. Self-employed persons and employers paid 16 percent of reported income. The growing deficit led the government to increase the amount of higher paid workers' contributions. The higher the wages, the larger the proportional contribution. The employer's share was increased to 10 percent. Both contributions and retirement and pension payments are limited to a maximum of twenty times the minimum wages. In the rural sector, contributions are mainly derived from a 2.5 percent levy on sales of rural products. The third component of receipts is marginal; it is derived from fines, financial gains, rents received, and so forth.

Receipts grew steadily during the 1970s, especially in the first years of the decade when rural employees and employers as well as domestic

Table 4-12. Social Security Contributors and Value of Receipts, Selected Years, 1971–83

Years	Contributions (billions of 1982 cruzeiros)	Contributors (thousands)	Per capita payments (1982 cruzeiros)
1971	693.8	9,680	71,669
1975	1,520.6	16,347	93,019
1980	2,291.9	23,782	96,371
1983	2,900.7	25,063	115,736

Source: SINPAS.

Table 4-13. Social Security Expenditure, Selected Years, 1971–83
(billions of 1982 cruzeiros)

Year	Total expenditures	Cash benefits
1971	915.2	557.6
1975	1,858.9	1,003.8
1980	2,799.5	1,777.5
1983	2,633.7	1,888.0

Source: Oliveira and others (1985), pp. 19–23; Montoro and Porto (1982), p. 160.

workers were brought into the system (table 4-12). From 1972 to 1979 the average real annual percentage increase was 16.0 percent, substantially higher than that of GDP, which increased very satisfactorily in the same period (8.4 percent annually). The good performance of receipts was partly due to the enlargement of the system, since the number of contributors almost doubled between 1971 and 1976. But average per capita payments also increased, from $72,000 cruzeiros in 1971 to $94,000 cruzeiros in 1976 and $119,000 cruzeiros at 1982 constant prices.

The rapid increase of receipts was followed very closely by the growth of expenditures (table 4-13). At constant prices, total expenditures went up by an annual average of 8.5 percent between 1971 and 1983.

The INPS in 1971 accounted for 66.0 percent of total social security expenditures. Its share grew to 74.0 percent in 1983, at the expense of the INAMPS (28 percent in 1971 and 22 percent in 1983).

The structure of the system and the growth in benefits are largely responsible for the increase in the expenditures of the INPS. With the

Table 4-14. Life Expectancy at Birth, by Region, Selected Years, 1950–80

Region	1950	1960	1970	1980
Brazil	45.5	51.6	53.5	60.1
Center West	51.2	56.9	58.9	63.9
Northern	44.9	53.6	54.7	63.6
Northe ast	39.0	41.1	45.6	51.0
South	53.5	60.4	60.7	67.2
Southeast	49.1	56.8	57.4	64.4

Source: FIBGE, Indicadores socials (1984), vol. 2, p. 213.

increase in life expectancy (table 4-14), periods of benefit grew correspondingly longer. The concession of benefits to those who have not contributed to the system (table 4-15) also raised the level of INPS expenditures, as did the progressive increase in the average value of benefits.

There has been widespread dissatisfaction concerning benefits. The LBA and the FUNABEM are chronically short of resources to meet the needs of their potential beneficiaries in a poor country characterized by severe inequality of income. But since neither of those agencies' beneficiaries have the means to express their dissatisfaction, it was against INAMPS- that the most vocal attacks were raised.

The medical assistance program has been plagued by shortages of hospital beds, material, equipment, and personnel. Thus INAMPS has turned to private clinics to complement the service it provides, but the contracting of services has led to rampant fraud and abuse. A great

Table 4-15. **Number of Social Security Beneficiaries in Various Categories, 1975 and 1983**

	Urban		Rural	
Category	1975	1983	1975	1983
Retirees who have reached retirement age	153,206	422,586	1,128,838	1,746,861
Retirees who have completed length of service retirement	384,025	897,867	0	0
People who have completed length of service requirement but continue to work	114,078	120,608	0	0
People who have had unhealthy or dangerous jobs	48,554	141,280	0	0
Handicapped benefits for retirees	705,455	1,359,948	80,975	409,464
Pensions	874,192	1,699,9 16	153,117	670,491
Sickness benefits	610,051	861,158	0	0
Work injury benefits	34,280	115,528	0	1,145
Partial incapacity benefits	0	56,369	0	0
Welfare payments for handicap	99,828	497,576	114,218	187,154
Welfare pensions for persons over 70	165,793	441,642	0	237,348
Total	3,189,462	6,558,109	1,477,148	3,252,463

Source: INPS.

many insured persons at lower income levels, who depend exclusively on the system for health assistance, have to endure long waiting lines and very poor services. Those insured persons who are better off generally resort to private physicians and clinics—often with the help of a private health insurance plan. In this sense, they pay for but do not use the services of the social security health assistance program.

The economic slump in the first years of the 1980s generated new demands on the system. Workers who lost their jobs resented the absence of unemployment benefits. While expenditures were growing at a much faster pace, reduction in the level of economic activity limited the growth of receipts.

Since the disequilibrium between receipts and expenditure, which had structural causes (a small deficit occurred in 1979 when GDP was still growing at an 8 percent annual rate), was aggravated by the economic crisis, a reform was conceived to boost contributions. At the end of 1981, under Law 6950, the wage ceiling used as the basis for assessment of monthly contributions was raised from ten to twenty times the minimum wage. Soon after, at the beginning of 1982, new rates were defined for contributions according to wage class.

It has been argued that the increased cost of contributions, to be paid by employers, places an excessive burden on the productive sector, creating new expenses for the use of labor, the most abundant productive factor in the economy. In fact, wage costs had already been affected by indirect benefits to workers collected by the employer, like the Fundo de Garantia por Tempo de Servico, FGTS. The expense of all these programs for the employer was the equivalent of about 40 percent of the wage paid, as shown in table 4-16.

Education

Public education in Brazil is highly decentralized, but tax revenues are concentrated on central government (see de Mello e Souza 1979). Primary and secondary education are the responsibility of state and municipal governments, whose tax revenue is not sufficient to cover their cost. University education, the central government's responsibility, is in a privileged position.

Since 1824, primary education (four years) has theoretically been free, and since 1934 it has also been compulsory. In 1967, the first eight years were made compulsory, but resources to meet these constitutionally prescribed objectives have not been available.

Funds are earmarked for education from five sources—constitutional provisions indirectly mandate certain revenues to education; states and municipalities, until recently, dedicated part of the participation funds, a compulsory transfer from the central government, to education; part of the net proceeds of lotteries is designated for education; private

Table 4-16. Social Charges as a Percentage Addition to Wage Costs

Benefit	Percent
IAPAS	10.0
SESI or SESC	1.5
SENAI or SENAC	1.0
INCRA	0.2
IAPAS (referring to the 13th wage)	0.6
Family allowance paid to IAPAS	4.0
Maternity benefit paid to IAPAS	0.3
FUNRURAL	2.4
FGTS	8.0
Fund for dismissal	0.8
13th wage (monthly prorata)	8.3
Insurance	3.0
Education wage	2.5
Total	42.6

Source: *Conjuntura* (April 1980, vol. 34, no. 4, pp. 73–76).

and certain funds from credit sources are earmarked to programs for educational infrastructure or for educational credit.

After 1970 firms were allowed to allocate up to 2 percent of their income tax to MOBRAL, the Campaign to Abolish Adult Illiteracy. However, as a result of poor performance, the agency was virtually abolished in 1985.

Two other important sources of funds for education are the taxes levied on the payroll of firms since 1942 to finance vocational training in industry through SENAI and in commerce through SENAC. This levy varies from 1 percent to 1.2 percent of the payroll of firms.

The activities of SENAI are carried out in more than three hundred training centers and in on-the-job training arrangements. One characteristic of its organization and management is its high degree of decentralization, which, together with its wide geographical coverage, explains why its courses differ in content, method, duration, and standards. Nevertheless, SENAI's courses enjoy a high reputation for their quality. A few Latin American countries like Colombia and Venezuela have imitated this vocational training system pioneered by Brazil.

Another important source of funds is the so-called education wage that was established in 1965. Firms that do not provide free first-level education to their employees or their employees' children have to pay this levy, which was initially 1.4 percent of the payroll and was increased to 2.5 percent in 1975. Two-thirds of the proceeds of the education wage goes to the states and the rest to the central government.

Earmarking is hardly necessary in the richer regions and in the poorer ones it is ineffective. Rules change so frequently that the future availability of resources is always in doubt. There is no assurance that the volume of loans to meet each year's educational needs can be maintained, for the decisions depend on the monetary authorities. However, earmarked resources from the education wage and lotteries have provided some element of stability in the flow of resources.

Expenditure per capita of the school-age population group almost doubled between 1960 and 1970 and more than doubled between 1970 and 1980. Total expenditure on education increased 736 percent in real terms from 1960 to 1982, in contrast with an increase in public budgetary expenditures of 429 percent. This raised education's share of total government spending from 10.2 percent in 1960 to 16.2 percent in 1982.

Table 4-17 indicates that the fraction of school-age population actually enrolled in school has been increasing steadily since 1960 and that public education has accounted for about 80 percent of total education.

Private secondary education, which in 1960 was more important than public, has lost ground relatively. The number of students in private secondary schools grew 112 percent between 1960 and 1970 while that in public schools grew more than 500 percent. Public university education lost ground to private between 1960 and 1980, the former showing a growth of 846 percent in the number of students, the latter more than 1,800 percent. Growth in higher education as a whole was much faster than that in primary and secondary education.

The student–staff ratio of 7.5 to 1 in 1980 for public university education in contrast with over 17 to 1 for private universities corroborates the well-known higher quality of the former. With a few exceptions, private university education became a profitable business without a commitment to quality.

Table 4-17. School-Age Population and Enrollment, 1960, 1970, and 1980

Item	1960	1970[a]	1980
Enrollment (thousands)			
Public schools	6,083	13,552	18,421
Private schools	1,560	2,942	4,629
Total	7,643	16,494	23,050
School-age population (thousands)	32,099	43,858	54,126
Total enrollment as share of school-age population (present)	23.8	37.6	42.6

a. Breakdown of higher education by private and public schools was estimated.
Source: FIBGE, Annuário estatístico; data supplied by Ministry of Education.

Statistics on the number of persons ten years old and older by level of education reveal that in 1980 the Northeast with 29.2 percent of total population, accounted, respectively, for 15.4 percent, 16.2 percent, and 17.3 percent of the number of Brazilians who had completed primary, basic, and middle education; the Southeast, with 43.4 percent of total population, accounted, respectively, for 54.2 percent, 55.9 percent, and 58.3 percent. In 1980 the Northeast, with 29.2 percent, and the Southeast, with 43.4 percent of total population, accounted, respectively, for 14.8 percent and 61.0 percent of people who had completed seventeen years or more of education.

Health

Public expenditure on health has been characterized by a growing emphasis on curative and a corresponding decline in preventive medicine (table 4-18). In the past, public expenditure was concentrated on control and eradication of communicable diseases like yellow fever, malaria, smallpox, Chagas's disease, tuberculosis, and leprosy. Resources were limited and health conditions were so poor that inoculation and educational programs, at relatively low costs, yielded satisfactory results.

With the unification of the several existing social security services and the creation of INPS there was a great increase in financial resources available. Since most of the insured population is urban, the type of medical assistance provided by the INPS is predominantly curative.

Public health services in Brazil are offered by INAMPS, by the Ministry of Health, and by the health secretariats of the states and of some municipalities. The INAMPS and the Ministry of Health operate autonomously, the former concentrating on the more developed and more

Table 4-18. Distribution of Public Expenditures on Health Services, Selected Years, 1949–82
(percent)

Year	Medical or hospital attention (curative services)	Primary attention (preventive services)
1949	12.9	87.1
1965	35.8	64.1
1975	70.2	29.7
1982	84.6	15.4

Source: Brazil, IPEA/IPLAW (1984), p. 14.

urbanized regions of the country, and the latter acting mainly in the least developed regions through preventive public health campaigns against endemic diseases and through medical-sanitary services. The Ministry of Health gives technical and financial support to state and municipal health secretariats.

A principal element of the INAMPS program is the coverage of medical and hospital services performed by accredited private hospitals. In 1981, health service contracts with the private sector accounted for 55.7 percent of INAMPS expenditure. Health services performed by INAMPS itself accounted for 18.5 percent, another 18.7 percent was spent on health through agreements with other government agencies and philanthropic entities, and the remaining 7.1 percent was spent on activities not related to health. In 1982 expenditure on public health was equivalent to about 2.5 percent of GDP. In real terms, public expenditure on health increased substantially at the beginning of the 1970s and leveled off thereafter. Per capita expenditures went from $23.52 in 1970 to $58.53 in 1980 and then declined to $54.76 in 1982.

The number of hospitals increased from 2,547 in 1960 to 6,680 in 1983, with the greatest growth in the number of public hospitals. Private hospitals, however, still constitute the majority (78 percent in 1983).

Para-hospital facilities—clinics, health units, and other facilities that perform medical services for outpatients only—grew enormously (more than eight times) between 1960 and 1983. Among them stand out public health units that spread out on the periphery of large cities and in most of the municipalities.

The number of people engaged in medical and hospital activities increased apace with the expansion of the physical infrastructure. One beneficial result of this was a decline in the ratio of inhabitants to hospital beds.

The effects of public expenditure on health cannot be directly measured by indicators of better health because those indicators are also influenced by improvements in income levels, education, and sanitary conditions. Whatever the causes, health conditions have improved significantly.

Housing

In contrast with other social sectors like education and health, the government spends little directly on housing. In 1983 the central government allocated only 0.2 percent of its budgetary expenditure to housing and urbanization, the states 1 percent. Municipalities spent 19 percent, but most of this went to urbanization and very little to housing.

State housing action is principally through the state financial institutions' financing of the purchase and construction of dwellings and through the provision of streets, electricity, sanitation, and water supply to facilitate the construction of new houses.

Practically all house financing is done through financial agencies under the control of the Banco Nacional de Habitação (National Housing Bank, or BNH). Together these BNH and public and private financial agencies constitute the Sistema Financeira da Habitação (Housing Financial System, or SFH). The source of the funds for the BNH and the other members of the SFH are the obligatory accumulations of employees' funds in the FGTS and passbook savings deposits. Together these are very large. All employees have individualized accounts in the FGTS, which they may use to finance purchase of their houses through payments to the SFH. Or they may use passbook savings accounts, which are guaranteed by the government and earn interest at the rate of 6 percent a year plus a correction for inflation.

The BNH became very important to the housing sector both through its direct action in housing and sanitation and as the executive agency for housing policy. It operated like a central bank for the Housing Financial System through its regulatory and supervisory action. It plays a relatively small role as lender since it channels most of its applications through other agencies. Even its direct loans are made through building societies or state housing cooperatives, and never to individuals as with other agencies.

The importance of the housing loans granted by state agencies is shown in table 4-19. Government institutions increased their share of loans from less than half of the total placed in 1974 to nearly two-thirds in 1984.

The Fiscal Structure and Its Distributive Impact

The Brazilian tax system is highly regressive and makes income more unequal after than before tax. Table 4-20 shows how the revenue struc-

Table 4-19. Outstanding Loans of the Housing Financial System, by Government and Private Institutions, 1974 and 1984

	1974		1984	
Institutions	Millions of cruzeiros	Percentage of total	Millions of cruzeiros	Percentage of total
Private	34,192	52.2	27,110,686	35.6
Government	31,262	47.8	49,110,630	64.4
Total	65,454	100.0	76,221,316	100.0

Source: *Boletim do Banco Central,* April 1983 and March 1986.

Table 4-20. Categories of General Government Revenue, Total Expenditure, and Overall Balance, 1970, 1982, and 1984

Category	1970 Millions of cruzeiros	1970 Percent of GDP at market prices	1982 Billions of cruzeiros	1982 Percent of GDP at market prices	1984 Billions of cruzeiros	1984 Percent of GDP at market prices
Indirect taxes	32,532	16.7	6,355	13.2	40,257	10.4
Direct taxes	5,900	3.0	1,902	4.0	17,217	4.4
Social security contributions	7,700	4.0	2,947	6.1	17,081	4.4
Provident fund contributions	2,500	1.3	1,229	2.6	6,977	1.8
Other direct levies	1,800	0.9	339	0.7	2,714	0.7
Other net income	2,139	1.1	−647	−1.3	−2,821	−0.7
Total revenue	52,617	27.1	12,125	25.2	81,425	21.0
Total current and capital expenditure	50,588	26.0	13,499	28.1	99,687	25.7
Overall balance	2,029	1.0	−1,374	−2.9	−18,262	−4.7

Source: Data supplied by FIBGE and Center for Fiscal Studies, Fundação Getúlio Vargas.

ture changed from 1970 to 1984. The system is striking for the modest proportion of direct taxation, the heavy reliance on indirect taxes, and the existence of social security levies that do not affect incomes beyond a certain level. The only element of taxation whose impact is significantly progressive is the personal income tax, but this is offset by the very regressive nature of other taxes.

In theory, income tax rises to 47 percent for the highest income group, but the top group (with disposable income more than one hundred times the minimum wage) actually paid only 5 percent of total disposable income (table 4-21).

In 1980, total gross income reported on tax returns was 3,246 billion cruzeiros, while nontaxable declared income reached 1,514 billion cruzeiros. Nondeclared income far exceeds income subject to taxation, partly because of evasion but also because the largest part of gains from the stock exchange and from agricultural activity is not taxable. Because income falls into four categories—declared taxable, declared nontaxable, nondeclared taxable, and nondeclared nontaxable—the real progressivity of income tax is much smaller than the theoretical.

The best study on tax incidence, in 1975, was done by Ibrahim Eris, who examined taxes at the federal level, income tax, all indirect taxes, and taxes (and transfers) for social security, and at the state level, the tax on the circulation of goods; municipal taxes were not included (Eris and

Table 4-21. Incidence of Major Taxes, by Level of Disposable Income, 1975
(percent)

Income as multiple of minimum wage	Income tax Individual	Income tax Corporate	Tax on goods (median rates) Industrial products	Tax on goods (median rates) Turnover	Social security tax	Total
Less than 1	0.00	5.0	5.4	18.2	8.7	37.3
1–2	0.00	4.5	5.2	14.6	7.8	32.1
2–5	0.00	4.0	4.5	11.9	3.9	24.3
5–10	0.00	3.8	4.5	10.0	4.4	22.7
10–15	0.27	3.6	4.1	8.5	4.3	20.8
15–20	1.06	3.4	3.8	7.7	4.3	20.3
20–30	1.96	3.2	3.6	7.1	4.3	20.2
30–40	3.58	3.0	3.1	6.4	4.0	20.1
40–50	4.71	2.7	2.7	5.7	3.7	19.5
50–75	5.09	2.5	2.5	5.3	3.4	18.8
75–100	5.77	2.1	2.1	4.5	3.1	17.6
More than 100	4.96	1.4	1.4	3.1	2.1	13.0

Source: Eris and others (1983).

others 1983). To estimate the incidence of indirect taxes, Eris used the National Study on Family Expenditures (ENDEF) of the Fundacão Instituto Brasileiro de Geografia e Estatística (Brazilian Institute of Geography and Statistics Foundation, FIBGE), from the Survey on Household Budgets of the University of São Paulo, and the 1970 input-output table of FIBGE (adjusted to a 1975 basis). He made several hypotheses on the transfer of taxes, which implied six alternatives for the simulated model. The most reasonable alternative assumed that taxes on total income are not transferred, taxes on profits are transferred, and taxes on wages and salaries and on sales are transferred. For social security, he used the net impact of contributions and benefits.

The study is a short-term static analysis, where implicitly the level of income of the economy is assumed to be given. Eris attempted to evaluate how the distribution of this income, among families, was influenced by the existence of taxes. He captured this influence by comparing two states of the economy—the observed state or the status quo (where all taxes are present), and the counterfactual situation that would arise in the absence of the taxes under study.

Table 4-21, summarizing Eris's findings, shows the obvious regressiveness of the system. The class that earns less than one minimum wage per month paid 37 percent of its disposable income, whereas the richest

Table 4-22. Categories of General Government Current and Capital Expenditure, 1970, 1982, and 1984

	1970 Millions of cruzeiros	1970 Percent of GDP at market prices	1982 Billions of cruzeiros	1982 Percent of GDP at market prices	1984 Billions of cruzeiros	1984 Percent of GDP at market prices
Personnel	16,117	8.3	3,563	7.4	21,832	5.6
Other current goods and services	5,889	3.0	1,494	3.1	10,155	2.6
Total current goods and services	22,006	11.3	5,057	10.5	31,987	8.2
Subsidies	1,497	0.8	1,254	2.6	6,147	1.6
Social security	8,400	4.3	2,612	5.4	16,832	4.3
Provident fund withdrawals	1,000	0.5	692	1.4	5,845	1.5
Public debt interest and monetary correction	2,500	1.3	1,667	3.5	24,247	6.3
Other transfers[a]	6,600	3.4	1,031	2.1	7,300	1.9
Total current expenditure	42,000	21.6	12,312	25.6	92,357	23.8
Total capital expenditure	8,588	4.4	1,187	2.5	7,330	1.9
Functional breakdown						
Education	5,529	2.8	1,589	3.3	—	—
Health (including some transfers)	4,168	2.1	1,247	2.6	—	—
Army, navy, and air force budgets	5,172	2.7	533	1.1	—	—

— Not available.

Note: General government refers to consolidated government spending at federal, state, and local level, excluding expenditure of public enterprises.

a. Includes credit subsidies.

Source: For broad categories, FIBGE; transfers supplied by Center for Fiscal Studies, Fundação Getúlio Vargas; for functional categories, unpublished estimates by A. Villela and Associates.

class, with a monthly income more than one hundred times the minimum wage, paid only 13 percent. Those who earned less than two minimum wages per month had a tax burden above the median. All other tax groups had a smaller burden.

The regressivity of taxation is offset only to a mild degree by the expenditure of government (summarized in table 4-22).

Note

1. The Instituto de Aposentadoria e Pensoes dos Maritimos (IAPM) was created in 1933, the Instituto de Aposentadoria e Pensoes dos Comerciários (IAPC) in 1934, the Instituto de Aposentadoria e Pensoes dos Bancários (IAPB) in 1934, the Instituto de Aposentadoria e Pensoes dos Industriários (IAPI) in 1936, the Instituto de Aposentadoria e Pensoes dos Empregados de Transportes e Cargas (IAPETC) in 1938, and the Instituto de Aposentadoria e Pensoes dos Ferroviários e Empregados em Servicos Públicos (IAPFESP) in 1953.

III Mexico

5 The Mexican Polity, Institutions, and Policy

The colonial experience in Mexico lasted 300 years. The main economic goal of the Spanish crown was to extract a fiscal surplus for transfer to Spain. Within Mexico the spoils of office were largely reserved for bureaucrats and clergy named to their offices by the Spanish authorities. Economic policy was closely regulated, particularly with regard to foreign trade. Social discipline was enforced inexpensively with the help of the religious orders and the Inquisition. The indigenous population was repressed economically, had the legal status of children, and remained psychologically in a state of depressive anomie.

In the first fifty years of Mexico's independence, half of its territory was seized by the United States, and the country suffered from U.S. and French invasions. Internal law and order broke down, church lands were seized by government and sold to large landowners, and there was virtually no economic progress.

Under the thirty-four-year dictatorship of Porfirio Diaz, 1877–1911, internal and external security was restored, railways were built, and the country's natural resources were exploited through foreign trade. However the government was administered by social Darwinists interested in modernization and so indifferent to popular welfare that the Indians' land rights were further alienated.

Interests, Ideology, and the Exercise of Power

The Mexican revolution of 1910–20 was unlike any other in Latin America. It was an inchoate outburst against the institutional heritage of colonialism and the Porfiriato. Initially it had no clear ideology, organization, or dominant leadership. In the 1920s and 1930s its nature began to be defined under the influence of two very strong presidents. Plutarco Elias Calles and Lázaro Cárdenas (table 5-1). Calles built a new party—Partido Nacional Revolucionario, or PNR—and a strong state. Cárdenas gave the party a leftist ideology, which involved land reform; state control of natural resources, banking, and insurance; the creation

Table 5-1. Presidents of Mexico, Percentage of the Population That Voted for Them, and Percentage of Poll They Obtained, 1920–88

Term	President	Vote (percent)	Poll (percent)
1920–24	Alvaro Obregón	7.9	95.8
1924–28	Plutarco Elias Calles	8.9	84.1
1928	Alvaro Obregón[a]	10.4	100.0
1928–30	Emilio Portes Gil[b]	0.0	0.0
1930–32	Pascual Ortiz Rubio[c]	12.0	93.6
1932–34	Abelardo Rodriguez[b]	0.0	0.0
1934–40	Lázaro Cárdenas	12.5	98.2
1940–46	Manuel Avila Camacho	12.6	93.8
1946–52	Miguel Alemán	7.5	77.9
1952–58	Adolfo Ruiz Cortines	9.4	74.3
1958–64	Adolfo López Mateos	19.5	90.4
1964–70	Gustavo Díaz Ordaz	20.0	88.8
1970–76	Luis Echeverría	23.4	86.0
1976–82	Joeé López Portillo	24.9	92.3
1982–88	Miguel de la Madrid	22.1	71.6
1988–	Carlos Salinas de Gortari	11.6	50.4

a. Assassinated before taking office.
b. Interim.
c. Resigned.
Source: Mexico, INEGI (1985a) and (for 1988) newspaper reports.

of a strong labor wing in the party; default on foreign debt; nationalization of foreign assets; and an independent foreign policy. With this ideology and a party organization with a solid power base of peasants, workers, and the new technocratic elite, Cárdenas greatly strengthened the legitimacy and power of the Mexican presidency. The interlocking control apparatus of party and state channeled huge spoils to privileged politicians and technocrats. There was, however, a predictable turnover of beneficiaries every six years, and law and order under this system has been maintained with minimal expenditure on the armed forces.

The revolution produced many basic institutional changes. The PNR, renamed Partido Revolucionario Institucional (PRI) in 1946, became an extremely powerful machine and has held a monopoly of political power since the 1920s, winning all presidential and gubernatorial elections. Rival parties exist but, until 1988, they won a very small fraction of the votes. The party is organized in a peasant section, a labor section (for the officially favored trade unions), and a section devoted to bureaucratic and professional interests. It plays the institutional role that the church or the army played in former times. The church now has no political power, and the armed forces absorb only 0.5 percent of GDP.

Enormous power is concentrated in the presidency. The president is elected by a popular vote as large proportionately as the vote in U.S. presidential elections, but the official candidate, whose election is guaranteed, is chosen by the outgoing president. There are no primaries and no other official candidatures. In Mexico, these would be construed as a limitation on presidential power. The president can veto any legislation, and the veto cannot be overridden. This concentration of power is limited by a regular six-year alternation and ineligibility for reelection. The last president who tried to be reelected was Alvaro Obregón, and he was assassinated.

There are no overt checks and balances in this system, and the legislature has no control over budgetary policy. The party and the presidency also wield considerable power of patronage in nominations to public office, in appointments to jobs in state enterprises and banks, and in allocation of government land for farming, public housing, and social security benefits.

There has been a clearly discernible political business cycle as each incoming president tends to inherit budgetary problems brought on by an end-of-term splurge in public spending by his predecessor. The biggest of these presidential spending booms was in the last year of José Lopez Portillo's administration when the public sector deficit was 17 percent of GDP.

Mexico's authoritarian and highly centralized political system has favored the growth of public enterprise. Both *dirigiste* momentum and a nationalistic reaction against the excessive privileges formerly granted to foreign investors in the natural resource sector account for this. The biggest public corporation is Petróleos Mexicanos (PEMEX), the oil company whose value added in 1983 amounted to 13 percent of GDP. The other public corporations accounted for 5 percent of GDP; they include most of banking and insurance, railways, electricity, telephones and other public utilities, as well as food retailing, fertilizers, and part of the motor vehicle industry. Public corporations are very capital intensive. Altogether they provide only 3 percent of employment. Salaries in the public sector are well above those in the private sector, as are such fringe benefits as social security and access to housing.

In spite of the leftist rhetoric of Mexican politics, there is a cozy cooperation between the state and private capitalists, both domestic and foreign. The bulk of manufacturing is in private hands and manufacturers receive fiscal privileges, protection, and favors from government if they stay in line. Direct foreign investment is important (the stock was about $17 billion in 1986), particularly in manufacturing. However, foreign interests are excluded from mining and agriculture and are virtually banned from banking, finance, and insurance.

Although Mexico is a country of high inequality, official policy has been more concerned with popular welfare than in Brazil. Standards of education and health seem somewhat better; and land reform has been under way since the 1920s. Social security payments have been somewhat smaller than in Brazil, but subsidies on important items of mass consumption have been much bigger. In 1982, government subsidies of all kinds in Mexico amounted to 11.3 percent of GDP compared with 2.3 percent in Brazil.

In general, Mexico has tended to be less market oriented in its policy instruments than Brazil. It has relied more on administratively allocated import controls, maintained unrealistic exchange rates longer, and has had less realistic price policies for agriculture. One exception is exchange controls—it has none.

On the face of it, Mexico looks like a predatory state, with its concentration of state power, use of regulation rather than price mechanisms, and spoils system for powerholders. Compared with the country's past political systems, however, it is quite benign, with a predictable and regulated alternation of power, mechanisms for accommodating to pressure, and demonstrated ability to change course between presidential regimes. Public employment of all kinds is only 14 percent of the labor force (including the 3 percent in public enterprises).

The ideology of Mexico emerged from the revolution against the Diaz dictatorship, well before the Soviet revolution or the creation of socialist states in the rest of the world. There is a powerful state sector, a privileged bureaucracy of party members, and a rhetorical official leftism about revolution, indigenism, and land reform. But the system is quite unlike that in Eastern European countries, and state ownership is smaller than in France, Italy, or Austria. People are free to emigrate and return, to hold their assets abroad, to run capitalist enterprises and attract foreign investment. The ideology of Mexico is largely a nationalist reaction to its position as a neighbor and former victim of the United States. Before the good neighbor policy of the Roosevelt administration in the 1930s and 1940s, it seemed quite feasible that Mexico would move much further to the left than it has done. As long as this sensitive relationship with the United States remains "neighborly," the official ideology is unlikely to change much, in spite of internal strains.

Major Interest Groups

Peter Smith (1979) has given a brilliant picture of the career structure of the political elite, which is confirmed by Camp's (1985) systematic analysis of political biographies. This elite consists of the president and his entourage, the politicians who hold elective office at the national and state levels, and the highly competent technocrats who make the system work. Smith's catechism for aspirants to the technocratic elite runs more or less as follows: go to university, join the PRI, go immediately into a government job, be on the lookout for better job opportunities, be willing to move frequently, make as many useful personal contacts as you can, make no enemies, demonstrate loyalty, do not rock the boat or make controversial public statements, use legal means to make yourself rich (such as buying land that will be used for roadbuilding), and be prepared to end your official career at an early state. The great contrast between the Mexican system and that in other countries where one party has dominated for long periods is the exceptionally high turnover of elites and the brevity of careers because of the tradition of not re-electing presidents. There is almost no career interchange between private business and government office. Generally members of the elite leave office rather prosperous because salaries are high and the legal opportunities for augmenting income and perquisites such as cheap loans are important. Virtually all members of the elite have some discretionary power in nominating people for jobs, thus facilitating their own access to credit or cheap housing, which are important in reinforcing their power and status.

Generally speaking, the technocrats come from prosperous families, are better educated, and advance more rapidly than the machine politicians. Their rapid rise to power is demonstrated by the fact that the last four presidents—Luis Echeverría, José López Portillo, Miguel de la Madrid, and Carlos Salinas de Gortari—were all men who had not held elective office previously.

Smith points to the fact that family background is an increasingly significant factor in acquiring a top job. The revolution has a history of seventy years, and there is now an important dynastic element within the elite. Twenty members of the cabinet and subcabinet of López Portillo, for instance, had such connections (including six relatives of López Portillo himself) (Smith 1979).

During and after the revolution, the military were a prominent part of the political elite, but this has not been the case since the 1940s when the military section of the party was disbanded. No president since Manuel Avila Camacho has had a military background, and the only military officers in the cabinet have been appointed to defense positions. The resources absorbed by the military have been small, though the armed forces increased in number and were modernized in the 1970s to police the border with Guatemala, deal with the drug traffic, and step up internal security after the Tlaltelolco massacre of 1968. The armed forces have a strength of 120,000 regulars, plus 250,000 reservists who turn up only eight weekends a year for practice. Ronfeldt (1984) suggests that there are more generals in the army than in the U.S. army, and commanders are regularly rotated from one zone to another. There is no close contact with the U.S. armed forces in terms of equipment and training. Apart from fairly marked anticommunist views, the military elite seems to be apolitical. Army officers are recruited from a lower social level than the technocrats and seem relatively happy with their pay and prospects for promotion.

Exclusion of the military from politics is a major virtue of the Mexican political system. Mexico has little interference from the military compared with most of Latin America, and even with advanced democracies such as France and the United States, where special military interest groups have wielded substantial power. Low military expenditure has released resources for more productive use in economic development.

Lower-level bureaucrats and administrators are rather poorly paid and make wide use of opportunities to augment their incomes by extracting bribes to provide permits or to overlook offenses in a system that gives some of them wide discretionary power.

Mexico's "official family" also embraces the two other groups that have their own sections in the party—the trade unions and the peasants. In much of Latin America relations between government and labor are hostile. This is not true in Mexico where there are few strikes or demonstrations against government policy, even though minimum wages are low, and wages have been squeezed more frequently than they have been favored by successive presidents.

About one-third of the work force is organized in 11,000 unions, most of which are members of the powerful Confederación de Trabajadores de México (CTM). The CTM was formed in the 1930s and subsequently integrated into the official party. The founding secretary general, Vicente Lombardo Toledano, proved too independent and leftist and was ousted by Fidel Velasquez, who has headed the federation since 1941. Velasquez cooperated with the American Federation of Labor in combating communist influence elsewhere in Latin America, and steadfastly backed the government, torpedoing any possible alliance with the student movement in 1968 (see Riding 1985). In return, the government has given unionized workers privileged access to social security and to housing (in a scheme whose highly subsidized beneficiaries are selected largely by the unions). The unions have also had control over access to government jobs and protection against loss of jobs.

The most privileged of the unions is the Mexican Oil Workers' Union (Sindicato de Trabajadores Petroleros de la República Mexicana, or STPRM), founded in 1935 with encouragement from Cárdenas as part of his campaign against foreign oil interests. Since nationalization of the oil industry in 1938, this closed shop of union workers has enjoyed privileged conditions. It has been dominated since the 1960s by Joaquin Hernandez Galicia ("a true godfather," in Riding's terminology). The union controls access to jobs, gets PEMEX contracts for oil drilling, and owns tankers, land, supermarkets, aircraft, and urban real estate. In 1983 the union's assets were conservatively estimated to be worth $670 million. The union also ensures that people in the 80,000 regular jobs (and as many more temporary ones) it controls get high wages and substantial perquisites.

The union section of the PRI, although loyal to the party, is the section with the greatest independent power. While the party can remove virtually any member of its political-bureaucratic and peasant units, this is not so of union members.

Apart from government unions, there has always been a leftist fringe in the labor movement including a variety of political parties. Although these parties are outside the official orbit, they are given a voice in Congress, where seats have been allotted to the opposition since 1977. As a result, the kind of labor group that is clandestine elsewhere in Latin America falls within the spectrum of respectability in Mexico, with outlets in the press and in university life.

The peasant section of the party caters mostly to the *ejidatarios*, a uniquely Mexican farming group whose land holdings were created by successive government distributions of land. Development of the *ejido* system provided a major element of legitimacy to the political system. Agriculture employs about one-quarter of the population, and about 60 percent of agricultural workers are *ejidatarios*. They do not own land but have been allocated plots that are under the control of the local administration. The more capitalist and prosperous rural element, the private landowners, are not such loyal supporters of the party as there are restrictions on the size of their holdings and they have from time to time been in fear of expropriation of their lands for distribution programs. Nevertheless, the capitalist sector has been a major beneficiary of government credit and irrigation investment.

Although Mexico has some of the characteristics of Eastern European countries, with a strong party apparatus and a powerful corporatist organization, it also has a strong private sector with dynamic entrepreneurs. For many decades, private businessmen have enjoyed unrestricted freedom to move their capital and their skills out of the country. Except in the natural resource sector, Mexico has generally welcomed and received foreign private investment in manufacturing and services (though banking and insurance are more or less taboo for foreign investors). There businesses have received many favors from government in the way of tariff protection and credit arrangements.

There is a formally corporatist organization of industry, particularly in Confederación de Cámaras Industriales (the Confederation of Industrial Chambers, or CONCAMIN). But this organization does not have a fraction of the power over its members that the CTM has over workers, and its deal-making with government has been much more limited.

Flavia Derossi (1971) provides a fascinating survey in *The Mexican*

Entrepreneur of the family background and attitudes of businessmen. A significant proportion of indigenous entrepreneurs comes from formerly prosperous families of the *ancien régime*, those large landowners or raw materials processors of the Porfiriato period who were dispossessed by the revolution and reacted by using their skills, contacts, and whatever capital they had left by going into industry. Another group that is unexpectedly large is the immigrants from various parts of Europe who arrived with skills and some capital. Derossi paints a picture where small family enterprises figure more prominently than in the United States and where there is room for upward social mobility and increasing development of professionalized management.

Most entrepreneurs learn how to work within the system. Using pressure to get tariff or quota protection or access to credit is the main activity that requires some political finesse. The principal drawback of the system is the inability to control the supply of imported parts that may suddenly become unobtainable or more expensive. By international standards, Mexican businesses pay low taxes and low wages.

In general the contact of business with the political system tends to be discreet and is closest with the technocrats in government banks.

There is only one business-oriented think tank, Instituto Panamericano de Alta Dirección de Empresa (IPADE), in Mexico, and overt affiliation of business groups with the main right-wing opposition party, Partido Accion Nacional (PAN), is frowned on. Thus the ideology of Mexican business is not something that has been very overtly formulated. The biggest shock to the business class in the past few decades was the nationalization of all banks in the last stages of the López Portillo presidency, which also had the effect of nationalizing many private firms that were controlled by private banks. This naturally created uncertainty in the business community that led to reduced investment and capital flight. To some extent it strengthened business support for the PAN, particularly in the northern part of the country, where business is most dynamic. However, the de la Madrid government quelled fears to some extent by a policy of gradual privatization of business and liberalization of economic policy.

Mexico has an intellectual climate more like that of France than that of the United States. Intellectuals have a relatively high status and are expected to take a position on political issues. Generally speaking, it is not respectable for intellectuals to hold right-wing views. Rather, there is wide scope for revolutionary and leftist positions, most of which pose no threat to the system. In the 1950s and 1960s the mainstream intellectual attitudes were consensual, and distinguished poets or writers were as likely to be appointed foreign ambassadors as were former presidents or ministers. After the 1968 uprisings, the intelligentsia became much more critical of government, which helps to explain Echeverría's leftist rhetoric and López Portillo's breakneck push for economic expansion.

Class Structure

Apart from the top political and bureaucratic elite, those who have benefitted most from growth in the past half century are generally referred to as the middle class. The term middle class may be an appropriate sociological concept for the United States, which has high average income levels and where the popular aspiration for success is to occupy a place in what is in fact a rather broad middle spectrum (because U.S. income distribution is relatively equal), but it is not very suitable for Mexico. People who tend to describe themselves as middle class in Mexico are not really in the middle. They are among the 15 percent or so who come immediately below the 0.5 percent who are the top elite. They are better described as a bourgeoisie in the southern European sense. They aspire to elegant housing, servants, private education, foreign travel, cars, and household durable goods in a country where poverty is widespread. Broadly speaking, the Mexican elite and bourgeoisie follow the same get-rich policy as did their counterparts under Louis Philippe in France. Their motto could just as easily be "enrichissez-vous." What is different is their capacity to diffuse resentment against the system by dispensing favors to lower social groups; those favors are as much determined by group pressure as by redistributive goals. In fact, welfare state expenditure is probably as high relative to GDP in Mexico as in the United States, but the highest benefits go to the best-organized groups.

The class in the middle—about half of the population, who have a high enough standard of living and access to social benefits to maintain a decent life and have aspirations for their children—could well be described as a working class, rather than a middle class. In any case, they should not be confused with the bourgeoisie.

The bottom third of society consists of the poor, who are generally illiterate, badly housed, in ill health, and often hungry. They are also lacking in political clout in a system where there is no urgency to remedy their situation. In general, as Oscar Lewis (1964) has shown, this group is trapped in an intergenerational cycle of poverty with little scope for upward mobility. Most of the poor are Indians, whose ancestors were regarded as social inferiors or outcasts in the colonial period and the Porfiriato. The revolution may not have raised them from poverty, but it did involve a major effort to remove status inferiority by stressing the indigenous origins of the country and by creating murals and museums that stress the Indian cultural heritage.

The Political Element in Macroeconomic Policy, 1940-85

There have been three main periods since 1940. From 1940 to 1970, there was a clear halt in revolutionary momentum and an unleashing of market forces within a framework of responsible fiscal policy and sound money. Technocrats played a major role in policymaking and their long terms in office made for policy continuity—between 1935 and 1970 there were only four ministers of finance (table 5-2) and three governors of the Bank of Mexico (table 5-3). The second period of populist presidentialism, 1970-82, pushed harder for growth, cared less about efficiency, and pushed the economy to disaster in 1982. After 1982 there was a reversion to older virtues, but the size of the external debt, the instability of oil prices, and the fiscal, monetary, and expectational legacy of the 1970-82 period brought poor rewards and created severe problems for the political acceptability of adjustment policies.

The New Economic Order of Avila Camacho and Alemán, 1940-52

Presidential elections that took place in 1940 promised to be difficult. The swing of Cárdenas toward land reform, his strong support of labor, the expropriation of oil resources, Cárdenas's stance on the Spanish Civil War, and the leftist leanings of many cabinet members aroused an

Table 5-2. Ministers of Finance, 1927-86

Finance minister	Term
Luis Montes de Oca	1927-32
Alberto J. Pani	1932-33
Plutarco Elías Calles	1933
Marte R. Gómez	1934
Narciso Bassols	1934-35
Eduardo Suárez	1935-46
Ramón Beteta	1946-52
Antonio Carrillo Flores	1952-58
Antonio Ortiz Mena	1958-70
Hugo B. Margain	1970-73
José López Portillo	1973-75
Mario Ramón Beteta	1975-76
Julio Rodolfo Moctezuma Cid	1976-78
David Ibarra Muñoz	1978-82
Jesús Silva Herzog	1982-86
Gustavo Petricioli	1986-

Source: Supplied by Victor L. Urquidi.

Table 5-3. Directors General of the Bank of Mexico, 1925–86

Director General	Term
Alberto Mascareñas	1925–28
Agustin Rodriquez	1929–34
Gonzalo Robles	1934–35
Louis Montes de Oca	1935–40
Eduardo Villaseñor	1940–46
Carlos Novoa	1946–52
Rodrigo Gómez	1952–69
Ernesto Fernandez Hurtado	1969–76
Gustavo Romero Kolbeck	1976–82
Miguel A. Mancera	1982
Carlos Tello	1982[a]
Miguel A. Mancera	1982–

a. Served from September to December.
Source: Supplied by Victor L. Urquidi.

articulate opposition. The opposition was, as usual, reputed to have support from foreign interests, including oil companies. Within the party, political debate was resolved in favor of pushing the pendulum toward center-right. The purity of the elections was much disputed, but the new president who took office in the last quarter of 1940, General Manual Avila Camacho, immediately announced a policy of "national unity" in the face of World War II and its possible implications. Economic and social policy had perforce to be turned back from the more extreme positions taken under Cárdenas. A more balanced approach was taken to development and to the broadly conceived, liberal social-democratic tenets of the 1917 Constitution. In fact, Cárdenas, in the last part of his administration, had already instituted policies favoring industrial development. Moreover, concern about shortages of imported manufactured supplies in case of war in Europe and the active involvement of the United States also pointed to the need to foster industrialization.

The administration of Avila Camacho attempted to meet many goals: to continue to legitimize the social and economic platform of the dominant government party; to safeguard the economy and the social programs from the unfavorable impact of the spread of international warfare; to tone down the domestically divisive positions taken by previous administrations (for example, land reform and "socialist" education); to improve relations with the United States; to promote industrialization and encourage investment in commercial agricultural expansion, and in general to restore confidence among private enterprise; to initiate a political transition toward civilian-dominated government; and in matters of finance, to lay the groundwork for stimulating domestic savings and capital formation. The financial policies included pursuing negotiations to settle the external debts on which Mexico had defaulted in the nineteenth and early twentieth centuries.

Avila Camacho moved the polity in the direction of social democracy rather than a radical transformation of society. It is no wonder that leading intellectuals during the 1940s wrote of the "end" of the revolution. Notable among them were Professor Jesús Silva Herzog, father of the finance minister, and Daniel Cosío Villegas, a prominent historian.

Avila Camacho held over a gifted minister of finance, Eduardo Suárez, from the previous administration. Suárez remained in office from 1935 to 1946 and left behind a school of financial and monetary managers who played a strong role in financial and economic policy until 1970. One of his first initiatives in 1941 was to strengthen the powers of the central bank—Banco de México—and to give substance to the development bank—Nacional Financiera (Nafin)—and other banks that had been created in the mid-1930s; he also obtained legislative approval for sweeping reform of the banking system.

There was much new investment during the 1940s, not only in manufacturing but also in modern commercial agriculture on irrigated land. Large industrial projects were promoted with the assistance of Nacional Financiera, notably in steel manufacturing (C. P. Blair in Vernon 1964). Mexico operated the first steel mill in Latin America, but the open-hearth facility in Monterrey had, even in 1940, a capacity of less than 200,000 tons of ingot a year and its main product was reinforcing bars for construction. Small foundries existed in a number of cities. It was a major decision, therefore (parallel to that in Brazil), to obtain equipment for a rolling mill, particularly under wartime conditions. The result was Altos Hornos de Mexico, the initiation of state-sponsored development of steel manufacturing, which, for all practical purposes, came to monopolize steelmaking after the bankruptcy of the leading privately owned mill. A sponge-iron, direct-reduction process was later developed by a private group in Monterrey, which has survived and grown to international status. Similar government-financed developments were undertaken in pulp and paper, small motors, and many other sectors, frequently with the participation of private domestic banks and foreign capital.

Alongside these government-inspired industries, independent small businesses were set up in many fields, including chemicals, domestic appliances, hand tools, farm machinery, and a legion of intermediate commodities. Their development was encouraged by wartime scarcity of imports and also by government financial and tax-incentive support. Most of these new manufacturing plants were small and inefficient.

They were organized for a limited captive market, sometimes hastily, and depended on the United States for essential equipment and spare parts. Mexico designated a special ambassador to Washington, Ramón Beteta, whose sole function was to wrench export permits from the U.S. wartime controls administration.

The "new industrialists," as Mosk (1954) called them, were highly protectionist. They feared postwar readjustment and foreign competition, and the government on the whole supported their position. In 1945, William Clayton, head of the U.S. delegation to the Inter-American Conference on Postwar Economic and Financial Problems (The Chapultepec Conference), outlined U.S. policies of suspending long-term contracts for strategic basic products and returning to pricing through the international market. Moreover, Latin American countries would be required to open their customs borders to U.S. manufactured goods and to eschew tariff protection. The outcry from the new industrialists was strong. U.S. policy clearly determined Mexico's decision in 1948 not to join the General Agreement on Tariffs and Trade (GATT) and to maintain a highly protectionist policy. Mexico believed that wartime industrialization had helped transform the economy, had generated employment, and had assisted in the process of modernization away from the peasant economy and the mining enclaves of the past.

The 1940–46 period, in sum, was one of fairly rapid change, with structural shifts toward industry under a broad industrialization policy and with consistent financial and monetary management under difficult wartime conditions and inflationary pressure. Only the merest stirrings of interest had been aroused with respect to income distribution and the extreme inequality that prevailed.

The next stage, under the leadership of President Miguel Alemán, an enterprising and flamboyant politician, was one of both political renewal and developmental policies. Alemán had been a federal deputy and state governor, popularly known at one time as a "young cub of the Revolution" (his father had been an army general). As a representative of a younger generation, a lawyer graduated from the National University, he intended to turn society in a new direction. He initiated a clearly defined policy of infrastructural development (irrigation, electricity, and roads) and of encouragement of private enterprise. To this were added friendlier relations with the United States and a more open attitude toward foreign direct private investment (table 5-4). Agriculture on private, medium-size farms was favored, and manufacturing industry was given all-out incentives. After the 1947–48 balance of payments and currency adjustment, government policy was directed to obtaining loans from the World Bank, the U.S. Export-Import Bank, and foreign suppliers.

Table 5-4. External Debt and Stock of Foreign Direct Investment Assets, Selected Years, 1889–1986

Year	GDP Millions of current pesos	GDP Millions of current dollars	External debt (millions of dollars)	Foreign direct investment assets (millions of dollars)	Ratio of external debt to GDP (percent)	Ratio of total foreign assets to GDP (percent)
1889	764[a]	398[a]	40	—	10.0	—
190	3,100	1,540	220	1,480[b]	14.3	110.4
1929	4,863	2,262	648	1,212[b]	28.7	82.2
1946	27,930	5,748	125	575	2.2	12.2
1975	1,100,050	88,004	20,100	5,017	22.8	28.5
1986	79,353,450	129,800	101,000	17,053	77.8	91.0

— Not available.
a. Estimate, based on 1895 prices.
b. Total foreign assets minus government debt.
Source: For GDP, Mexico, INEGI (1985a). For public debt in 1889–1946, Bazant (1968), pp. 169, 206, 224; in 1975–86, table 5-5. For foreign direct investment, in 1910–29, Goldsmith (1966), p. 73; in 1946, Evans and Gereffi in Hewlett and Weinert (1982), pp. 158–9; in 1975–86, table 5-5.

Expansionary policies were adopted from the start, with little regard for financial orthodoxy. Mexico rode the world cotton boom, for which it opened up much new land. In December 1946, legislation was passed to protect private landholdings (freeholds) against outright expropriation, allowing the holders the right to injunction, which had previously been denied. In contrast to the limited support that was provided for the *ejido*-type peasant holdings, liberal farm credit was made available to private freeholders. Many of the latter turned out to be politicians, highly placed bureaucrats, and their cronies, so-called nylon, or artificial farmers. Government banks, including the Bank of Mexico and Nacional Financiera, were forced to bend toward the interests of private business, especially the groups associated with the politicians in power.

In spite of Alemán's advocacy of private enterprise, he actually strengthened the role of the state in controlling the economy. He also launched state-supported industrial projects. This industrialization and agricultural development policy was not very discriminating; almost anything was regarded as good and worthy of support. Excesses were the order of the day, but public relations took care to present a progressive image at home and abroad.

Alemán's policy, while essentially developmental and employment-creating, was somewhat antilabor. His long-time enmity toward the leftist former labor leader and still influential public figure, Vicente Lombardo Toledano, probably hardened his position. He was also encouraged by private business groups who favored low wage costs and who benefitted from a great variety of policy advantages. It was during this time that concern among economists and statisticians led to the first attempts to measure the distribution of personal income. Imperfect as the calculations were, they showed extreme inequality, with the lowest 40 percent of the population earning 10 percent of the income, and the top 10 percent earning 40 percent—a distribution that has, by and large, not changed to this day.

Although Alemán's policies were unconcerned with income distribution and paid scant attention to social welfare, he did implement legislation (passed in 1943) that set the National Social Security Institute (Instituto Mexicano del Seguro Social, or IMSS) in motion. Applicable only to wage earners and their families in the formal sector, IMSS offered social security benefits and free health care, though not family allowances or unemployment insurance. The system helped modernize the health sector, and a similar institute was later established for federal and state civil servants. Other, narrower, systems were set up for petroleum, railroad, and bank employees and workers, as well as for armed forces personnel. These benefit arrangements were supposed, partially, to offset income inequality and extend social welfare. Under Alemán, sizable contributions were made to education, and new facilities were built for the National University on the outskirts of Mexico City.

Financial policies were not as cautious as they had been under the preceding administration. The minister of finance, Ramón Beteta, a "cardenista" turned developmentalist under Alemán, was less consistent and less careful to guard against the inflationary and financially destabilizing effects of government policies. In fact, financial and budget information was seldom accurate and many expenditures were beyond strict budgetary control. It was only in 1950 that statistical analysis of government finances began to be developed in such a way that it could be integrated with the national accounts (Beteta 1951). The accounts, entrusted to the Bank of Mexico as far back as 1945, did not become fully available until the late 1950s.

The record of the Alemán administration, as reconstructed from national accounts data, was an average annual GDP growth of 5.7 percent; with population growth of 2.9 percent, per capita GDP increased by 2.8 percent a year. By 1952 the central government's deficit was 2–3 percent of GDP. Net external borrowing per year was less than $100 million, and total "new" external debt was of a small order, largely in the form of medium- to long-term loans for development.

Ruiz Cortines, 1952–58

As the election season approached, the "alemanistas" tried to impose a close ally and relative of Alemán's as the presidential candidate. But a revolt within the inner chambers of the PRI resulted in the last-minute choice of the minister of interior, Adolfo Ruiz Cortines. An unknown quantity, he started his term of office with a lackluster but down-to-earth campaign strategy invoking the need for moderation, honest government, concern for the poor, and a touch of radical nationalism. He was less open than his predecessors to blandishments from private business groups or the United States.

The administration began on a pragmatic note, with retrenchment in public expenditure and investment plans. The director general of Nafin, Antonio Carrillo Flores, became minister of finance. He was well known in World Bank and New York financial circles.

By mid-1953, other members of the government, paying little heed to the impending international economic recession, started a series of declarations on the evils of direct private foreign investment. Their nationalistic assertions reinforced the already cautious attitude of the post-Alemán domestic business groups.

Meanwhile, the peso had drifted into a moderate overvaluation. A rising deficit in the current account led to speculation as to the stability of the currency and consequently to capital flight. By early 1954 the Bank of Mexico had been pushed into its traditional corner: it did not hold enough gold and foreign exchange reserves to guarantee stability of the exchange rate. After much hesitation, but choosing the right moment (Easter weekend), a new parity of 12.50 pesos to the U.S. dollar was adopted with the concurrence of the International Monetary Fund (IMF); this meant a devaluation of 30.8 percent. This move was widely regarded as a deliberate undervaluation to allay fears of currency instability and to provide exports with a safe margin, while at the same time helping to restrict excessive imports. The impact on the domestic price level was relatively small. Fiscal revenues increased almost immediately.

The 1954 devaluation turned out to be the cornerstone of a new development thrust. The initial impact was absorbed within a few months and the devaluation ushered in a long period of growth with a relatively stable price level, accompanied by good financial management. This was a period that by 1969 was designated as one of "stabilizing development"—*desarrollo estabilizador*—a well-defined growth strategy with consistent macroeconomic policies.

By 1958 Mexico's GDP was rising 5 percent annually, and that year a fairly smooth political transition took place. The new president-elect, Adolfo López Mateos, was a seasoned politician who had held congressional posts and been minister of labor. On taking office on December 1, he appointed Antonio Ortiz Mena as minister of finance and Antonio Carrillo Flores as ambassador to Washington. The two Antonios worked hand in hand, and Ortiz Mena quickly took firm control of the whole financial system. The Bank of Mexico, under the able direction of Rodrigo Gómez, played its part in the strategy adopted.

Development with Price Stability, 1958–70

A slowdown, however, ensued in 1959–60, at the start of the López Mateos administration, resulting from the usual dip in public investment during the first few months of a new presidency, as well as from the mild international recession of that time. Exports stagnated and the balance of payments weakened; a makeshift, almost day-to-day policy analysis working group, reporting to Ortiz Mena, was made responsible in 1959 for guiding short-term policy. Development goals were maintained for industrialization, modern agricultural development, expansion of the tourist industry, changes in the financial and banking system, upgrading of skills through educational expansion and training, vastly expanded health and welfare programs, and the like. In particular, improvement in real wages was to be sought and efforts were to be made to promote raid absorption of the labor force into urban manufacturing.

Once more, external events intervened to create uncertainty and discourage private investment. An attempt at tax reform in 1961–62, partly based on recommendations made in 1960 by Nicholas Kaldor, coincided unfortunately with a rise in the private business sector's distrust for overall policies, especially foreign policy, that had much to do with the Cuban revolution. Fidel Castro's rise to power had generated echoes among Mexican politicians who wished to renew the revolutionary rhetoric of the past. That rhetoric ran counter to the pragmatism of the López Mateos administration, which attempted to steer a middle, development-oriented course that would enjoy support from the multilateral financial agencies in Washington and from the U.S. government. Domestic political dissent began to rise, the main actors taking sides with reference to Cuba, U.S. pressure, deviation from Mexico's longstanding revolutionary path, and so forth.

The year 1961 was fateful in many ways, largely in favor of the administration's policies. Mexico had veered toward a position of aloofness from the Cuban revolution while maintaining formal relations with the Castro regime in line with the traditional policy of self-determination and nonintervention. The early policy decisions of the Kennedy administration clearly favored the Alliance for Progress framework.

When the 1961 Punta del Este Charter on inter-American cooperation was adopted, Mexico quickly put together an Immediate Action Plan for 1962–64 (at that stage a formal development plan would have been politically impossible). The three-year program set out goals for public sector investment and, on the basis of hurriedly carried out surveys, listed and encouraged private industrial investment projects. The Ministry of Industry, headed by a well-known economist, Raúl Salinas Lozano, who had been director of the National Investment Commission under Ruiz Cortines, shortly reversed some of the government's policy statements and came out clearly in favor of support for the private business sector.

At the same time, the government was able to argue that the main objectives and instruments of the Alliance for Progress—land reform, fiscal reform, health, sanitation, educational targets, enhanced food production, and so on—had always been prime elements in Mexican development policy. The stage was set for stimulation of domestic private investment and unhampered access to multilateral funding, suppliers' credits, and a moderate volume of commercial bank financing. The manner in which the electric power sector had been nationalized in 1961—through purchase of its assets by the government, with the help of a loan from a U.S. insurance group—worked in Mexico's favor. In 1963, the government welcomed both a special evaluation mission of the Alliance for Progress's Committee of Nine and an overall evaluation mission from the World Bank. The two missions, working in close liaison through the Ministry of Finance, established the basis for external loan policies to back up the development efforts over the medium-to-long-term period. The immediate needs were indeed modest: for 1964, a net inflow of external credit of not more than $150 million. Foreign exchange reserves had reached a healthy level, exports had revived, with a rising component of manufactured products, and tourism was booming.

Three issues stand out, nevertheless, as having dimmed the prospects for steady growth and development. First, industrialization concentrated on import substitution, paying little attention to the expanding international market for manufactured goods. Overprotection and gradual overvaluation of the currency were undermining what little competitiveness could be claimed. Stability of the currency had become an article of faith, even with mild cumulative inflation indicating that an adjustment of the parity would sooner or later have to be made. Second, highly unequal income distribution, both in terms of personal income and in factor shares, continued to prevail, only slightly offset, for a narrow range of incomes, by nonwage policies and benefits. A survey of family income and expenditure conducted in 1962–63 showed little change had taken place in the inequality of incomes since the early 1950s, although the middle-income deciles seemed to be gaining a slightly larger share (Bank of Mexico 1974).

The third issue was political. The incumbent president, López Mateos, was known to be suffering from serious illness toward the end of his administration. A strong-willed minister of interior, Gustavo Díaz Ordaz, a politician with little training in economic and financial matters, was chosen as the PRI candidate in late 1963. He set out to campaign on a hard line toward any form of dissidence, especially from labor and students.

On his election in mid-1964, Díaz Ordaz did not formulate any major change in development strategy to take account of underlying changes in society. When he took office in December, he retained Ortiz Mena as minister of finance, which assured some continuity in economic and financial policies. On the political side, the PRI structure showed signs of rigidity, an inability to revitalize itself. Díaz Ordaz was also hard on higher education; during his administration grants for universities (with the exception of the powerful National University) were frozen in current terms. Then came the 1968 political shock, just before the scheduled Olympic Games. Within a short period, between July and October, there was a political disturbance on a scale not witnessed since the Revolution. Not only students but middle-class families took to the streets to protest repression. The government was convinced that the student movement was part of an international conspiracy and it was anxious to clean everything up before the October Olympics. Poor negotiating ability on both sides, and perhaps deeper division than appeared on the surface, led to the October 2 massacre, for which the president later assumed full responsibility. The effect on the economy was necessarily dampening, and the rest of Díaz Ordaz's six-year term was spent healing the wounds opened up in 1968. It was hardly surprising that the minister of interior, Luis Echeverría, another hard-liner, became the next PRI candidate.

The year 1968 was in many ways the end of an era of stable development that had relied on broad-based consensus or fairly widespread acceptance of the government's strategies. Over the whole 1950–70 period, average annual GDP growth was 6.6 percent, which resulted in a mean 3.3 percent annual per capita GDP increase. Profit-sharing legislation was enacted and a national minimum wage commission was established. But inequality had not been reduced, and the absolute numbers of the poor, of the uneducated, and of the illiterate actually rose. Population policy had not yet been formulated; as late as 1967 the minister of health had refused to send a representative, even as an observer, to a technical conference on population and development planning convened at Caracas by the Organization of American States (OAS), on the grounds that President Díaz Ordaz was satisfied that GDP was growing faster than population. Family planning was almost a dirty word and its promotion was left to small, pioneering private organizations. The lack of birth control decisions at the family level resulted in a large volume of illegal abortions that were responsible for a high death rate among women of childbearing age in low-income families, while middle-class women took care of themselves through prescription or free purchase of contraceptives.

The Beginning of Destabilizing Economic Policies, 1970–76

With the events of 1968 still fresh, the administration of Luis Echeverría that took office on December 1, 1970, attempted to break with the past. Echeverría had spent most of his political life working inside government. His ideas on development were not known. As his political campaign got under way in late 1969, he quickly showed his independence from the incumbent and his concern for political and social problems that the government had failed to tackle or had neglected. He announced a new strategy of "shared development"—*desarrollo compartido*—in contrast with the "stabilizing development" of the long Ortiz Mena stretch at the Ministry of Finance. Echeverría went so far as to demand Ortiz Mena's dismissal several months before the new administration took office and his replacement by a man of Echeverría's choosing, Hugo B. Margain, a mid-level administration official who had some experience in tax reform. This unusual change was meant to indicate that new development and financial policies, with a strong distributive bias, were to be adopted.

The new government seemed committed to a vast, complex series of changes in policy. It is not clear how much was carefully thought out and how much improvised in response to the events of 1968 and the need to legitimize the political system. What is crystal clear, however, is that Echeverría thought that by increasing public expenditure and enlarging the public sector, he could set the economy on a fast pace and that the benefits of shared development would rapidly trickle down. He was immediately set back, however, by lack of response from the private business sector, which had no confidence in his approach and in his "personal style" of governance. He brought everything up for drawn-out discussion in untidy groups at his offices in Los Pinos, the presidential quarters. He had also appointed a number of young and inexperienced economists and other technocrats to key ministerial posts and high office. He was extremely active and worked almost around the clock. And he soon developed a strong interest in international economic organization through the U.N. system—the "third" world was the order of the day.

In macroeconomic terms, Echeverría, after the 1971 doldrums, launched a public investment expansion that was to have extraordinary consequences. By late 1972 government spending had been stepped up and was generating unusual inflationary pressures and requiring a vast increase in imported equipment. The cost-of-living index rose by 12 percent in 1973, and the current account deficit was 2.4 percent of GDP. The pace increased in the following years, with a widespread and seemingly chaotic expansion of the public sector corporations, joint ventures, and trust funds. In 1972, Echeverría also attended the meetings of the United Nations Conference on Trade and Development (UNCTAD) at Santiago, Chile, stated his sympathies for the Allende government, and announced his proposal for a U.N. charter of economic rights and duties of states. Shortly thereafter he was instrumental, with Venezuela, in creating a new agency, the Latin American Economic System (Sistema Economico Latinoamericano, or SELA), to coordinate trade and economic policies toward the industrially advanced nations. He managed to create considerable animosity among Mexican businessmen.

In the field of energy, the policy of the government, through PEMEX, had been to make oil products as cheap as possible for domestic agricultural and industrial development, as well as for urban and interurban transportation and for electricity generation. The government refused to allow foreign private capital to participate in oil exploration (though a few risk-sharing projects of limited scope were authorized, and later canceled). As a major state corporation, PEMEX found itself in a quandary, unable to generate enough of its own resources for its development, and at the same time becoming an important charge on the federal budget.

In 1973, because of the high rate of growth of domestic energy consumption and the slow development of the nationalized oil industry, Mexico became a net importer of crude petroleum (70,000 barrels a day), precisely at the time of the first oil shock. This did not restrain expansion. It must be surmised that Echeverría knew that Mexico was sitting on, and about to discover for commercial purposes, huge oil and natural gas reserves, so that he was able to gamble on a heavy inflow of foreign exchange in the latter half of his administration (1974–76). Meanwhile, in the face of mounting inflation, and to maintain the fixed parity of 12.50 pesos per dollar, the government had begun to borrow abroad from commercial banks and in the Eurodollar and petrodollar markets. Public external debt had stood at a mere $4 billion when Echeverría took office; by the end of 1976 it had multiplied by a factor of five, to $21.6 billion (table 5-5), and the share of short-term commercial borrowing had risen substantially compared with loans from the multilateral financial agencies. Private sector debt reached $6.3 billion.

The Bank of Mexico became a printing press to finance rising budget deficits and public sector enterprises. It lost both power and respectability. During the early part of the administration, a correction of the parity for overvaluation would have been sensible and would have done much to help promote exports. The president himself, however, or his close advisers, failed to understand the implications of a policy that raised aggregate demand rapidly while holding on to an increasingly overvalued currency. The gamble on oil potential did not pay off im-

Table 5-5. External Debt and Debt Service, 1970 and 1975–88

Year	External debt (billions of dollars) Public sector	External debt (billions of dollars) Private sector	External debt (billions of dollars) Total	Interest on total external debt (billions of dollars)	Ratio of interest payments to exports of goods and services (percent)	Net debt to IMF (millions of dollars)[a]
1970	4.3	—	4.3	0.3	13.7	0
1975	14.4	5.6	20.1	2.2	34.9	0
1976	21.6	6.3	27.9	1.7	21.5	0
1977	23.9	6.4	30.3	1.9	21.5	0
1978	27.9	7.2	35.1	2.5	22.3	299
1979	31.9	10.5	42.4	3.7	22.7	136
1980	37.5	16.9	54.4	7.5	33.5	0
1981	59.1	21.9	81.0	11.3	40.3	0
1982	68.5	19.1	87.6	13.3	47.5	220
1983	74.7	19.1	93.8	10.5	36.3	1,255
1984	78.1	18.5	96.6	12.1	36.8	2,367
1985	79.8	16.7	96.6	10.6	34.4	2,943
1986	84.9	16.1	101.0	9.2	38.0	4,028
1987	92.4	15.1	107.5	9.1	29.8	5,119
1988	90.9	10.0	100.9	9.9	30.8	5,250

— Not available.
a. Included in external debt, public sector.
Source: Bank of Mexico and Wharton (1959).

mediately. As 1976, the last year of the administration, approached, there was a loss of confidence, followed by a stampede of capital to U.S. bank accounts once the current account deficit for 1975 became known (4.7 percent of GDP).

In September 1975, Echeverría, in authoritarian fashion and making a mockery of the PRI's institutional procedures, arranged for the major labor confederation to announce his choice for the next presidential candidate; José López Portillo, his friend since adolescence and now minister of finance. Perhaps this choice was meant to ensure continuity of populist policy. But unfortunately, inflation got out of hand in 1976, as did the external disequilibrium, and capital flight increased, amid all sorts of rumors of political instability. By August 1976, devaluation became inevitable, and the country was subjected to a strong jolt—the 12.50 parity turned without warning into a float up to 19.85 pesos per dollar. A further fall occurred shortly thereafter. The last few months of the administration were chaotic. Echeverría still managed to play to the gallery at the very end, by expropriating farmland in the rich Northwest irrigation districts.

Nevertheless, Echeverría managed to carry out some reforms. He opened the political system to broader minority party representation in Congress. There was a vast expansion of the education and health systems. The government adopted a population policy (judged by some to have been perhaps ten years too late) favoring a decline in the rate of fertility, mainly through officially sponsored family planning programs. And several large industrial projects, such as steel and petrochemicals, were undertaken.

On the other hand, Echeverría alienated foreign opinion and elicited deep distrust in the domestic private sector. He thought of himself as a latter-day Cárdenas, a redeemer; but his administration brought about economic and financial instability, was affected by corruption, and thus jeopardized the development objectives of the PRI and of the government itself. His initial aim was to improve income distribution, but the 1977 family expenditure and income survey showed no noticeable improvement over conditions existing in 1973, in 1963, and as far back as 1950 (Mexico, INEGI 1977).

Oil Boom and Bust, and External Indebtedness, 1976–82

Oil deposits were found in abundance, around 1972–73, at great inland depths and offshore. They were to be the touchstone of recovery for the López Portillo administration. In his inaugural address on December 1, 1976, the president carefully avoided all reference to the "third" world and put his emphasis on reestablishing domestic business confidence. He also "begged forgiveness" of the people for the failure of past administrations to raise living standards of the poor. The regime was "in debt" to the people, and he committed his government to redeeming that debt.

Among President López Portillo's first measures was an agreement with the IMF to tide over the foreign exchange crisis brought about by overspending in the previous administration. Given the expected crude oil exports, the IMF agreement seemed reasonable. After adjustments in 1977, a mild boom started, based on higher oil exports and further borrowing abroad, mostly from commercial banks. This enabled public investment to increase rapidly. Initially the strategy was to expand investment between mid-1978 and 1980, with the petroleum industry itself as a priority and with the launching of vast public sector industrial projects, electric power expansion (including two sizable nuclear plants), port development, and rebuilding of the urban infrastructure and transportation. Private business was also encouraged to develop, with the assistance of external borrowing. Oil and natural gas in the subsoil were considered sufficient guarantee for limitless external borrowing by the public sector and private business (and by the banks, for limitless lending), and currency stability inspired the confidence of the international financial community. The years 1981 and 1982 were to be used for consolidation of the gains achieved in the middle two years of the administration, and thus Mexico would face boundless opportunities with widespread prosperity for all.

All of these objectives were set out in a National Development Plan for 1978–82, with details spelled out in a large number of sectoral plans, some quite unrealistic (those for manufacturing industry and energy, for instance). Gross domestic product was expected to grow at an average rate of 8 percent a year.

But far from creating a phase of "administered wealth," which the president himself announced, the economy quickly became overheated. Aggregate investment—both public and private—rose at an annual average rate of 16.8 percent during 1978–80, and aggregate consumption increased at the unusual pace of 8.3 percent a year. It did not require very sophisticated analysis to foresee that the expansion in real demand would spill over into higher imports, especially for the large development projects (for example, the oil industry program itself).

Rising overvaluation of the peso also induced imports; inflation was consistently above official forecasts. A prominent cabinet member evoked the Brazilian syndrome, saying that it was better to grow with inflation than not to grow at all, not realizing perhaps that these were not the horns of the Mexican dilemma. Inevitably, a high pace of growth invited waste and corruption, and as crude oil output rose to 2.7 million barrels a day and the value of exports expanded from a mere $400 million in 1974 to almost $2 billion in 1978, with promise of further rapid increases, general commodity imports went up accordingly. In 1978–80 commodity imports rose at an average annual rate of 49.1 percent!

The Ministry of Finance did not take advantage of the boom to institute real tax reform. A value added tax of 15 percent was introduced to replace cascade-type turnover taxes, but it fed inflation and was poorly administered. The U.S. dollar became the cheapest commodity. The evils of overvaluation and excess liquidity, of which there was abundant experience in recent Mexican history, again went unheeded.

With the second oil shock of 1979, and its distinct impact on foreign exchange receipts from oil—which reached $9.4 billion in 1980—all caution was thrown to the winds. As the current account deficit mounted, further external loans were obtained to finance it, for a while at negative real rates of interest. The consolidation biennium was converted swiftly into an all-out finish, a veritable boom-and-bust. By 1980, the public sector deficit had grown to 6.5 percent of GDP and it kept on rising. By mid-1981, warnings that the international price of crude oil was weakening went unnoticed by the administration. The president brushed off the question by noting that the U.S. dollar was in a strong position, which benefitted oil exports. Overexpansion of the economy, the lag in adjustment of the rate of exchange to real parity, a generalized feeling that inflation was unstoppable, all contributed—once more at a critical political moment when the new PRI candidate to the presidency was about to be announced (September 1981)—to setting the stage for a loss of confidence and, as it turned out, violent capital flight. Liquidity was at its highest and interest rates in the United States were attractive even to the unsophisticated holder of small amounts of such liquidity. Never before had Mexico seen such swarms of people standing in line at bank counters day after day to buy dollar banknotes and drafts.

The peso floated down in early 1982, and an attempt was made in the spring to stem the avalanche, without benefit of an agreement with the IMF. The PRI presidential candidate, Miguel de la Madrid, who as minister for budget and programming had been in charge of the development strategy, became alarmed and required—emulating Echeverría—that "his own" minister of finance take over. This was Jesús Silva Herzog, an experienced economist who had made his career at the Bank of Mexico, in the Inter-American Development Bank (IDB), in the Ministry of Finance, in the National Workers Housing Institute, and in academic life. He improvised a weak stabilization program, but one in which he had no real control over budget expenditure or over the expansion of the public enterprise sector. It was all to no avail, for in August he was forced to announce to the IMF, the U.S. Treasury, and the world financial community that Mexico was practically insolvent (although he termed it "illiquid"). During 1981, short-term borrowing had been obtained in jumbo packages, totaling $20 billion, to offset the current account deficit, capital flight, and interest on debt. The private sector had still been able during the first six months of that year to borrow an additional $6 billion net.

By mid-1982 no more fresh money was available. The April adjustment measures were too little and had come too late. Confidence was completely shattered. López Portillo reacted with desperation, announcing to the utter surprise of all, in his address to the Congress on September 1, that the banks were to be nationalized that day, and that full and comprehensive exchange control was to go into effect immediately (partial and ineffective measures of control had been taken earlier). But the government persisted in maintaining a grossly overvalued exchange rate, so that a parallel market developed at once. No account was taken of the special problem of Mexican–U.S. border transactions. Because the new incumbent at the Bank of Mexico, Carlos Tello, a well-known economist identified with the left, decided to lower domestic interest rates, the whole bank lending process tended to be carried out outside the banking system (financial disintermediation). Foreign confidence in Mexico had been further diminished, shortly before, by the forced conversion of U.S. dollar accounts, which had been legal and had attracted short-term funds from abroad, into pesos at an artificially high (dollar) rate.

Table 5-6. Economic Indicators for the Adjustment Period, 1981–88

Indicator	1981	1982	1983	1984	1985	1986	1987	1988
Annual change in GDP (percent)	8.8	−0.6	−4.2	3.6	2.6	−4.0	1.4	−0.2
Annual change in population (percent)	2.4	2.3	2.3	2.2	2.2	2.1	2.0	2.0
Rate of inflation (percent)[a]	26.0	60.9	90.5	59.1	56.8	74.3	143.0	49.4
Real exchange rate (1981 = 100)	100.0	138.0	142.8	125.8	120.8	174.4	171.1	142.7
Export oil price (dollars per barrel)	33.18	28.69	26.39	26.89	25.33	11.84	16.06	12.25
Oil exports (millions of dollars)	13,305	15,623	14,793	14,967	13,309	5,508	7,877	5,860
Nonoil exports (millions of dollars)	6,797	5,607	7,519	9,229	8,355	10,451	12,779	14,788
Imports (millions of dollars)	23,948	14,437	8,551	11,254	13,212	11,432	12,223	18,683
Trade balance (millions of dollars)	−3,846	6,793	13,761	12,942	8,452	4,599	8,433	1,965

a. GDP deflator.
Source: Wharton (1989).

The Adjustment Policies of 1982–88

When Miguel de la Madrid, a lawyer with considerable experience in public administration, particularly in the financial sector, took office on December 1, 1982, inflation was running at an annual rate of more than 100 percent. The new president had no alternative but to cut down public sector expenditure and prepare for hard negotiation with the IMF, as a basis for rescheduling the external debt.

The public sector deficit which had reached 17 percent of GDP in 1982, was the prime target of adjustment policy. Subsidies were reduced, investment was postponed, and real wages and salaries in the public sector were reduced. Recession set in at once, and brought a sharp decline in imports.

It was necessary to cut real wages, with the help of an understanding with organized labor. The immediate prospect of reducing the rate of inflation was fulfilled, though not to the extent foreseen. Mexico had entered a phase of inertial inflation not experienced before in which the economic and business sectors readily discounted inflation to protect themselves. A sliding, controlled rate of exchange was introduced for trade and official transactions, with a parallel so-called free rate.

The real economy declined sharply during the first half of 1983. The prospect of a weak revival of public and private investment, or no revival at all, in the face of a rapidly growing labor force, meant a dim outlook for employment and for maintenance of the real income of wage earners and lower-income groups in general.

The government devoted considerable effort to negotiating new agreements with the IMF as a basis for rescheduling a large part of the public sector external debt. The first of these was successfully achieved in 1983, involving some $23 billion, and the second in 1984 for $48 billion.

In order to help the private sector reduce external debt, the Bank of Mexico established a trust fund (FICORCA). Enterprises could deposit pesos with an exchange guarantee on the part of the Bank of Mexico, which in turn would transfer the payments to creditor banks at later specified dates. Table 5-5 shows the striking reduction of private sector foreign indebtedness from a peak of nearly $22 billion in 1981 to $10 billion in 1988, mostly brought about by this scheme.

Although rescheduling provided relief on amortization, the interest bill remained very high and its financing required a large trade surplus. A surplus of $6.8 billion was achieved in 1982 and a major surplus of $13.8 billion in 1983 (table 5-6). Since aggregate exports were over $21 billion a year in 1982–83, interest payments were made possible by the fairly steady market for oil and by the drastic fall in imports, the latter reflecting the decline in GDP as well as the impact of currency depreciation.

In 1984 and 1985 there was a resumption of economic growth and public sector spending rose beyond targeted figures. Private consumption was allowed to increase by 2.5 percent and was substantially higher than agreed with the IMF, and the real exchange rate was allowed to fluctuate.

By mid-1985, more radical measures of adjustment had to be taken. In July the controlled peso was devalued by 19 percent and set on a daily market-adjusted sliding scale rather than being depreciated by a fixed nominal daily amount. A cut was announced in public expenditure, including the dismissal of thousands of government workers. At the same time, the government announced its intention of joining the GATT and abolished import licensing on a large percentage of tariff items. All of this had a clearly dampening effect on the real economy. The GDP fell during the rest of the year, with both private and public investment declining rapidly.

The central government's budget proposals for 1986 were made on the assumption that the average price of crude oil would be $22 a barrel. But the price hit bottom at less than $10 by the following April and the volume of oil exports also declined. The net outcome was a loss in projected foreign exchange receipts of about $8 billion, and a shortfall of tax revenues, equivalent to 4 percent of GDP. The year 1986 was one of major setback, with GDP down 4 percent and the rate of inflation reaching 74 percent. Real income per capita was 14 percent below that of 1980. Relief could only come from new external debt negotiations.

The negotiations, undertaken in the second half of the year, were not finalized until March 1987, so that the implementation of domestic recovery policy had to be postponed. A $12 billion package of fresh money was finally obtained, of which $6 billion was to be provided by the creditor banks and $6 billion by the multilateral financing agencies.

The external prospect improved toward the end of 1986, with the better-than-forecast price of crude oil and an appreciable rise in exports of manufactured goods. There was also a moderate return flow of private financial assets held abroad, partly induced by speculation in the domestic stock exchange and by high real rates of interest. Gross gold and foreign exchange reserves stood by mid-1987 at some $13 billion to $14 billion.

In December 1987 the government embarked on a new course, an attempt to break inflationary expectations with an income and price policy. Its effort was strengthened in February 1988, with a voluntary "pact" between government, business groups, trade unions, and peasant organizations to freeze basic prices and maintain wage stability. The government pledged to maintain fiscal austerity, maintaining a so-called primary budget surplus of 8 percent of GDP, (that is, before accounting for interest payments). The government also abolished most import licensing, rationalized tariffs, and abolished more than half of the 1,200 state enterprises. To provide an anchor for expectations, the exchange rate was frozen.

This approach succeeded in cutting inflation sharply during 1988, but at a high cost. The freeze in the exchange rate reduced competitiveness in external markets, induced higher imports, produced a big fall in the trade surplus and a major rundown in reserves. The domestic interest rate had to be very high in real terms (2–3 percent a month) to discourage capital flight and this created extra difficulties in establishing fiscal equilibrium. The pact also had a high political cost. The new president obtained only a very narrow majority in the 1988 elections and the PRI barely scraped through in Congress.

The government now has several concepts of fiscal balance. The "primary" balance was in substantial surplus, but the "financial" balance, which includes interest payment on debt, was in substantial deficit (interest payments in 1988 were 17.2 percent of GDP, 12 percent for domestic debt and 5.2 percent for foreign). In the "operational" deficit the government treats the erosion of the face value of debt through inflation as if it were government revenue (that is, as an inflation tax). The Bank of Mexico calculated that the operational deficit was reduced to 0.9 percent of GDP in 1988, but the public sector borrowing requirement (the financial deficit) was 12.3 percent of GDP.

This kind of inflation accounting is obviously necessary to separate real from monetary developments, but the differential between the financial and operational deficits will have to be greatly reduced if the country is to return to noninflationary growth. The very high real rates of interest that the government has had to pay to domestic lenders (who are free to move their capital over the border) show that expectations about the success of policy are still highly uncertain.

The Outlook

There has been a substantial reduction of the foreign debt burden as a result of the plan introduced by U.S. Treasury Secretary Brady, and the associated renegotiation of debt, and if the price of oil holds up, there is some hope that Mexico may be able to resume a more promising growth path. In the meantime, the new president, Carlos Salinas de Gortari, has renewed the main lines of the "pact" with the modification of a steady depreciation of the currency. Prices of basic wage goods and of public utility services have been adjusted periodically, and real wages have lagged, by agreement among the parties concerned.

It is clear that the crisis has had major social effects. Real GDP per capita declined by 15 percent from its 1981 peak to 1988 and real income was further squeezed by worsened terms of trade and debt service. Most categories of Mexicans have suffered. The 1987 minimum wage in real terms was 41 percent below the 1981 level. The quality of social services deteriorated. People working in the public sector had their real earnings cut substantially by government austerity. The private financial sector was hit badly by the bank nationalization, and the depressed level of activity hit many businesses badly. The wealthy and relatively prosperous persons who transferred their assets abroad were sheltered from these losses. It is in fact very difficult to make a careful assessment of how the misery has been shared. The minimum wage has limited significance as a guide to real earnings, and the processes of real exchange rate depreciation, import liberalization, and nationalization followed by privatization have redistributed the flow of profits and rents between industries. The fluctuating incidence of inflation and adjustment policies has had myriad effects that are difficult to trace.

6 Mexican Growth Performance since 1950

During the forty years between 1940–80, Mexico's GDP grew by 6.3 percent a year and its per capita product by 3 percent. By world standards, this performance was bettered only by Brazil. In 1980–87, performance worsened sharply—GDP grew only 0.8 percent a year, GDP per capita fell substantially, and factor productivity was negative.

Quantification of the factors underlying growth performance can only be rough, but nevertheless, it tells an interesting story.

The Overall Growth Accounts

Table 6-1 breaks down the main expenditure categories of GDP. Here it is clear that there was a massive mobilization of resources for investment and for government use, which together rose from 19.3 percent to 37.2 percent of GDP from 1950 to 1980. These expenditures were considered by government to be key channels in its growth strategy. The main burden of the switch in resource allocation was borne by private consumption, whose share fell from 80 percent to 65 percent. Foreign finance also played a significant role as the external balance on goods and services moved from surplus to deficit. Since the debt crisis of 1982, the picture has changed drastically. The capital inflow stopped abruptly. Investment, imports, and public consumption have had to be cut to carry the burden of debt service.

Policy between 1950 and 1970 had a strong inward-looking bias. Exports of goods and services fell from 17 percent to less than 8 percent of GDP, and imports were also substantially constrained. Since 1970, thanks mainly to oil, the export share has risen back to 1950 levels.

Tables 6-2 and 6-3 show the significant items affecting growth performance, including the growth of irrigated land and education, which are not part of our simple estimate of total factor productivity. Table 6-4 gives a crude indication of the sources of growth. In the 1940s land expansion played the most dynamic role, but in the succeeding three decades it was the expansion of physical capital inputs that was most

143

Table 6-1. Main Expenditure Categories of GDP, Selected Years, 1950–87
(percent)

Year	Private consumption	Public consumption	Gross capital formation	Exports of goods and services	Imports of goods and services
1950	80.3	5.2	14.1	17.2	16.7
1960	76.7	6.3	19.7	11.3	14.0
1970	71.9	7.3	22.7	7.7	9.7
1980	65.1	10.0	27.2	10.7	13.0
1987	64.4	8.7	20.8	18.5	12.4

Source: For 1950–60, Bank of Mexico, *Indicadores económicos* (July 1986); for 1970, Mexico, INEGI (1983), p. 17; for 1987, Wharton (1989).

Table 6-2. Indicators of Growth Performance, Selected Years, 1940–85

Year	Index of net fixed reproducible capital stock[a] (1950 = 100)	Rainfed cropland (thousands of hectares)	Irrigated land (thousands of hectares)	Equivalent rainfed land (thousands of hectares)	Employment (thousands)	Average education level of labor force (years)
1940	76.4	5,642	271	6,045	5,858	1.7
1950	100.0	7,752	1,300	9,702	8,345	2.3
1960	162.9	8,372	2,300	11,822	10,213	2.7
1970	301.7	12,713	2,765	16,861	12,956	3.7
1980	624.4	12,067	3,709	17,631	19,440	4.9
1985	703.6	(14,000)	(4,200)	(20,300)	(21,130)	(5.0)

a. Figures are for midyear. As the 1950–67 estimates were for the whole capital stock, and the 1967–85 estimates excluded agriculture, dwellings, general government, and a substantial part of transport, figures for the latter years were adjusted roughly by a coefficient intended to offset for the fact that it covered sectors where the capital stock had grown faster in 1950–67.

Source: For capital stock, in 1940–50, Selowsky (1967), p. 37; in 1950–67, Bank of Mexico (1969), table 175; in 1967–85, Villalpando Hernández and Fernández Moran (1986 and associated diskettes). For cropland, Mexico, INEGI (1985a), p. 348; for irrigated land, Mexico, INEGI (1985a), p. 845. Relative weights (1:1.5) for cropland derived from section on agriculture. Employment from table B-4. Education of labor force from table 7-2.

Table 6-3. Indexes of Basic Indicators of Growth Performance, Selected Years, 1940–85
(1950 = 100)

Year	Net fixed reproducible capital stock (weight = 25.0[a])	Land (weight = 10.0[a])	Employment (weight = 65.0[a])	Combined factor input (weight = 100.0[a])	GDP	Total factor productivity
1940	76.4	65.3	70.2	71.2	56.1	78.8
1950	100.0	100.0	100.0	100.0	100.0	100.0
1960	162.9	117.9	122.4	132.1	180.7	136.8
1970	301.7	171.0	155.3	193.4	338.4	175.0
1980	624.4	174.3	233.0	325.0	641.2	197.3
1985	703.6	201.1	253.2	360.6	694.9	192.7

a. Share of 1950 national income at factor cost (Bank of Mexico, *Indicadores económicos* [May 1986]). National income was 36,676 million pesos, of which 11,104 million pesos was remuneration of wage and salary earners. Altimir (1974), pp. 78, 80, shows that wage and salary earners were 47 percent of employment in 1950; imputed labor component of other incomes is assumed to be the same per capita as for wage and salary earners. Thus total labor income was 23,732 million pesos and total property income 12,944 million pesos. The share of agricultural land in tangible assets excluding consumer durables was taken from Goldsmith (1985), p. 264.

Source: First three columns derived from table 6-2; the fourth is a weighted average of the first three. For GDP, tables B-1 and B-2.

striking. Factor productivity growth, which provides a rough proxy for the efficiency with which resources are used, was at its peak in the 1950s. It declined sharply after 1970 when the government abandoned the old policies of stabilizing development in favor of more ambitious goals and policy weapons that involved substantial distortion in relative prices. In 1980–85, total factor productivity performance was substantially negative, partly because capital was under-utilized after 1982, and there were substantial efficiency losses in the superboom and subsequent recession.

Table 6-5 shows growth experience in major sectors of the economy. For all major sectors the period of revolution and institutional change, 1910–40, was one of relatively slow growth. This was particularly true in agriculture where there was a major change in landownership and property rights. In petroleum, foreign companies managed to isolate production from the effects of the revolution so that output in 1921 was fifty-three times as high as in 1910; in the 1920s and 1930s, disputes over property rights caused a fall in output. By 1940, petroleum output was less than a quarter of its 1921 peak.

It is clear that the 1940s belong to the golden age of fast growth, which lasted until 1982. The agricultural sector did particularly well in the

Table 6-4. Sources of Growth, by Period, 1940–85
(annual average compound growth, in percent)

Period	Net fixed reproducible capital	Land	Employment	Combined factor input	GDP	Total factor productivity	Labor productivity	Capital productivity
1940–50	2.7	4.4	3.6	3.5	6.0	2.4	2.3	3.1
1950–60	5.0	1.7	2.0	2.8	6.1	3.2	4.0	1.0
1960–70	6.4	3.8	2.4	3.9	6.5	2.5	4.0	0.1
1970–80	7.5	0.2	4.1	5.3	6.6	1.2	2.4	−0.9
1980–85	2.4	2.9	1.7	2.1	1.6	−0.5	−0.1	−0.8

Source: Table 6-3.

Table 6-5. Growth of Real GDP, by Major Sector, Selected Periods, 1910–85
(percent)

Factor and period	Agriculture, forestry, and fishing	Mining	Manufacturing, construction, and utilities	Services	GDP
Overall growth[a]					
1910–40	0.6	2.2	2.7	1.1	1.3
1940–50	5.8	3.5	7.5	5.7	6.0
1950–80	3.5	6.5	7.6	6.5	6.4
1980–85	2.9	4.4	1.1	1.5	1.6
Share of growth increment[b]					
1910–40	9.9	9.5	31.7	49.0	100.0
1940–50	18.9	3.3	25.1	52.7	100.0
1950–80	6.9	3.3	33.6	56.2	100.0
1980–85	16.6	9.3	21.7	52.4	100.0
Share of growth in employment					
1910–40	54.4	0.6	9.4	35.6	100.0
1940–50	41.6	−0.4	27.5	31.3	100.0
1950–80	7.0	3.4	31.7	57.9	100.0
1980–84	37.9	4.6	−23.7	81.2	100.0
Growth per person employed[a]					
1910–40	0.4	2.1	2.5	0.7	1.1
1940–80	3.1	1.8	2.5	1.3	3.1
1980–84	0.5	2.5	1.7	−1.5	−0.3
Productivity level per person employed					
1984	32.0	148.4	137.1	123.4	100.0

a. Annual average compound growth rate.
b. Based on 1960 market prices.
Source: Tables B-3, B-4, B-5.

1940s. This was partly the fruit of investment in irrigation but it must also have reflected a restoration of more normal cultivation and rebuilding of livestock after all the transitional costs of changing property rights.

Although modernization and growth in Mexico have often been attributed to industrialization, it is clear that the service sector accounted for the biggest share of growth (table 6-5). Part of the growth occurred in technically advanced areas like transport, communications, and financial services, but there was also growth in government employment in administration, health, and education—as well as in privately financed health and education. Employment in commerce increased its

Table 6-6. Structure of Employment and Gross Value Added, 1950 and 1986

(percent)

Sector	Employment 1950	Employment 1986	Share of GDP including intermediate financial services 1950	Share of GDP including intermediate financial services 1986
Agriculture, forestry, and fishing	58.3	27.5	20.0	9.3
Manufacturing	11.8	11.0	21.2	24.3
Mining and utilities	1.5	1.7	6.6	4.8
Construction	2.7	8.7	2.3	4.2
Trade	8.3	14.4[a]	29.5[a]	26.3[a]
Transport and communications	2.5	4.8	4.4	7.0
Other services[b]	14.9	31.9	16.1	24.1
Total	100.0	100.0	100.0	100.0
Intermediate financial services	—	—	−0.8	−1.3

— Not available.
a. Includes hotels and restaurants.
b. Includes unspecified services.

Source: For GDP, in 1950, Bank of Mexico (1969); in 1986, Mexico, INEGI (1987a), p. 33. For employment, in 1950, Mexico, INEGI (1985a), vol. 1, p. 252; in 1986, Mexico, INEGI (1987a), p. 35.

share, as the urbanization process meant a relative intensification of distributive networks.

In terms of labor productivity (table 6-5) agriculture showed the most growth over the four decades 1940–80, at 3.1 percent a year; manufacturing grew at 2.5 percent, mining at 1.8 percent, and services lagged at 1.3 percent. The subsequent slowdown in productivity growth in the 1980s was drastic in all sectors except mining. It was most pronounced in services, which, having a lot of self-employment and government employment, are prone to labor hoarding in time of recession.

Overall productivity (GDP per person employed) grew faster than that in most individual sectors in 1940–80. At 3.1 percent a year, it was matched only by agriculture. The overall figure reflects not only within-sector growth, but the effect of shifts in the relative importance of employment between sectors. The level of productivity was low in agriculture, and much higher in other sectors whose share of employment was growing. The positive effect of the intersectoral shift boosted aggregate productivity growth in the golden age. The reverse was the case in the 1980s.

The level of productivity in agriculture, forestry, and fishing in 1984 was about a third of that in the economy as a whole, and a quarter of that in industry (table 6-5). The highest productivity was in mining where the natural resource advantage lies.

Table 6-7 shows the changing pattern of labor productivity by region. The spread is quite wide, with the highest levels in the metropolitan and the North Gulf regions—in and around Mexico City and Monterrey—and the lowest performance in the South Pacific region. From 1950 to 1980, there was some narrowing in the regional spread from 2.7 to 1 to 2.5 to 1, and the most successful region in 1950, the North Pacific, had reverted to the mean by 1980.

The quality of statistical information on Mexican growth is seriously limited. Shortcomings are greatest in the case of employment (particularly in agriculture), where long-term series have to be derived from successive censuses that have varied in their definitions and reliability, the 1980 census being one of the worst. The adjusted employment estimates used here for each period are from the analyst who seems to have tackled the problems in that period most successfully (for 1900–10, D. P. Keesing in Wilkie and Ruddle 1977; 1950–70, Altimir 1974; 1940 and 1980, Gregory 1986). Nevertheless, the figures for employment and labor productivity by sector are rough—robust enough for broad conclusions, but not fit for more refined growth accounts. (Problems with

Table 6-7. GDP per Employed Person, by Region, 1950 and 1980
(percent)

Region	1950	1980
National average	100.0	100.0
Metropolitan	117.8	139.2
North Gulf	146.2	137.0
North	146.4	105.6
North Pacific	153.1	101.3
Central North	94.3	67.6
Central Pacific	75.6	86.7
Central Gulf	137.4	101.6
Central	55.7	68.5
South Pacific	64.5	55.1
Peninsular	87.2	77.2
Ratio, highest to lowest	2.7:1	2.5:1

Source: For 1950, van Ginneken (1980); for 1980, Mexico, INEGI (1985c).

The Role of Government on the Supply Side

Government has been important in mobilizing resources for growth—in raising the rate of domestic saving, in restoring international creditworthiness, in encouraging foreign investment, and in fostering technical change. It has also played a major role in allocating resources to particular purposes by elaborate regulatory measures, controls, investment and pricing policy for public enterprises, subsidies, and tax incentives. The tightest control, over imports, reflects a strong commitment to national autonomy, self-sufficiency, and import substitution. This attitude, fairly general in Latin America, has been reinforced in the Mexican case by deep feelings of national pride and a desire to break with the long experience of foreign intervention and influence.

MOBILIZATION AND ALLOCATION OF CAPITAL. Over the course of four decades, in considerable measure through government macromanagement, the rate of fixed investment was raised steadily and by impressive proportions (table 6-8). In 1939, gross fixed investment was a meager 5.3 percent of GDP, which may well be fairly representative of the depressed situation in the 1920s and 1930s. By the end of the golden age it had risen to nearly 23 percent. Part of the rise was financed by government itself, either directly or by foreign borrowing, but private domestic investment was also greatly encouraged by the nature of policy after 1940—reestablishment of international creditworthiness, noninterference with basic property rights, gradual encouragement of private saving by a policy of cautious public finance, moderation of inflation,

Table 6-8. Public and Private Gross Fixed Investment as a Proportion of GDP, Selected Periods, 1939–85
(percentage of GDP in current prices)

Year	Total	Public	Private	Financed externally
1939	5.3	2.9	2.4	−2.6
1940–49	8.6	4.2	4.4	0.0
1950–59	15.3	5.2	10.1	2.8
1960–70	17.5	6.6	10.9	2.3
1971–76	19.8	7.2	12.6	3.2
1977–82	22.7	10.1	12.6	4.0
1983–85	17.9	7.1	10.8	−2.2

Source: For 1939–69, Bank of Mexico; thereafter, Mexico, INEGI.

exchange rate stability, complete freedom for capital movements, high real rates of interest on domestic savings, and low taxes. These policies reached their peak of success in the period of stabilizing development in 1958–70 in the presidencies of López Mateos and Díaz Ordaz, when Ortiz Mena was finance minister, but the tone and intent of policy was clear from 1940 onward. In fact there were only four finance ministers over the thirty-five years from 1946 to 1970, and effective power over economic policy was more or less delegated to them and their associated technocratic elite.

Although the government role in capital formation has been substantial and has involved favored terms for borrowers in segments of the market to which the government gave priority, Mexico generally was given fairly high marks for the efficiency of its mechanisms for allocating capital funds before the 1970s. Thus Little, Scitovsky, and Scott said: "Much attention was and is still paid in Mexico to the evaluation of competing investment projects and their profitability. This probably has to do with the important role played, and influence on investment policy exerted by the state development bank, Nacional Financiera, which naturally takes a banker's attitude in applying economic criteria and calculating rates of return on the various projects considered" (1970, p. 36).

After 1970, the basic policy tradeoffs changed. Government continued to increase public investment, but there was a clear move away from fiscal and monetary caution, greater emphasis on public ownership, a bigger departure from realistic pricing in the public sector, and three serious infringements of private property rights—expropriation of land in the Northwest in 1976, compulsory conversion of domestic dollar accounts to pesos, and bank nationalization in 1982. All of these reduced the effectiveness of investment and posed threats to its level once confidence in the system was broken. They also induced the massive capital flight in the 1980s.

Some idea of the inefficiency of resource allocation in the capital market by the 1980s can be obtained from table 6-9, which shows the variation in real rates of return between various instruments in 1985 and 1986. In 1985 these varied from minus 27 percent on savings accounts to plus 23 percent on petroleum bonds, and the spread in 1986 was even wider. In earlier periods, these spreads were much smaller—in 1960–67 around 5 percent and in 1974–79 up to 16 percent, compared with a 50 percent spread in 1985 and 58 percent in 1986.

GROWTH AND ALLOCATION OF LABOR SUPPLY. With regard to labor, the other major factor input, government policy played a smaller and more indirect role than in capital flow. Inflows to the labor market mainly reflect the growth of population around fifteen years earlier. Because government encouragement of family planning did not start until 1974,

Table 6-9. Annual Yield of Various Financial Instruments, 1985 and 1986

(percent)

	1985 yield		1986 yield	
Instrument	Nominal[a]	Real[b]	Nominal[a]	Real[b]
Savings accounts	20.0	−26.7	20.0	−41.7
Certificates of Deposit				
1 month	70.0	3.8	106.7	0.5
3 months	65.9	1.3	111.5	2.8
6 months	54.2	−5.8	94.2	−5.6
1 year	39.6	−14.7	40.1	−31.9
Treasury bills				
28 days	79.9	9.9	130.1	7.9
91 days	77.5	8.4	122.0	7.9
Bank Acceptances (30 days)	82.0	11.2	133.9	13.7
Petroleum-bonds	102.0	23.4	138.6	16.0

a. Assuming capital and interest reinvestment for equal periods of time.
b. Deflated by the increase in the consumer price index from December to December.
Source: Reyes Heroles G. G. (1987).

the falling birth rate thereafter has not had a direct effect on the flow of young workers, but it has probably contributed to a rising rate of female employment. The rate for male employment dropped, partly as a result of increased schooling and partly because growth in social security permitted older workers and the handicapped to obtain pensions. The activity rate in Mexico is extraordinarily low by international standards. In 1950 the labor force was only 30.5 percent of the population and the figure was down to 28.9 percent in 1980 (table 6-10). This is undoubtedly a result of high fertility rates, which have produced a large dependent population of children and women whose main pursuit is motherhood.

The average education of the labor force rose from 2.3 years in 1950 to 4.4 years in 1980, as older uneducated cohorts left the scene and were replaced by workers who had benefitted from the spread of education. Apart from formal education, the government increased expenditure on vocational training. However, the 1980 census showed that 27 percent of the population between the ages of six and fourteen was not attending school, and for those twelve to fourteen years old the ratio was 51 percent. The proportion of those who had never attended was of course a good deal higher for older people, already in the labor force. A fifth of the labor force in the 1980s could not even read or write, and the level of literacy and numeracy of those who could do so was poor. No reasonable measures of the quality of education suitable for international comparison are available, but it is clear that most Mexicans think the quality of public education is poor. Those who can afford it spend a good deal of money sending their children to private schools. In 1978, 17 percent of total expenditure on education was in private institutions.

Although the government party, Partido Revolucionario Institucional (PRI), has a strong labor wing, and the relatively small number of workers in public enterprise have favorable pay and perquisites, government action has had only a marginal effect on wage levels. That is true despite the existence of minimum wage boards since 1934 and a great deal of ostensible prescriptive activity. There are no unemployment benefits; evasion of minimum wage legislation is extensive, and the minimum wage clearly does not provide an effective floor to wages. Gregory (1986) cites figures for Mexico City in 1970 showing that 65 percent of unskilled construction workers and 78 percent of unskilled service workers earned less than the minimum wage. The minimum wage has moved erratically and has borne little relation to the growth of real per capita GDP. It fell by half in real terms in the 1940s and rose very little in the boom years 1976–82. In any case, wage and salary earners are somewhat less than half of those employed. Gregory argues that wage flexibility has been a major reason for the lack of significant unemployment. He concludes: "The labor market has proved to be an efficient mechanism for reallocating labor resources in response to changes in sectoral and regional demands for labor. By avoiding institutional interventions that seriously distorted the price of labor, Mexico has also avoided misallocation of labor.... Because the labor market was allowed to price labor at its opportunity cost, labor-intensive productive activities have been able to thrive alongside a more capital-intensive productive sector that requires a substantially different class of labor. The flexibility of the labor market has thus facilitated a high level of employment and utilization of the labor force" (1986, p. 268).

A major easement of the labor situation has been the possibility of migration to the United States. Gregory (1986, p. 171) quotes figures

Table 6-10. Ratio of Labor Force to Total Population in Three Countries, 1950 and 1980

Country	1950	1980
Brazil	33.0	36.5
Mexico	30.5	28.9
United States	40.5	45.0

Source: For Mexico, table B-8; for Brazil, FIBGE, *Anuário Estatístico;* for United States, OECD, *Labour Force Statistics.*

showing legal migration of more than 1.2 million Mexicans over the period 1951–77, and, after sifting the conflicting and murky evidence, he arrives at a figure of between two million and three million undocumented Mexican immigrants in the United States in the mid-1970s (p. 185). Most of these migrants were people of working age, so even on a conservative estimate the Mexican labor force might well have been 10 percent bigger by 1980 if this escape valve had not existed.

EMBODYING TECHNICAL PROGRESS. As a country that lagged well behind the world's best technological practice, Mexico enjoyed considerable opportunities for growth by adapting foreign technology. It was effective in attracting large-scale foreign investment and in promoting industrial research. Research on new seeds, which pioneered the world's Green Revolution, explains a significant part of Mexican agricultural success.

Inefficiency in Product Markets

Government intervention in product markets has aroused more criticism than has intervention in factor markets, and there is certainly substantial evidence of microeconomic inefficiency here. Estimates of the impact of particular measures on growth forgone do not seem to exist and would be difficult to construct. But there is good evidence on intervention in foreign commerce, on the pricing policy of public corporations, and on the manipulation of input and output prices to the disfavor of agriculture and in favor of heavy industry.

INTERVENTION IN FOREIGN COMMERCE. In the early postwar years, Mexican tariffs were low. Little, Scitovsky, and Scott (1970) still characterized tariff protection as moderate in the mid-1960s, by Latin American standards. However, Mexico did not become a member of the General Agreement on Tariffs and Trade (GATT) until 1986, so the scope for tariff manipulation was unlimited, and the legal short-cut to quick tariff changes (bypassing congressional approval) by calculating incidence on the basis of artificial "official prices" was frequently used. Moreover, trade barriers did not have to be on a most-favored-nation basis but could involve discriminatory bilateral arrangements.

More important than tariffs was the extensive use of quantitative import controls. During the period 1954–76, when the exchange rate of 12.50 pesos to the dollar was fixed, the peso became increasingly overvalued. Mexico's price level rose faster than that of its main trading partner, the United States, and the relative level of internal demand was often much higher. As a result, the commodity export share fell from 14.3 percent of GDP in 1950 to 3.8 percent in 1970 (table 6-11). The current payments deficit widened, and there was increased reliance on foreign

Table 6-11. Elements in the Current Balance of Payments, Selected Years, 1950–85

	Share of GDP in current prices (percent)					
Year	Merchandise exports	Other current earnings	Merchandise imports	Other current expenditures	Current balance	Real exchange rate $(1950=100)$[a]
1950	14.3[b]	6.1	11.4	5.6	3.4	100.0
1960	6.3[b]	5.0	9.3	5.3	−3.3	76.9
1970	3.8[b]	5.3	6.6	5.9	−3.4	62.6
1982	12.7	4.1	8.6	11.9	−3.7	97.0
1985	12.3	4.7	7.6	9.1	0.3	84.9

a. From table B-10.
b. Includes exports of nonmonetary gold and silver.
Source: Bank of Mexico, *Indicadores económicos* (May 1986).

borrowing. Tariffs were raised four times between 1956 and 1962, and 80 percent of tariff positions were subject to licensing in 1973 as opposed to 33 percent in 1956 (table 6-12). The number of individual items subject to import controls rose from 1,376 in 1956 to 12,800 in 1973 and, according to King (1970), more than thirty government committees were required to issue about 3,000 individual import licenses each week. Import licenses were not auctioned, so the scope for inefficiency, collusion, corruption, smuggling, and windfall gains and losses was extraordinary. This kind of distortion was present throughout the golden age of high growth in the 1960s; it was not an innovation of the later period in which total factor productivity fell so sharply.

Table 6-12. Evolution of Import Licensing, 1956–85

	Tariff positions		
Year	Total	Number controlled	Percent controlled
1956	4,129	1,376	33
1962	5,204	2,313	44
1970	12,900	8,400	65
1973	16,000	12,800	80
1980	7,776	1,866	24
1983	8,032	8,032	100
1985[a]	(8,500)	425	5

a. July.
Source: Bueno (1987).

In August 1976, there was a major devaluation, a temporary check to demand as the new López Portillo government carried out a stabilization exercise in 1977 and liberalized imports. However, the old pattern was soon repeated. The exchange rate grew increasingly overvalued between 1976 and 1982 because of the differences in price inflation in Mexico and the United States and the huge pressure of internal demand built up by the government's expansionary public spending. In spite of very large foreign borrowing and booming oil exports, the government had to buttress the payments position by raising tariffs and quantity restrictions in 1981 and again in 1982. In 1982–83, import controls reached their peak, and all imports were subject to license.

PRICING POLICY OF PUBLIC ENTERPRISES. Public enterprises have always been conceived to have social objectives. There has been a deeply ingrained tendency to assume that these objectives could be best attained by selling the products of public enterprises cheaply, sometimes below cost. This practice has caused losses that had to be made good by claims on the general budget, and benefits have been random and untargeted, which has resulted in significant inefficiency and waste in resource use—for example, unusually high levels of consumption of gasoline, electricity, water, and sugar.

The propensity to distribute largesse by underpricing grew from 1970 onward, as the growth in the government budget deficit indicates, but even if it had remained unchanged over time, the importance of this phenomenon would have risen simply because the number of public enterprises rose so fast (Trejo 1987):

Year	Number	Year	Number
1917	2	1970	391
1930	12	1982	1,176
1940	47	1986	744
1950	158		

The output of non-oil public corporations rose modestly, but that of PEMEX, the state oil monopoly, jumped from 1.3 percent of GDP in 1973 to 8.2 percent in 1980. If PEMEX had been allowed to charge world prices domestically, its value added would have risen from 2.1 percent to 13.8 percent (table 6-13). The hidden subsidy to domestic consumers rose from 0.8 percent of GDP in 1973 to 5.6 percent in 1980 (table 6-14). PEMEX did generate increased tax revenue for the government which rose from 0.17 percent of GDP in 1973 to 3.8 percent in 1980. It also had a modest operating surplus after tax, which rose from 0.4 percent of GDP in 1973 to 1.4 percent in 1980, but in both years its investments were more than double the after-tax operating surplus, so that it was forced to borrow abroad to finance them.

Table 6-13. PEMEX Finances, 1973 and 1980

Item	1973	1980
Income and expenditure (billions of pesos)	18.0	95.4
Internal sales revenue		
Foreign sales revenue	0.3	261.9
Wages and salaries	5.2	20.1
Other current expenditure	9.3	111.3
Gross operating surplus	3.7	220.8
Tax Payments	1.2	162.3
Investment	5.9	121.8
Gross value added	8.9	240.9
Subsidy to domestic consumption	5.4	350.9
Potential gross value added	14.3	591.8
Value added (percent)	1.3	8.2
Share of GDP		
Potential as share of GDP	2.1	13.8
Employees (thousands)	79,100	112,300

Source: S. C. Rizzo in Aspe and Sigmund (1984).

Apart from their pricing policy, public corporations tended to have inflated labor costs because of the political clout of government unions. It has been argued that PEMEX workers enjoyed labor compensation 50 percent higher than workers in comparable industries in 1973 and twice as high in 1980. Costs were also inflated by poor management and corruption, though to a much smaller degree than the inflation caused by pricing policy, because employment in public sector firms was only 3.3 percent of total employment in 1980.

Table 6-14. PEMEX Subsidies to Domestic Consumers, 1980

Product	Price (pesos per equivalent cubic meter of crude oil) Consumer	International	Ratio of international to consumer price (Consumer price = 1.0)	Subsidy (billions of pesos)
Natural gas	295.6	3,728.5	12.6	58.7
Fuel oil	265.7	4,092.4	15.4	64.3
Diesel	872.6	7,101.1	8.1	90.3
Liquid gas	2,088.6	6,706.9	3.2	23.0
Gasoline	3,365.0	7,706.9	2.3	75.0
Kerosene	510.9	7,794.4	15.3	14.9

Source: S. C. Rizzo in Aspe and Sigmund (1984).

MANIPULATION OF RELATIVE PRICES. Government manipulation of prices has worked against agriculture and in favor of heavy industry. In agriculture, producer prices for livestock products have been squeezed to the point where farmers have slaughtered their cattle rather than sell milk at a loss; the result was a surge in imports of powdered milk. In sugar markets low prices to producers and subsidized prices to consumers transformed the country from a sugar exporter to an importer in the 1970s. In industry, a combination of discriminating rates of protection and subsidized loans gave heavy favors to capital goods.

Demand Management and Growing Macroeconomic Disequilibrium, 1970–82

Apart from the mobilization of factor input and its efficient allocation, the government needs to ensure a reasonable overall equilibrium between demand and supply through effective management of the fiscal-monetary mix. If the economy is not kept on a reasonably smooth growth path but is allowed to gather too much steam, inflation will emerge, external payments will fall into deficit, and crises of confidence may develop. The sharp and damaging adjustment measures necessary to restore balance have greater costs than the output forgone if less ambitious policies were pursued at an early stage. The full consequences of the sharp deterioration in 1970–82 in the management of Mexico's economy were felt only in the 1980s.

Until 1970, Mexico's fiscal policy was reasonably cautious and its growth path very smooth in real terms (table 6-15). There was a steady decline in the rate of inflation from the 1940s to 1970 and external public debt was modest. From 1970 onward the situation changed substantially. Fiscal and monetary policy became much more expansionary, with a sharp rise in the ratio of government expenditure to GDP (from 20 percent in 1970 to 47 percent in 1982) and a huge public sector borrowing requirement in the López Portillo administration, which peaked at 17 percent of GDP in 1982 (table 6-16). The average real interest rate became negative and there was a capital flight of around $30 billion in face of an increasingly unrealistic exchange rate. The growing external deficit was met by subjecting all imports to licensing and by massive foreign borrowing.

Between 1976 and 1982, the number of people employed in general government grew by 60 percent (table 6-17). Some of this represented a growth in education and health services, but there was also a big increase in general administrative personnel and a rise of 53 percent in the number working for public enterprise. Deficits of public corporations were increased by the policy of random subsidies to those consuming their products. Government credit agencies increased the subsidy element in loans.

Table 6-15. Indicators of Macromanagement Performance, 1941–87

President	Period	Public sector borrowing requirement (percentage of GDP)	Annual real interest rate on deposit accounts (percent)	Average annual change in GDP deflator (percent)	Average annual growth of GDP (percent)	External public debt at end of period (billions of dollars)
Avila Camacho	1941–46	1.3	−9.0	15.5	6.1	n.a.
Alemán	1947–52	0.5	−4.8	7.7	5.7	n.a.
Ruiz Cortines	1953–58	1.2	−1.0	7.5	6.4	n.a.
López Mateos	1959–64	2.1	4.8	4.0	6.7	2.1
Díaz Ordaz	1965–70	3.4	5.5	3.3	6.8	4.3
Echeverría	1971–76	7.2	−3.2	13.7	6.2	27.9
López Portillo	1977–82	9.9	−7.7	30.0	6.0	68.5
de la Madrid	1983–87	12.7	—	81.5	−0.4	89.4

n.a Not applicable.
— Not available.
Source: For 1941–82, Titkin (1984); for 1983–87, Bank of Mexico and National Accounts.

The López Portillo policy performance was a catastrophic case of macroeconomic mismanagement and microeconomic waste engendered by populistic ambition, the new oil wealth and unlimited faith in the efficacy and wisdom of government action (table 6-18). The final gesture, the nationalization of the banking system, exacerbated the crisis, struck a major blow at the confidence of the private sector, and encumbered the government with private foreign liabilities. Adverse external factors, such as the sharp rise in international interest rates in real terms and the fall in oil prices, worsened Mexico's problems. But the inflation and debt crisis were in large degree self-inflicted. Whatever the judgment on causality, the 1986–82 crisis was as big a shock for Mexico as the 1929–32 world crisis.

Table 6-16. Public Expenditure as a Share of GDP, Selected Years, 1965–82
(percent)

Year	Transfers	Interest	Other	Total
1965	4.2	0.8	14.4	19.4
1970	4.5	1.9	13.8	20.2
1976	6.3	3.0	21.1	30.4
1982	12.2	8.6	25.9	46.7

Note: Includes general government and public corporations.
Source: Titkin (1984).

Table 6-17. Government Employment, 1975-86
(thousands)

Year	Public education	Public health services	Public administration, defense, and security[a]	General government, total	Public enterprise, total[b]	All government employment, total
1975	727	195	701	1,623	529	2,152
1976	850	212	721	1,783	564	2,347
1977	938	232	716	1,885	592	2,477
1978	1,017	240	769	2,026	631	2,657
1979	1,134	266	826	2,226	675	2,901
1980	1,253	293	919	2,465	738	3,203
1981	1,394	318	989	2,701	801	3,502
1982	1,469	345	1,029	2,844	865	3,709
1983	1,589	352	1,051	2,992	1,013	4,005
1984	1,702	353	1,121	3,176	1,049	4,225
1985	1,768	370	1,148	3,287	1,060	4,347
1986	1,846	384	1,152	3,382	1,032	4,414

a. In 1980 there were 120,000 regulars and 250,000 conscripts in the armed forces.
b. Figures cover the 212 major public enterprises.
Source: Mexico, INEGI (1985a, 1988).

The de la Madrid presidency was fully occupied cleaning up the aftermath of the previous administration. It had to cope with inflation on a scale unknown since the Revolution, which was probably a necessary cost in facing the burdens of adjustment. It greatly reduced imports, increased and diversified non-oil exports, joined the GATT and liberalized trade, kept the exchange rate realistic, serviced the foreign debt more fully than other Latin American debtors, built up reserves,

Table 6-18. Government Share of Value Added and Employment, by Sector, 1975 and 1983
(percent)

Sector	Gross value added at current prices 1975	1983	Employment 1975	1983
Agriculture, forestry, and fishing	0.0	−0.4	0.7	1.1
Industry	16.8	42.6	11.2	16.1
Construction	0.0	0.0	0.0	0.0
Services	17.6	19.7	25.8	34.2
Total	14.4	25.8	14.1	20.4

Source: For public sector, Mexico, INEGI (1985b); totals, Mexico, INEGI (1983, 1984c).

cut down domestic spending, raised taxes, rationalized public sector price policy to some degree, eliminated half of the public sector corporations, rebuilt private business confidence to some extent, and contained capital flight. The real cost of these actions was a drop of per capita income by 2.5 percent a year from 1982 to 1987, compared with a growth of 3.1 percent a year in the forty-two years from 1940 to 1982.

Conclusion

It is not possible to provide a detailed counterfactual account of alternative and better policies for growth. But the evidence marshalled here indicates that if there had been a more realistic exchange rate policy, a more liberal trade policy, a different pricing policy for public enterprise, and a more cautious fiscal-monetary mix, growth in 1970–82 might have been a little smaller, but the whole growth process would have been much smoother and more efficient and the readjustment problems of the 1980s would have been mild. Mexico had unusual opportunities, because of its new oil wealth, and they were recklessly squandered. More sensible policies would not have conflicted with the basic constraints of the political system and institutions.

Agricultural Policies

Land reform and its consequences are the elements essential to understanding the politics and economics of the Mexican farm sector. Mexico is proud of being the first developing country—in 1915—to enact radical agrarian reform legislation. At that time, land was held in large units, many of them over 100,000 hectares in size, and owned either by descendants of the colonial Spanish or by new, and often foreign, proprietors, who had obtained estates cheaply during the Porfiriato. Working on these estates were several million landless peons, lowly paid, many of them permanently in debt to their landlords and thus unable to leave. Since the estate owners cultivated only small portions of their holdings, it seemed sensible to transfer some of their unused land to the land hungry. Production would be increased while land capital would become more equally distributed.

Land Reform

The Agrarian Reform Act of 1915 pursued two objectives, giving land to the rural poor and limiting the size of the large holdings. Some intellectuals and political leaders favored the establishment of small owner-occupied family farms on the European model. Majority opinion, however, accepted the fashionable doctrines of the communist-utopists, notably those of Enrique Flores Magón, whose writings depicted a happy society in which all property was held in common, and everyone worked for the common good. It was also believed (not entirely correctly) that communal cultivation had prevailed in Aztec times.

The new legislation provided that the inhabitants of any village could join together and collectively request land from the government. The grant was made to the organized village, or *ejido*, which became the legal owner. The *ejido* in turn, while retaining the pasture and forest areas for common use, allocated to its members—*ejidatarios*—parcels of arable land (*parcelas*), usually 5–10 hectares, to be held as long as they were farmed. The *ejidatario* can pass his *parcela* to his sons but cannot sell, rent, or divide it. If he leaves—migrates to a city, for example—his *parcela* reverts to the *ejido* and he receives no compensation, even if he has made improvements such as terracing or drainage. This has discouraged land improvements and has given the president, or local boss, of the *ejido* wide powers to manipulate the occupancy of *parcelas* so that his friends secure the more fertile units.

In parts of Mexico where villagers had lost their farmland to private buyers during the Porfiriato but still worked as communities to tap resin and cut timber in communally held forests, their lands, when satisfactorily identified, were restored to them under the Reform Act. Today the organization of those communities (*communidades agrarias*) largely resembles that of *ejidos*, except that many of their assemblies have permitted outright individual ownership of *parcelas*. These communities are found mainly on poor-quality land in remote regions of the west and south. They occupy only 6.6 percent of the total land area, whereas *ejidos* have 43.3 percent.

Legal texts tend to be ambiguous about the limitations on the size of private farms. The provisions for arable farms differ from those for pasture and livestock farms, and a landowner has to register for one or the other. An arable farm can have a maximum of 100 hectares of irrigated land (150 hectares for cotton) or 200 hectares of rainfed land (300 hectares for coffee), exceptions that have no technical or economic justification. A livestock farmer is permitted a maximum of 500 head of cattle or its equivalent in minor animals (pigs, sheep, goats, poultry), though the equivalent is nowhere defined. He is further entitled to a pasture area sufficient to support 500 cattle, though elsewhere the act puts the pasture limit at 800 hectares. However, in the arid zones of the north, 50 or more hectares per head of cattle is the norm—in other words, on the interpretation of "sufficient pasture" the rancher would be entitled to 25,000 hectares, not 800!

A crop or livestock farmer obtains a certificate of inalienability—that is, exemption from expropriation—only if his property conforms to the provisions of the act. In addition to these and other legal ambiguities, the fact that no official property surveys exist and that property boundaries are therefore a matter of local tradition opens opportunities for land seizure by ambitious local politicians—hence the feeling of insecurity among private farmers.

Despite the revolutionary fervor of 1915, expropriation proceeded remarkably slowly. Only some 8 million hectares, or 6 percent of the total farm area, had been transferred to *ejidos* by 1930. Then the pace quickened, under President Cárdenas, to cover another 20 million hectares in the 1930s, 15 million between 1940 and 1960, and 16 million in the 1960s (Mexico, INEGI 1985a). Grants to communities increased at a more modest rate; in 1970 they held 9 million hectares compared with 61 million in *ejidos*.

The number of *ejidos* rose to 21,461 and the number of *ejidatarios* above 2 million (table 6-19). The *ejidos* grew in size, from an average of 2,000 hectares in 1930 to nearly 3,000 hectares in 1970. But this increase was mainly in pasture and forest; the average arable land per *ejido* rose only from 419 to 495 hectares. The goal of 10 hectares per *ejidatario* was never attained, the average holding of arable land being 5.4 hectares in 1940 and very little better at 6.1 hectares in 1970. At that date, only 16,710 *parcelas*, or 1 percent of the total, exceeded 20 hectares in size, and then not by very much. *Ejidos* and communities predominate in the center and south of the country, exceeding 60 percent of the total area counted in the census, whereas they occupy only 30–40 percent in the northern states.

Table 6-19. Ejidos and Ejidatarios, by Decade, 1930–70

Category	1930	1940	1950	1960	1970
Ejidos					
Total number	4,189	14,670	17,579	18,699	21,461
Total area per *ejido* (hectares)	1,992	1,970	2,213	2,380	2,821
Arable area per *ejido* (hectares)	419	447	444	469	495
Average number of *ejidatarios* per *ejido*	128	109	88	85	94
Ejidatarios					
Total (thousands)	537	1,601	1,553	1,598	2,013
Without land (thousands)	—	378	175	74	—
With land (thousands)	—	1,223	1,378	1,524	1,733[a]
Arable land per *ejidatario* with land (hectares)	3.3	5.4	5.7	5.8	6.1

— Not available.
a. Number of *ejidatarios* with individual *parcelas*.
Source: Decennial agricultural censuses.

For a time, more equitable land distribution seemed compatible with expansion of output, largely because land unused but of good quality was being given to *ejidos*. From the 1960s onward, only very poor or already cultivated private land has been available for transfer, the expansion of food production has slowed, and a conflict between policies of economic growth and policies of more equal land distribution has become apparent.

But the continuing nature of the transfer, together with the political slogan "the revolution is never finished," encouraged the rural poor to believe that land distribution would go on forever. When transfer activities diminished in the 1970s, activists resorted on many occasions to violence, forcibly occupying private farms, slaughtering cattle, and destroying buildings.

Farm People

As subsistence agriculture and single crops predominate in many regions, it is difficult to determine the number of persons actually engaged in farming. Work is heavy at seedtime and harvest, with months of near idleness between. Many farm people then take other jobs and derive more than half their income therefrom. Since farm labor peaks occur at different seasons in different districts, family members may migrate to pick cotton, cut sugarcane, or harvest coffee and thus be counted twice as part of the farming population. Juridical problems in counting *ejidatarios*, because of differences in the legal definition of their status, can cause the registered number to vary between 1 million and 2 million. Moreover, thousands of *ejidatarios* work almost all year in cities but carefully retain their registration so as not to lose the right to their *parcelas*.

Hence it is not surprising to find widely divergent estimates of the farm labor force. For instance, in 1970 the population census enumerated 5.1 million persons occupied in agriculture, while the agricultural census reported 7.8 million. Moreover, the population census included persons whose principal occupation was hunting, forestry, or fishing, which the agricultural census excluded. In some states the agricultural census figure was more than double the population census figure, and indeed in six states the "occupied in farming" total exceeded the total working population. Similar anomalies had occurred in earlier censuses but were more pronounced in 1970. They can be partly explained by the confusion of concepts, but they also derive from careless enumeration and (in 1970) from the first use of computers for tabulation. In the 1980 population census the tabulation of occupations contains such a high percentage of "unspecified" (over 30 percent in several states) that the breakdown by sectors is meaningless. Hence the 1970 data remain the latest reasonable figures available.

In light of all this, and because of the difficulty in determining the status of individuals (for example, whether hired workers are classed as family members) the numbers reported here are farm *families* whose incomes come principally from agricultural activities (table 6-20). Thus, in round numbers, the 2 million *ejidatarios* reported in 1970 must be reduced by the 200,000 who reported that their principal activity was nonagricultural; there may well have been more. A further 200,000 also owned private farms; it does not matter which way they are classified, but they must not be counted twice. That leaves some 1.6 million "pure" *ejidatarios* plus 200,000 *comuneros*, members of communities. The number of private farmers, when calculated in a similar way, ranges from 900,000 to 600,000. Some 400,000 hired laborers were permanently employed on farms, and another estimated 500,000 were seasonal but farm work was their principal source of income. Effectively, the number of seasonal workers was much higher because it included many sons of *ejidatarios* and other farmers but including them would be double counting; in any case, it is families that are being considered.

Table 6-20. Number of Families Mainly Dependent on Farming, 1960 and 1970

(thousands of families)

Item	1960	1970
Ejidatarios	1,598	2,013
Minus *ejidatarios* with mainly nonfarming activities	151	200
Full-time *ejidatarios*	1,447	1,800
Minus *ejidatarios* also having private farms	288	200
Full-time *ejidatarios* without private farms	1,159	1,600
Comuneros	200	200
Private farmers	1,146	900
Minus private farms with mainly nonfarming activities	382	300
Full-time private farmers	764	600
Full-time hired workers	—	400
Seasonal workers dependent mainly on farm wages	—	500
Hired workers, total	900	900
Grand total	3,023	3,300

— Not available.
Source: Lamartine Yates (1978).

With an average of six persons per family, which censuses indicate is the rural norm, a total of almost 20 million people were in the farming sector in 1970. That number is consistent with the population census finding of 39.4 percent of a national population of 50.6 million in that year. Since 1970 there has been some increase in the number of *ejidatarios*(small in the case of full-time ones) and a continuing decline in the number of private farmers, especially of those occupying holdings of less than 5 hectares.

Information on the size of farms is most realistic when based on the *arable* area rather than the *total* area of farms. That is true partly because *ejido* pasture and forest lands are collectively owned and partly because the semidesert ranches of the north, though large in extent, support relatively few cattle. Hence the more meaningful picture is drawn from the arable *parcelas* of *ejidatarios* and the private arable farm (few of the latter contain nonarable land, which could contravene the agrarian legislation).

In 1970 there were 608,300 arable farms of less than 1 hectare which must be considered part-time units, almost equally divided between *ejidatarios* and private owners. Most of the arable land of full-time *ejidatarios* was in units ranging from 1 hectare to 20 hectares, whereas most of the privately farmed arable land was in units larger than 25 hectares (table 6-21).

Over the 1940–70 period, private farms were becoming progressively larger within the permitted limits, the area in units of 25 hectares or more rising from 64 percent to 73 percent of the total (table 6-22). Simultaneously, the *ejidatarios' parcelas* were becoming smaller, the number under 10 hectares rising from 44 percent to 55 percent of the total and their area from 16 percent to 23 percent of the total, chiefly because the *ejido* population was increasing faster than the quantity of *ejido* arable land.

Unfortunately, no census has ever been taken of cattle ranches, the large farms composed of pasture and perhaps some forest but little or no arable land. According to one estimate (Lamartine Yates 1978) 14,450 such ranches existed in 1940 covering 80 million hectares. By 1970 the number had increased to 17,300 while their area had fallen to 46.8 million hectares—that is, from an average of 5,500 hectares per ranch to some 2,700 hectares, of which about 2,000 hectares were pasture. If the typical carrying capacity was 10 hectares per head, this suggests around 200 cattle per ranch, though undoubtedly some ranches were and are very much larger.

Farm Capital and Inputs

Estimates of farm capital in the agricultural censuses show the value of land, the most important element, constitutes around 65 percent;

Table 6-21. Number and Arable Area of *Parcelas* and Arable Farms, by Size and Type of Tenure, 1970

			Family units			Larger farms (over 100 hectares)	Total
Type of farmer	Part time (less than 1 hectares)	Mini units (1–5 hectares)	Small (5–10 hectares)	Medium (10–20 hectares)	Large (20–100 hectares)		
Land parcelas and arable farms (thousands)							
Ejidatario	280.5	792.8	484.0	144.6	16.7	0.0	1,718.6
Comunero	46.7	64.1	13.6	3.3	1.3	0.0	129.0
Private farmer	281.1	286.0	99.9	80.3	60.6	17.0	825.0
Total	608.3	1,1 42.9	597.5	228.2	78.6	17.0	2,672.6
Arable area in parcels and arable farms (thousands of hectares)							
Ejidatario	191.5	2,487.3	3,723.0	2,184.0	624.5	0.0	9,210.2
Comunero	32.0	176.1	103.3	58.9	58.1	0.0	428. 4
Private farmer	166.1	788.7	766.7	1,339.7	3,117.2	4,207.7	10,385.6
Total	89.6	3,451.6	4,593.0	3,582.6	3,799.8	4,207.7	20,024.2

Note: In the family units the individual *parcelas* are 5–10 hectares, 10–20 hectares, and 20 hectares and over; the private farms are 5–10 hectares, 10–25 hectares, and 25–100 hectares. Fully collectivized *ejidos* and communities are excluded because they do not have individual *parcelas*.
Source: Decennial agricultural censuses.

livestock some 25 percent; and machinery, buildings, and irrigation works the remaining 10 percent. In each census arable land has been valued separately from "other land" and is worth about ten times more per hectare than "other," which comprises pasture, forest, and waste areas. Arable land values are differentiated by type and size of farm. Thus in the 1970 census, arable land of less than 5 hectares in private farms was valued at 3,764 pesos per hectare, that of the larger private farms at an average of 2,453 pesos, and the *ejidatarios'* arable land at 2,601 pesos.

The high *ejido* figure is difficult to believe. *Ejido* land, which, being inalienable, lies outside the market, has in the censuses been attributed a value equal to the value of land of similar quality in private ownership. That implies that, on average, *ejidatarios'* arable land in 1970 was of better quality than the privately owned land, which is exactly contrary to what is generally believed. Moreover, in 1970 the value of crop output per arable hectare was 50 percent higher on the larger private farms than on *ejidatarios'* holdings.

Arable land is of higher value in the northwest, where there is irrigation, than in most other regions. But the highest figures of all are found

Table 6-22. Distribution of *Parcelas* and Arable Farms, by Size, 1940 and 1970

(percent)

Year	Part time (less than 1 hectares)	Mini units (1–5 hectares)	Small (5–10 hectares)	Medium (10–20 hectares)	Large (20–100 hectares)	Larger farms (over 100 hectares)	Total
Parcelas							
1940	9.1	34.9	43.7	9.8	2.5	0	100
1970	16.3	39.1	35.2	8.4	1.0	0	100
Arable area in parcelas							
1940	1.0	14.9	47.8	22.4	13.8	0	100
1970	2.1	20.6	46.8	23.7	6.8	0	100
Arable farms							
1940	42.8	44.2	6.2	5.0	3.1	0.7	100
1970	34.0	34.6	12.1	9.7	7.4	2.2	100
Arable area in farms							
1940	2.1	14.9	7.0	12.1	22.3	41.6	100
1970	1.5	6.9	6.7	11.7	27.3	45.9	100

Notes: In family units, individual *parcelas* are 5–10 hectares, 10–20 hectares, and 20 hectares and over; the private farms are 5–10 hectares, 10–25 hectares, and 25–100 hectares; *Parcelas* are those of *ejidatarios* only; no 1940 data for *comuneros parcelas* are available. Fully collectivized *ejidos* are excluded because they do not have individual *parcelas*.

Source: Decennial agricultural censuses.

in states such as México (5,478 pesos in 1970) and Morelos (8,808 pesos) where, although most of the land is of low fertility and gives low yields, population is dense—Mexico City is nearby—and land hunger considerable.

Nevertheless, by international standards farmland is cheap—only half the U.S. average price. This can be accounted for by low productivity of the land in the regions that suffer from poor soils and insufficient rainfall, and partly by the reluctance of investors to buy land in the private sector with the ever-present danger of expropriation.

During agriculture's golden age of expansion, private farmers made considerable investments in improving their properties. Even *ejidos* invested, at least in the years immediately following their establishment. But since 1970 the situation has changed. *Ejidatarios*, being virtually tenants, invest little. *Ejidos* can invest in the improvement of their communally owned grasslands and forests only by the general consent of their governing assemblies, which seldom occurs. Hence, new investment is synonymous with public works, mainly irrigation. At a rough calculation, some 60 billion pesos (at 1970 prices) were thus invested between the mid-1930s and the mid-1970s. This was a major factor in boosting agricultural output during those forty years.

Farm credit has had a checkered history. Allegedly to improve efficiency, the three competing agricultural credit banks, all of which had been public institutions, were merged in 1975 into the National Rural Credit Bank. Although recent information is not available, it is believed that about 80 percent of all loans are short term, 75 percent being crop loans; two-thirds of the total goes to *ejidatarios* and *ejidos*. A major portion of the lending benefits the northern and northwestern regions where commercial farming predominates even among *ejidatarios*. In the rest of the country less than half the *ejidatarios* are considered creditworthy. An alarming proportion of the Credit Bank's loans is considered unrecoverable, in spite of its large army of supervisors and extension workers who compete and clash with those of the Ministry of Agriculture.

The role of the farm inputs—fertilizers, machinery, and so on—varies according to region and type of farm. In the irrigated Northwest it resembles in importance that of the inputs on California farms, whereas on the arid central plateau such expenditure is minimal, especially among *ejidatarios*.

Consumption of fertilizers, both nitrogenous and phosphatic, has trebled in volume in each recent decade. On private farms of more than 5 hectares the per hectare consumption is double that on *ejidatarios' parcelas*; in the northwest it is three times the national average. Fertilizer prices are generously subsidized, so that in the 1970s and 1980s their cost to farmers rose at only one-third the rate of inflation.

Mechanization, which proliferates when farms increase in size, when wages rise rapidly, and when animal traction becomes costly, has proceeded relatively slowly in Mexico, where these conditions do not obtain. Between 1950 and 1980 the number of tractors only quadrupled, while in Brazil it increased twentyfold (FAO *Production Yearbook*). In the central districts of Mexico 90 percent of *ejidatario* land in 1970 was cultivated with animal power, which implies that a sizable proportion of the limited crop output has to be devoted to feeding work animals. But as long as the *ejidos* remain overpopulated and the *parcelas* small, their mechanization will remain uneconomic. The Rural Credit Bank provides subsidized credit for the purchase of tractors and other farm machinery, though this principally benefits private farmers, plus a few *ejidatarios*, in the north and northwest.

Irrigation

Where rainfall is insufficient, as in most parts of the country, irrigation assumes major importance. When the Revolution broke out in 1910 there were about 1 million hectares of land under irrigation, created in previous years by (mostly American) land companies to grow cotton and sugarcane. The 1917 Constitution nationalized all water sources, but the government's lack of money and the continuing civil disturbances inhibited development of new irrigation schemes. In 1940 only 1.8 million hectares were supplied with water. President Alemán (1946–52) and his successor Ruiz Cortines provided substantial funds and technical staff, so that by 1960 there were 3.5 million hectares supplied with water. Some further expansion has occurred since 1975, though confused statistics make it impossible to say how much.

Of the total irrigated area about half is located in *ejidos*. Two-thirds of the irrigated land is still in the northwest and northern regions, which formerly were virtual deserts. Over the country as a whole, about 30 percent of the harvested area is irrigated, and these areas provide half the nation's crop output, in value terms. But irrigation's contribution to marketed output is much higher, because a major part of the rainfed production is retained for consumption in subsistence farmers' families.

Many of the older irrigation districts are deteriorating because of poor maintenance of canals, insufficient water supply, or, in coastal zones, overpumping and thus infiltration of seawater. Prospects for further expansion focus on the major rivers of the southeast where, unfortunately, construction costs are high. Moreover, they are tropical regions that cannot produce the temperate zone crops such as wheat and oilseeds that the Mexican consumer increasingly demands.

Crop Yields

Until the mid-1960s the areas of almost all crops were increasing, but in the 1970s and 1980s there was little change. The chief exceptions were some increase in wheat at the expense of maize, a marked decline in the cotton area, and a rapid expansion in oilseeds (soybeans and safflower), grain sorghums (for livestock), and fruits. Cotton, wheat, soybeans, safflower, alfalfa, and most fruits are grown principally under irrigation, maize and beans mainly on rainfed land, and sugarcane on both.

Yields per hectare of major crops show steady increases according to official data; for instance, comparing the 1980–84 average yield with that of 1930–34, maize registers 317 (1930–34 = 100), wheat 519, barley 437, and cotton 316. Yet the long-term series of yields as published by Mexico's Ministry of Agriculture is rendered somewhat suspect by revisions in the methods of crop reporting. A particular crop may be showing an upward trend in yield of, say, 1.5 percent a year, when suddenly the yield jumps 40–50 percent in one year and then resumes the previous trend. This has occurred from time to time with regard to most of the basic crops, giving some long-term rates of growth in yield that are difficult to believe. For example, in the mid-1970s the reported maize yield suddenly increased by 50 percent. It is perhaps significant that much more modest increases in yield have been recorded in fruits and vegetables which are not politically important.

The International Center for Maize and Wheat Research—Centro Internacional de Mejoramiento de Maíz y Trigo, or CIMMYT—established with Rockefeller funds just outside of Mexico City shortly after World War II, has undoubtedly played a valuable role with its plant selection and breeding program. In the case of wheat, thanks to the different climates in different parts of the country, it became possible to sow and harvest two crops successively in one year, thus greatly accelerating the seed selection process. The researchers increased wheat yields so significantly that Mexico's hitherto massive wheat imports were eliminated by the 1960s. Later, Mexican-bred wheat varieties were exported to other developing countries—the origin of the so-called Green Revolution. Unfortunately, maize cannot be harvested twice in one year; hence the yield improvement was slower and less spectacular.

Livestock

Fragile though the estimates may be, it seems clear that the livestock sector has been expanding somewhat more slowly than the crop sector and has signally failed to match the rising demand for meat and milk. As a consequence, exports of beef and live cattle have fallen, sheep are being imported for slaughter, while imports of dried and condensed milk now contribute 15 percent of the milk supply. This is in part a result of price controls that have permitted much smaller increases in producer prices for meat and milk than in those for crop products. Partly also it stems from the tenure system, under which ranchers cannot easily expand their operations without violating the agrarian legislation, while *ejidos* do nothing to improve their pastures that might enable them to carry more animals.

Moreover, the productivity of *ejido* livestock leaves much to be desired. According to the 1970 census, the value of livestock output per animal unit average 721 pesos on private farms but only 282 pesos in the *ejidos* and communities. Since then the situation has not materially changed and the gap in values is even more dramatic than the parallel productivity difference in the crop sector.

Prices

In most countries government intervention in the pricing of farm products is widespread; the practice exists partly to protect small-scale producers from exploitation by middlemen and partly because the farm vote is considered important. In Mexico, for a number of crops, intervention takes the form of establishing guaranteed prices with or without some state purchasing activity, though a few products are subject to administered prices—tobacco and henequen, for example, are entirely purchased by semigovernmental agencies.

Guaranteed prices were first introduced in the 1950s for maize, wheat, and beans and subsequently extended to other products. In the 1960s, when the farm sector appeared to be heading for surpluses, these prices were effective and shielded small producers in weak bargaining positions. In the 1970s and 1980s, when shortages were general, prices on the free market almost always exceeded the guaranteed level. The government has an agency, Compañía Nacional de Subsistencias Populares (CONASUPO), that buys, partly for stockpiling, a small portion of certain major crops, acting as purchaser of last resort; it is also responsible for bulk imports of foodstuffs that it sells in its chain of supermarkets at discount prices. However, most of the purchase, manufacture, and distribution of foodstuffs remains in the private sector.

For some agricultural commodities the government sets ceiling prices at the wholesale or retail level. Where the ceiling price is so low that distribution costs cannot be covered, the government provides subsidies (to manufacturers or wholesalers), notably for so-called basic products. The subsidization of sugar has been quite remarkable—between 1971 and 1985, thanks to the subsidy, its wholesale price rose at less than half the inflation rate. Prices of other major foodstuffs have also been held down artificially.

The retail price subsidy on sugar has been sufficiently generous to put Mexicans among the highest per capita sugar consumers in the world, with damaging effects on dental health. And because of stagnating sugarcane production, Mexico has moved from being a major sugar exporting country into an importing one. In 1985 the government began reducing price subsidies, which led to some sharp price increases; and in the case of sugar, the action reduced consumption and eliminated the need for imports.

Fixed prices cause problems largely because the governmental machine responds slowly to changing situations. For instance, the sale of milk at wholesale and retail level is subject to a ceiling price. When faced with rapidly rising production costs because of inflation, milk producers and processors submit a documented claim for a price revision, but the bureaucratic deliberations may take eight or nine months, and only a proportion of the claim may be granted; meantime, costs may have risen still further. Many dairy farmers caught in such predicaments in recent years slaughtered their cows and went out of business, so that the government has had to import large quantities of processed milk.

Though no index of farm prices is published by the government, it is feasible to construct one using data on volume and value of output. Indexes of the value of output show that in real terms neither crop nor livestock product prices have ever regained the levels they had around 1950 (table 6-23). The crop index fell significantly during the 1950s and 1960s, but not much further after 1970. Livestock prices fell less during

Table 6-23. Indexes of Producer Prices, Nominal and Real, Selected Years, 1950–84
(1950 = 100)

Year	Index of crop prices Nominal	Index of crop prices Real	Index of livestock product prices Nominal	Index of livestock product prices Real	Combined index (real)
1950	100.0	100.0	100.0	100.0	100.0
1960	165.7	83.9	169.9	86.0	85.2
1970	207.9	74.5	225.7	80.9	77.5
1975	421.0	83.7	415.3	82.5	83.2
1980	1,034.9	73.0	919.3	64.9	70.0
1981	1,333.1	73.9	1,111.8	61.6	69.4
1982	1,980.9	68.1	1,566.8	53.9	62.2
1983	3,842.4	68.8	2,765.7	49.5	60.3
1984	6,773.2	73.1	5,138.5	55.4	64.8

Note: Nominal prices are current values divided by current volumes (at 1970 price); real prices are nominal prices deflated by gross domestic product implicit price index; combined index is weighted average (by value) of crop and livestock indexes.

Source: For 1950–74, Mexico, Ministry of Agriculture, *Annual Crop Report* for value and colume of crop production; *Annual Livestock Report* for livestock product prices; unofficial estimate of livestock products production (Lamartine Yates [1978]). For 1975–84, Bank of Mexico, *Informe anual.*

the earlier period but very substantially after 1975. The combined index fell from 100 to 85.2 between 1950 and 1960, to 77.5 by 1970, to 70.0 by 1980, and to 60.3 by 1983.

For a few years after 1950, as the benefits of irrigation and technology were making themselves felt, unit costs were falling, but in the 1970s and 1980s the influence of these factors weakened progressively so that farmers indeed were being squeezed. Thus Mexico conforms to the developing world pattern of underpaying her farmers so that the (more vocal) urban consumers may enjoy cheap food.

Prices of farm inputs are also kept artificially low through subsidies for fertilizers, pesticides, fuel, electricity, and the like, but these are income-regressive subsidies benefiting chiefly the larger-scale commercial farmers who could operate comfortably without them.

Agriculture and the Economy

For almost three decades after 1940 Mexican agriculture grew at a phenomenal rate and was regarded as one of the great success stories of the developing world. Though the official sources (censuses and Ministry of Agriculture data) differ somewhat as to the actual figures of crop production and though only private estimates exist for livestock production, it appears that over the period 1940–70 crops were expanding at more than 5 percent a year and livestock products at close to 4 percent, this lower rate due partly to the catastrophic outbreak of foot-and-mouth disease in the late 1940s. These rates refer to gross output, which includes the fodder crops fed to livestock.

The principal technical factors responsible for the farming boom were increases of about 3 percent a year in the harvested area, much of it a result of new irrigation; increases of nearly 2 percent yearly in per hectare yields; and—less important—a gradual shift to higher-value crops. The harvested area peaked in 1965, and the scope for substituting higher-value crops has diminished, leaving only the yield increase as a continuing positive factor.

Thus the growth rates have been lower in recent years. The national accounts show that gross crop output increased at 3.4 percent between 1970 and 1980 and livestock products at 3.8 percent (table 6-24). Increases in the net output rates were lower, 3.3 percent for each group. For the period 1975–85 the Bank of Mexico, apparently using Ministry of Agriculture material, gives net output growth rates of 3.5 percent for crops and 2.5 percent for livestock. The sudden upward revisions of some crop output and livestock numbers by the Ministry of Agriculture suggest that published rates may be somewhat better than reality.

Some states have shown much greater agricultural progress than others. For instance, between 1950 and 1970 gross crop output (at constant 1970 prices) expanded nearly fivefold in Sonora and fourfold in

Table 6-24. Annual Growth Rates of Agricultural Output, at 1970 Prices, Selected Periods, 1940–85
(percent)

Period	Crops	Livestock	Combined
Gross output			
1940–50	5.4	4.5	5.0
1950–60	4.5	2.3	3.4
1960–70	4.9	4.4	4.7
1970–80	3.4	3.8	3.6
Net output			
1970–75	2.5	3.6	3.0
1975–80	4.1	3.0	3.6
1980–85	3.0	2.0	2.6
1975–85	3.5	2.5	3.1

Source: For 1940–50, from agricultural censuses; for 1950–85, for crops, 1950–70, Mexico, Ministry of Agriculture, *Annual Crop Production Reports*; for 1970–85, Mexico, INEGI (1984c; 1987b). For livestock, in 1950–70, unofficial estimate of volume of production from Lamartine Yates (1978) valued at producer prices as published by Ministry of Agriculture; in 1970–85, same as for crops.

Sinaloa (both states have massive irrigation works) and more than threefold in Colima, Guanajuato, and Querétaro. Growth was slower in southern states, which did not benefit from the irrigation projects. By contrast, animal husbandry expanded more in southern than in northern states, gross output increasing fourfold in real terms in Tabasco and threefold in Chiapas.

Since 1970 the situation has changed radically. Progress has been most rapid in some of the more backward states. Thus between 1970 and 1980 the gross value of crop production more than doubled in the states of México, Hidalgo, Tlaxcala, Puebla, and Campeche. All of these states except Campeche are adjacent to the rapidly expanding market of Mexico City. Meanwhile, the impetus of new irrigation having ended, and the existing canal networks having been physically neglected, crop output in Sonora, Coahuila, and Guanajuato actually declined.

During the same decade of the 1970s, gross output of livestock products doubled in Aguascalientes, Querétaro, Tlaxcala, Campeche, and Quintana Roo. In the north, because many ranches had been overgrazed, livestock output stagnated in Sonora, Chihuahua, Nuevo León, and Zacatecas.

Another factor in the decline of agricultural growth rates has been and is the land tenure system. The fact that the per hectare crop output of *ejidatarios* averages only two-thirds of that on private farms, and output of livestock products per animal unit only 40 percent, did not greatly matter as long as more and more land was being brought into cultivation. Livestock numbers could be easily increased. But since the 1960s most of the new *ejidos* have been established on land previously in technically advanced private cultivation, a transfer that has held back the increase in arable productivity and the expansion of fodder production for farm animals. Bearing in mind that *ejidos* and communities now possess over 60 percent of the nation's arable land and the majority of its animals (except cattle), the continued existence of this regime threatens to impede future progress in physical productivity.

In addition to the physical productivity of land and animals, the efficiency of the farming community in using capital is important. Even during the agricultural golden age the trends were discouraging (table 6-25). Thus, between 1950 and 1970 the value of agricultural production per 1,000 pesos of farm capital fell from 402 pesos to 316 pesos, a decline experienced in almost all regions of the country. These are gross output figures; the value added results would be worse, since during that era of technical advances, purchased inputs such as feed and fertilizers were becoming increasingly important. Moreover, the calculation excludes public investment in irrigation, unrecovered farm credit, and expenditures on research and extension.

Over recent decades labor productivity in the primary sector has hovered around 30 percent of national average productivity. The farm sector includes many thousands of relatively prosperous private farm-

Table 6-25. Value of Agricultural Production at 1970 Prices, Selected Years, 1950–85

(pesos)

	Crops		Livestock	
Year	Gross value	Net value	Gross value	Net value
1950	13,219	—	14,909	—
1960	20,571	—	18,808	—
1970	33,148	—	29,005	—
1970	37,281	31,515	31,734	19,515
1975	42,766	35,679	38,658	23,295
1980	52,252	43,628	46,515	26,968
1985	—	50,241	—	29,968

— Not available

Note: Gross value is total output valued at producer prices. Net value is the contribution to GDP—that is, gross value minus inputs.

Source: Same as for table 6-24.

ers, and the disappointing sectoral average thus conceals a very much lower productivity on the part of *ejidatarios* and *comuneros*. To express this from another angle, 40 percent of the nation's labor force in 1970 was producing 10 percent of GDP, while it can be guessed that in 1985 about 35 percent was producing less than 9 percent of GDP.

From this evidence some observers would conclude that a principal consequence of the agrarian reform has been to distribute poverty. Others would argue that it was better to keep a sizable population on the land, even if producing very little, rather than have too many rural people migrate to become urban unemployed.

Today, the *ejido* system seems hallowed and untouchable. Yet sooner or later more flexible tenure arrangements may emerge. Many *ejidatarios* are already illegally renting their *parcelas* and purchasing farms in the private sector. Some day a government may legitimize these operations and legislate even greater flexibility. In this direction lies the major hope for improvement in the living standards of the rural poor and for a more adequate contribution to the nation's food supply.

Policies toward Industry and Services

Mining

Under the Porfiriato, mining was dominated by foreign interests. The reestablishment of national control was an important goal of the revolution, which was not finally accomplished until the nationalization of oil interests in 1938. Before nationalization, constant disputes about exploration rights and transfer of dividends had caused foreign companies to switch their new oil exploration and development activities to Venezuela. As a result, oil output had by 1940 fallen to a quarter of its 1921 peak, and exports had fallen even more (table 6-26). There was a revival of demand from the United States during World War II, and after 1950 expansion in mining was fairly similar to that in manufacturing, with an extra spurt from the mid-1970s to the early 1980s when the boom in oil prices raised the profitability of production. However, the 1921 level of oil output was not surpassed until 1974.

Since 1938 oil output has been the responsibility of the biggest public corporation, PEMEX. It faced political pressure to keep domestic prices low, which restricted its capacity to invest until the mid-1970s. Thereafter it financed its giant investment program by foreign borrowing. Table 6-27 shows that the oil bonanza of the 1970s and early 1980s was not a gift from God but the result of an enormous investment effort. In fact the growth of capital stock in petroleum gas and petrochemicals was considerably bigger than in all other manufacturing from 1970 to 1982. A second (and lesser) problem of the oil monopoly was that its labor force enjoyed political protection and therefore could demand very high pay and perquisites.

Table 6-26. Crude Petroleum and Natural Gas Production, Selected Years, 1901–87

Year	Crude petroleum (thousands of metric tons)[a]	Natural gas (millions of cubic meters)
1901	1	n.a.
1910	496	n.a.
1921	26,384	n.a.
1940	6,009	926
1950	9,880	1,762
1970	21,362	18,832
1976	39,989	21,855
1982	136,846	38,893
1985	131,020	37,247[b]
1987	126,538	—

n.a. Not applicable.
— Not available.
a. Data for 1901–82, given in thousands of barrels, have been converted to metric tons at 7.33 barrels per metric ton.
b. Preliminary.
Source: For crude petroleum, in 1901–82, Mexico, INEGI (1985a), table 12.1; in 1985–87, Wharton (1989). For natural gas, in 1940–50, Mexico, INEGI (1985a), table 12.2; in 1970–85, PEMEX.

Table 6-27. Net Fixed Tangible Capital Stock in Mining and Manufacturing, 1970 and 1982
(millions of 1970 pesos)

Year	Petroleum and natural gas	Other minerals	Petrochemicals	Other manufacturing
1970	19,646	4,294	5,128	65,356
1982	97,732	6,174	31,908	149,425
Increase, 1970–82	78,086	1,880	26,780	84,069

Source: Villalpando Hernández and Fernández Moran (1986).

Utilities

Since 1960, electricity has been a completely nationalized sector. Production and distribution were started by foreign firms under the Porfiriato. In the 1920s there was an increase in government control over the companies and growing disputes over their pricing policy. The Federal Electricity Commission (Comisión Federal de Electricidal, or CFE) was created in 1937 to increase the government's role. Pressure on the companies increased thereafter, with CFE gradually increasing its share in production (with loans from the World Bank). By 1960 the only private companies left were Mexican Light and Power (Belgian owned) and the American and Foreign Power Company (U.S. owned), which were mainly concerned with power distribution. They were bought out by the government in 1960 on reasonably favorable terms. The problems with public ownership of electricity, similar to those of PEMEX, have been political pressure to keep rates low, growing indebtedness, the need to cover deficits out of the public purse, and special concessions to unionized workers.

In Mexico, the gas industry is not a separate public utility but is part of the nationalized mining sector as far as production is concerned. The distributive network is small because most consumers use canisters rather than piped gas. Distribution of water supplies is largely a municipal activity and is treated in the national accounts as part of general government.

Manufacturing

In manufacturing (table 6-28) the bulk of activity is in private hands. Government enterprise is concentrated on a few capital-intensive operations such as fertilizers, steel, railway rolling stock, part of the motor industry, and some shipyards where it was felt the development job was too big for the private sector. Government also dominates the sugar industry, having taken over bankrupt private firms, and it controls the import and distribution of newsprint, presumably as a weapon to influence the press. Government capital is probably about a quarter of the total engaged in manufacturing. Employment in government manufacturing plants was 119,000 in 1975 and 215,000 in 1985—6 percent and 8 percent, respectively, of total manufacturing employment. In terms of value added, the public share in manufacturing rose from less than 4 percent in 1975 to 10 percent in 1982. In 1975 public corporations of all kinds in all sectors numbered about 500, but there were almost 119,000 establishments in manufacturing, and the vast majority were private.

Government has played an important role in promoting private industrial development. Nacional Financiera, which is probably the biggest development bank in the world, was set up in 1934 and has helped finance a vast array of industrial activities in both the public and the private sectors. It issued domestic bonds at reasonably high interest rates and borrowed from the World Bank to facilitate Mexican entrepreneurs' access to credit. The absence of exchange controls and the stability of prices and exchange rates in the 1960s also favored access to this kind of finance for private firms who made substantial use of their own bond issues. Apart from its role in facilitating access to credit, Nacional Financiera and other state credit agencies have also helped industry by giving credit at rates below the market.

Industry has benefitted from special incentives since 1925 and these gradually grew in extent to a peak in 1975. They included exemptions from or reductions in sales taxes and import duties spread over a wide variety of industries and involving a good deal of administrative dis-

Table 6-28. Growth of Subsectors within Manufacturing, 1950–85
(percent)

Subsector	Average annual compound growth rate	Share of total manufacturing growth
Food, drink, and tobacco	5.9	25.3
Textiles and clothing	4.8	11.9
Wood products	5.1	2.0
Paper and printing	6.2	5.5
Chemicals, rubber, and plastics	10.0	22.7
Stone, clay, and glass products	7.0	3.6
Basic metals	8.0	10.2
Machinery and transport equipment	9.7	17.0
Other	6.6	1.8
Total	6.9	100.0

Source: Bank of Mexico, *Indicadores económicos* (May 1986).

cretion. After 1975 the relative importance of these incentives declined in favor of outright subsidies and the implicit subsidy derived from purchase of inputs such as electricity and gasoline from public corporations that charged less than market rates.

In 1980, according to World Bank estimates, total government favors to manufacturing were worth more than 10 percent of value added in the sector, of which 1.8 percent were fiscal incentives, 0.9 percent were credit subsidies, 1.6 percent were straight subsidies, and 5.8 percent were the implicit subsidy due to underpricing of inputs supplied from public corporations. Most of the subsidies went to large firms, and a sizable proportion of the recipients were themselves public corporations or foreign firms. In the chemical sector (largely public) these various subsidies were nearly 14 percent of value added and in basic metals they were nearly 23 percent.

In addition to these domestic subsidies, official policy has treated most of manufacturing as an infant industry and shielded it from external competition. Quantitative restrictions, which covered less than 10 percent of total imports in 1950, applied to all imports in 1982. There was also substantial tariff protection, which was differentiated by product and had its biggest protective effect on capital goods and durable consumer goods. Some of the tariff protection was redundant in the sense that goods were sold in Mexico below the foreign price plus the tariff, but there were very substantial rents accruing to Mexican producers. One way of estimating the global impact of protection and subsidies is to measure the implicit protection by the difference between prices in Mexico and prices of potential imports (table 6-29). This measure incorporates the impact of changes in the effective exchange rate.

As a result of the combination of protective policies, Mexican competitiveness in manufactured goods weakened in the 1970s and about half of Mexican industry was not competitive at the exchange rates prevailing in the early 1980s. Since then, readjustment policies have moved to provide more competitive markets by changes in the real

Table 6-29. **Implicit Nominal Protection for Manufactured Goods, 1960, 1970, and 1980**
(percent)

Goods	1960	1970	1980
Consumer	19.5	17.7	6.0
Intermediate	14.6	11.1	11.0
Capital and consumer durable	36.4	34.4	45.0

Source: World Bank data.

exchange rate, abolition of most quantitative restrictions, reduction of implicit subsidies, modification of public procurement policies, and membership in the GATT. Ten Kate (1988, p. 18), has estimated that in 1984–86 effective protection (as measured by the average dispersion between foreign and Mexican prices for nearly 1000 items) was increasingly negative. At the end of 1986 the only items that were effectively protected to any degree were cement, certain wood products, electrical goods, and automobiles.

The major effort to promote labor-intensive manufacturing was the creation of an in-bond (duty free) area along the border with the United States. This is Mexico's Hong Kong. Output has grown rapidly, and growth has been financed largely by foreign investment. In 1986, there were 900 factories in this area, providing 255,000 jobs—about 10 percent of manufacturing employment (see Banamex 1986).

Apart from foreign investment in the frontier area, a large amount of direct investment has been attracted from many foreign countries, which has brought in valuable know-how and capital resources. Mexico has had a larger volume of such investment than any other country in the developing world except Brazil. The inducement was partly the tax incentives, but perhaps more important was the closure of the domestic market to imports, which forced firms that wanted a market share to choose direct investment. In the motor vehicle industry, most of the

Table 6-30. Evolution of Direct Foreign Investment, 1973–86
(millions of dollars)

Year	New investment	Cumulative total investment
1973	287.3	4,359.5
1974	362.2	4,721.7
1975	295.0	5,016.7
1976	299.1	5,315.8
1977	327.1	5,642.9
1978	383.3	6,026.2
1979	810.0	6,836.2
1980	1,622.6	8,458.8
1981	1,701.1	10,159.9
1982	626.5	10,786.4
1983	683.7	11,470.1
1984	1,442.2	12,899.9
1985	1,871.0	14,628.9
1986[a]	2,424.2	17,053.1

a. Preliminary.
Source: Mexico, SECOFI.

risks of new investment and cost of training personnel have been borne by foreign investors. By 1986, the total stock of foreign direct investment was valued at $17 billion (table 6-30). In that year, there were 7,302 firms with foreign participation; 607 had less than 25 percent foreign ownership, 3,744 had 25–49 percent, and 2,951 had higher foreign participation. Generally, over time, such firms come under pressure to Mexicanize higher management and to provide for a higher percentage of Mexican ownership. But this pressure does not seem to have caused serious friction.

Services

Although Mexico's modern growth is popularly considered to have been a process of industrialization, the dominant sector has in fact been services. Services already represented 54 percent of output in 1921, and

Table 6-31. Government Employment, by Sector, 1975 and 1986

Sector	Number of employees 1975	Number of employees 1986	Percent of total employment in sector 1975	Percent of total employment in sector 1986
Agriculture, forestry and fishing	30,658	73,094	0.7	1.2
Mining and related industries (includes petroleum refining and basic petrochemicals)	83,053	158,259	43.0	61.3
Manufacturing	119,375	186,341	5.8	7.8
Electricity	48,526	73,004	93.3	72.3
Construction	0	0	0.0	0.0
Commerce, restaurants, and hotels	9,984	35,960	0.4	1.2
Transport, storage, and communications	203,246	277,800	33.8	27.0
Financial services and real estate	27,540	217,594	9.8	46.2
Public administration and defense	701,000	1,152,168	100.0	100.0
Education and health	928,500	2,229,400	80.0	85.0
Other services	0	0	0.0	0.0
Total Services	1,870,278	3,912,922	25.8	35.5
Grand Total	2,151,890	4,414,495	14.1	20.4

Source: For total employment, Mexico, INEGI (1983), p. 12, (1987a), p. 35; for government employment, Mexico, INEGI (1985b, 1988).

in 1985 the service share was 56 percent. In every subperiod of growth the service sector has represented well over half of growth.

Government employment in services was a quarter of the total in 1975 and rose to a third in 1986 (table 6-31). Government is important in transport and communications (with state railways, air transport, and telephones) as well as in banking, insurance, and housing finance (where its stake was doubled by the bank nationalization of 1982). The government's extensive involvement in storage, import, and retailing of food items began in the 1930s and was consolidated in Compañía Nacional de Subsistencias Populares (CONASUPO) in 1961; however, government employment in commerce is very small.

Generally speaking, government corporations in transport and communications and food retailing have shown the same tendency to subsidize prices and protect their employees that is so strong in PEMEX. But government banks have generally been run efficiently on a profit-making basis, even though in their lending policy they have discriminated in favor of activities the government wanted to support.

The public sector commitment in the service industries is of long standing, dating back to the 1930s when Cárdenas was pushing Mexico to the left and the country was beleaguered by world depression and by its creditors. Foreign interests in banking and insurance were squeezed out in the 1930s, and private domestic banking was eliminated by the general bank nationalization of 1982, which has since then been partially reversed.

In education and health services, government does not hold a monopoly, but it accounts for 85 percent of employment.

It is more difficult to assess the impact of government policy intervention in services than in agriculture and industry. Most are nontradable services, so foreign trade distortions are not really operative, but government has considerable influence on relative price structures and resource allocation, not always in a manner favorable to efficiency and equity.

7 Mexican Outcomes in Terms of Equity and Alleviation of Poverty

The Dimensions of Income Inequality and Poverty

Analysts of Mexican inequality have faced considerable statistical problems. Total income reported in household surveys is well below that in the national accounts, and all of the surveys have had to make major adjustments for undercoverage, particularly for upper and lower extremes of income.

The survey material goes back to 1950. Some observers, like D. Felix (in Hewlett and Weinert 1982) and van Ginneken (1980), have detected a worsening of income inequality since 1950, Bergsman (1980), dealing with a shorter period, suggests that changes in inequality between 1963 and 1977 were small or nil, though he disregards the estimates of higher inequality in 1975 as freakish. P. Aspe and J. Beristain (in Aspe and Sigmund 1984) felt that income distribution had remained "basically unaltered" between 1950 and 1977. Nobody has suggested that there has been any improvement in income distribution in the postwar period.

Table 7-1 shows the outcomes of three analyses. There is no reason why any two observers should get exactly the same result even with unadjusted survey material because the Gini coefficient will vary with the degree of disaggregation. But what stands out unequivocally is that all three sets of adjusted Gini coefficients are in a range from 0.5 to 0.6, whereas for advanced capitalist countries Ginis range from 0.3 to 0.4. Thus Mexico is a country of high inequality.

Mexico is also a country with a great deal of poverty. When its golden age of economic growth began, in 1940, poverty was deep and very widespread—54 percent of the population was illiterate, 27 percent habitually went barefoot, 23 percent wore sandals rather than shoes, and life expectancy was only forty-one years. Two-thirds of all Mexicans were engaged primarily in agriculture, and their productivity was only marginally higher than that in 1910. The Indian population was probably worse off than it had been under the Aztecs.

185

Table 7-1. Three Summary Measures of Inequality of Income, Selected Years, 1950–75
(Gini coefficient)

Analyst and year	Unadjusted for underreporting	Adjusted for underreporting
Felix		
1950	0.432	0.526
1963	0.543	0.555
1968	0.529	0.577
1975	0.570	0.579
van Ginneken[a]		
1950	n.a.	0.50
1963	n.a.	0.55
1968	n.a.	0.56
1975	n.a.	0.58
Bergsman		
1963	0.527	0.584
1968	0.522	0.584
1975	0.557	0.628
1977	0.496	0.569

n.a. Not applicable.
a. After-tax income.
Source: Bergsman (1980), p. 15; D. Felix (in Hewlett and Weinert 1982), p. 267; van Ginneken (1980), p. 18.

By 1985, average per capita private consumption was probably triple that in 1940, and there is evidence that some of the benefits trickled down to those in the lowest income groups. This cannot be monitored with any accuracy, but labor productivity rose faster in agriculture than in the rest of the economy, the productivity spread between richer and poorer states narrowed, and all of the social indicators show substantial progress (table 7-2). Life expectancy has risen from forty-one to sixty-eight years and the rate of literacy from 46 percent to 83 percent, calorie consumption per capita has risen substantially, and household amenities such as piped water, sewerage, and electricity are much more widely spread.

Almost all analysts agree that, over the long run, absolute poverty has declined. This is the case with Wilkie's (1970) index, which is a crude composite of indicators such as illiteracy, proportion of the population going barefoot or wearing sandals instead of shoes or eating tortillas instead of wheat, and households without sewerage for 1910–60. Bergsman (1980) suggests that the proportion of households in poverty fell from 57 percent in 1963 to 30 percent in 1977, using the 1977 minimum

Table 7-2. Social Indicators for Mexico, Selected Years, 1940–85

Indicator	1940	1950	1960	1970	1980	1985
Crude birth rate (births per thousand population)	44.3	45.6	46.1	44.2	31.9	28.0
Crude death rate (deaths per thousand population)	22.8	16.2	11.5	10.1	6.6	5.9
Percent of deaths caused by infectious disease	43.1	34.6	25.5	23.1	13.7	—
Life expectancy at birth (years)	41	50	59	62	66	68
Infant mortality (deaths per thousand births)	125.7	96.2	74.2	68.5	53.1	51.2
Literates as a percentage of population 15 years old and older	46	57	66	76	83	—
Years of education of people 15 years old and older	1.7	2.3	2.7	3.7	4.9	5.0
Education enrollment as a percentage of population	8	11	16	22	30	—
Calorie consumption per capita per day	—	2,166	2,522	2,619	2,803	—
Percent of households with						
Piped water	—	17.1	32.3	49.4	65.8	—
Sewerage connection	—	20.3	28.9	41.5	51.0	—
Electricity	—	—	—	58.9	74.9	—
Owner-occupied house	—	—	—	—	68.0	—
Passenger cars per thousand population	—	6.3	12.9	24.1	61.3	63[a]
Telephones per thousand population	—	—	14.1	29.6	72.4	81.9[b]
Television sets per thousand population	—	—	17.5	58.5	108.1	—

— Not available.
a. For 1983.
b. For 1982.
Source: CEPAL (1984, 1986).

wage level as a criterion. Van Ginneken (1980) suggests that the proportion of poor families fell from 60 percent of all families in 1950 to 20 percent in 1975 (using a poverty line of 10,000 pesos of 1970 per family per year), though his figures (table 7-3) do show decidedly smaller growth of income for the poor than for the rich. Felix (in Hewlett and Weinert 1982) is the only observer whose figures (but not his text) suggest an increase in absolute poverty of the bottom fifth of the population from 1950 to 1975, a result that seems improbable.

Bergsman has analyzed the structure of poverty as it emerged from a 1975 household survey. He felt that the survey exaggerated poverty as it classified 4.6 million of the 11 million families as poor—that is, 42 percent of the total, compared with his finding of 30 percent in 1977.

The findings derived from the 1975 survey are shown in tables 7-4 and 7-5. Only 12 percent of the poor were unemployed; the rest had jobs or a source of work income. Over half were in agriculture, a fifth had household heads who worked in services, and 10 percent had their occupation in manufacturing. In sectors dominated by government employment—mining, petroleum, electricity, and administration—poverty was negligible because governmental pay and perquisites are generally better than those in the private sector.

For those who fall within the poverty gap—a measure of the below the poverty threshold—the concentration on agriculture is even greater; 59 percent of the poverty gap was in that sector, as opposed to 1 percent in government employment.

Table 7-3. **Average Annual Family Income after Taxes, 1950 and 1975**

Decile	Income (1958 pesos) 1950	Income (1958 pesos) 1975	Annual compound growth rate (percent)
Bottom	3,096	4,884	1.9
Second	3,900	7,364	2.6
Third	4,356	8,172	2.5
Fourth	5,052	9,804	2.6
Fifth	5,520	12,240	3.2
Sixth	6,312	12,288	3.2
Seventh	8,028	16,872	2.6
Eighth	9,876	26,904	2.8
Ninth	12,396	55,584	6.2
Top	56,244	144,144	3.8
Average	11,484	30,036	3.9

Source: van Ginneken (1980), p. 18.

Table 7-4. **Locus of Mexican Poverty, by Occupation of Household Head, 1975**

Occupation	Number of families (thousands)	Percent of population in poverty[a]	Average annual income (dollars)	Total poverty gap (millions of dollars)
Agriculture	2,410	52.4	492	2,564
Mining	26	0.5	1,037	13
Petroleum and electricity	6	0.2	1,077	3
Manufacturing	491	10.7	762	390
Con struction	135	3.0	894	89
Commerce, services, transport	921	20.0	776	718
Government	52	1.1	851	37
Unemployed and unspecified	558	12.1	593	537
Total	4,599	100.0	610	4,351

Note: Totals have been adjusted slightly to equal sum of shares.
a. Annual income less than 19,452 pesos ($1,556).
Source: Bergsman (1980).

The finding that poverty is concentrated in agriculture is not surprising, since productivity there is only a third of that in the economy as a whole. One factor that intensified rural poverty was government policy in squeezing the farm sector's terms of trade. Controlled prices for some farm products were kept low in order to favor urban consumers. This bias was partially offset by subsidization of farm inputs. Unfortunately it is not possible to measure the government contribution to the agricultural price squeeze, but the total phenomenon has been so big (a 40 percent loss between 1950 and 1983, according to table 6-23), that it obviously contributed to poverty in this sector.

Table 7-5. **Link between Education and Poverty by Education of Family Head, 1975**

Education of family head	Percent of poor families
None	47.7
1–3 years	30.6
4–6 years	18.8
7 years or more	2.9

Source: Bergsman (1980).

The fact that there is poverty among people employed in manufacturing in spite of government subsidization is not really surprising as the subsidies have gone to entrepreneurs and into profits rather than to workers and wages.

In 1975 the total poverty gap was equivalent to $4.4 billion—4.9 percent of a GDP, or $88 billion. This compares with the 14.7 percent of GDP going to government subsidies by the end of the López Portillo administration, none of which was targeted with a view to its distributive impact.

One striking fact that emerges from Bergsman's poverty analysis is the very strong link between poverty and low levels of education (see table 7-5). Nearly half of the poor had no education at all, and 97 percent of them had less than six years of education. All investigators of Mexican poverty have found this strong link (Bergsman cites van Ginneken and Felix in this context). There are therefore strong grounds for thinking that greater expenditure on education would be a powerful weapon for reducing poverty over the long run. As there are high economic returns from education, there are also strong efficiency arguments for a bigger push in this direction.

Government has taken many actions that were intended to mitigate poverty and social injustice, and these have brought about some improvement in popular welfare. Since the Revolution about 40 percent of land has been confiscated from its previous owners and redistributed. Without this, the fruits of agricultural progress would not have filtered down. However, there is substantial evidence (see chapter 6) that the system of land redistribution to collective *ejidos* has hindered incentives and productivity growth, while the opposite has been true of small peasant ownership.

Because the land redistributed to *ejidos* is not the personal property of those who receive it and cannot be sold or mortgaged, the incentive to use it productively is weaker than if it were private property. On the whole, the land that the government distributed is of poorer quality than that in private ownership. Moreover, the benefits of government irrigation work, credit, extension services, and seed development have also gone disproportionately to private landowners. The reasons for the continuation of the *ejido* system are mixed. It is partly because of the feeling that unrestricted private property rights would lead to sale of land and reconcentration of ownership, but *ejido* rights have also become a pillar of the political system, and the residual power over allocation of land which is in the hands of local politicians is a major instrument of social control.

Government action has contributed greatly to the spread of education facilities. In 1940 only 8 percent of the population was enrolled in school as compared with 30 percent in 1980, and in 1980 about 90 percent of enrollments were in government-financed schools. But the number of dropouts in basic education is large, and if six years of education are to become universal, scholarship assistance will have to be given to children of poor families.

Other social programs have had a rather weak redistributive impact. Preventive programs in public health such as water treatment and control of infectious diseases played a role in improving health, but the much more expensive programs providing facilities for curative treatment are heavily concentrated on favored client groups (such as state employees). This is also true of social security benefits and government credit to encourage home ownership.

Action to subsidize food prices through government shops (CONASUPO) and other subsidies for electricity, fuels, gasoline, transport, and water supply have not been targeted toward the needy. Their distributive effect has been a random churning process, with adverse effects on economic efficiency. The net impact of government action on poverty relief has been a tiny fraction of its total social spending.

Minimum wage legislation has had little real significance for the poor. Evasion of the law is virtually universal for those who hire unskilled labor, and only half the population are wage and salary workers in any case.

Thus most of the progress in reducing poverty in Mexico has been achieved by the poor themselves, seeking work opportunities in a rapidly growing economy and being willing to migrate within the country or to the United States.

The Distributive Impact of Social Welfare Programs

Social security arrangements in Mexico are much better for government workers and for insured blue- and white-collar workers than for the rest of the population. Over half of the population are not insured and fare rather poorly because the component of social security benefits devoted to welfare is very small.

Social Security

Between 1925 and 1942 federal laws were enacted granting pensions and other benefits to federal civil servants, the military, and teachers. Collective agreements, which made workers eligible for pensions, health care, and other benefits, were signed by unions and employers in petroleum, railroads, and electricity production and federal banks.

The general Social Security Law enacted in 1943 created the Mexican Institute of Social Security (Instituto Méxicano del Seguro Social, or IMSS) as a federal, autonomous agency to administer social security for all blue- and white-collar employees. Insured workers were to be eligible for old-age, disability, and survivor's pensions, workmen's compensation, and health and maternity care. In practice, the coverage of health services began in 1944; it was at first limited to the Federal District and then slowly expanded to other major cities. At the end of 1946 IMSS covered only 2 percent of the population and 3 percent of the labor force.

During Alemán's presidency (1946–52) IMSS coverage was extended to the most developed states Nuevo León, Veracruz, Jalisco, and México) and to those close to the Federal District (Puebla and Tlaxcala). By 1952, IMSS still covered only 4 percent of the population and 5 percent of the labor force. In 1954–55, coverage was extended to include permanent wage earners, small farmers, and those *ejidatarios* in the agricultural sector who were members of cooperatives or credit associations. Coverage began in the developed state of Sonora and by 1958 had expanded to ten states, practically all in the north and characterized by large plantations, relatively modern agriculture, and rapid economic development. By 1958 IMSS coverage had increased to 7 percent of the population and 9 percent of the labor force.

At the end of 1959 the General Office of Civil Pensions was transformed into the Institute of Social Security and Services of State Employees (Instituto de Seguridad of Servicios Sociales para los Trabajadores del Estado, or ISSSTE). This autonomous federal agency is in charge of administering the social security system for federal civil servants and the Federal District; coverage was extended later to state civil servants, employees of universities, and many public enterprises. This system includes pensions for old age and disability, survivors' benefits, health and maternity care, life insurance and funeral expenses, indemnification for layoff, day-care centers, loans at low interest rates, and a housing program, as well as other benefits such as tax-free stores, free or low-priced entertainment, and sports and recreational facilities.

Under López Mateos (1958–64), temporary and seasonal workers employed in agriculture were included in the IMSS program. By the end of his term, IMSS coverage had jumped to 17 percent of the population and 18 percent of the labor force. During Diaz Ordaz's presidency (1964–70) no significant social security laws were passed, but coverage of the IMSS increased to around 25 percent of the population and the labor force (table 7-6).

Political events in the late 1960s and early 1970s stimulated Echeverría's commitment to redistributive goals. In 1973 social security legislation proposed the extension of coverage to all municipalities in the country (in 1971, 78 percent of them still did not have any coverage), to include marginal groups in the rural and urban areas. Implementation, however, was left to future decrees, and the promises of the law were not fulfilled. However, as a consequence of the law, the IMSS started the social solidarity program in 1974, which did provide some sort of surrogate for the promised programs.

Table 7-6. Share of Population Covered by Social Security, Selected Years, 1965–80
(percent)

Year	Social security program		Insured	Uninsured	Total
	IMSS	ISSSTE			
1965	16.0	2.4	20.0	80.0	100.0
1970	19.5	2.7	24.4	75.6	100.0
1975	26.4	5.8	34.9	65.1	100.0
1980	33.2	7.5	43.0	57.0	100.0

Source: Mexico, COPLAMAR (1982), table 4.12.

During López Portillo's administration (in 1977) a decentralized agency, Coordinación General del Plan Nacional de Zonas Deprimidas y Marginadas (COPLAMAR), was created to promote agricultural, agroindustrial, and handicraft development in poor rural areas. It was given responsibility for social action in the areas of nutrition, housing, education, health, and environmental protection (E. Lozoya in Aspe and Sigmund 1984, p. 431). In 1979 the COPLAMAR and the IMSS signed an agreement to coordinate their efforts in marginal areas, especially in the sphere of health care. At that time the social solidarity program sponsored by the IMSS had 30 field clinics and 310 medical units providing services to about 3.8 million people. By 1981–82 there were 71 field clinics and 3,024 medical units (Lozoya in Aspe and Sigmund 1984, p. 433).

TYPES OF BENEFIT. The IMSS and the ISSSTE together cover over 90 percent of all insured. There are a dozen additional systems, most of which were created through collective bargaining in state monopolies (railroads, electricity, petroleum, and so on). The regulation and supervision of social security is not centralized; there is no overall agency in charge of coordinating the different systems.

The most important institution, in terms of insured population, has been and still is the IMSS. In 1980, 80.1 percent of the total active insured population belonged to the IMSS, and the absolute number had risen from 356,000 in 1944 to 24 million in 1980. Until 1954 there were no rural beneficiaries in the IMSS, and since then the number has risen only slowly. In the case of the ISSSTE, the total number of beneficiaries (active plus passive) went from about 0.5 million in 1961 to 3.9 million in 1976.

The uninsured are concentrated in agriculture and comprise mainly independent peasants, small farmers, and *ejidatarios* not associated with cooperative or credit unions. The other large group of uninsured are the urban self-employed, domestic servants, small businessmen, and unpaid family workers.

Inequalities in social security coverage by occupation, sector, and rural or urban location all indicate that benefits are oriented to the better-off segments of the labor force and do not adequately cover the neediest groups (tables 7-7 and 7-8). Coverage of municipalities is positively correlated with level of development. In 1970, all of the municipalities in the relatively well-developed Federal District and the state of Baja California were covered by the IMSS; but only 8 percent of municipalities in the backward state of Yucatan and 4 percent of those in the least developed state, Oaxaca, were covered.

There are important social benefits in addition to social security—for example, stores that sell at reduced and tax-exempt prices, mortgage loans at low interest rates, subsidized houses for sale, vacation centers, free or very cheap funeral services, sports fields, day-care centers, arts and crafts and vocational training schools, and theaters. These benefits are particularly important for people covered by the ISSSTE and for the armed forces. On the other hand, there are no unemployment benefits (except a lump sum in case of layoff) and no family allowances. The absence of unemployment insurance may be one reason why open unemployment appears to be relatively low and did not change much in the economic stagnation after 1982.

FINANCE AND EXPENDITURE. The IMSS and the ISSSTE have four main sources of finance: contributions from employees and from employers, transfers from the general government, and returns on investments of the agencies themselves. In the case of petroleum, railroad, electricity, and sugar workers, employees contribute little or nothing, and the employers (practically all of them state monopolies) absorb most of the cost.

Table 7-7. Rural and Urban Population Covered by Social Security, 1960, 1970, and 1976
(percent)

Year	Urban	Rural
1960	23.0	0.6
1970	41.2	4.1
1976	55.9	6.1

Note: Population insured by IMSS and ISSSTE as a percentage of the total population in rural urban areas. According to NAFINSA's definition, urban population includes inhabitats of towns of 10,000 or more; this definition may not be identical to that used by IMSS and ISSSTE.

Source: Calculated from NAFINSA (1978), pp. 5, 410, 411.

Table 7-8. Population Covered by Social Security, by State, 1978
(percent)

State	Share of population	State	Share of population
Oaxaca	16.6	Colima	31.5
Tabasco	18.7	Jalisco	35.3
Guerrero	19.8	Quintana Roo	36.1
Michoacan	19.9	Baja California Sur	36.9
Chiapas	22.5	Tamaulipas	37.3
Puebla	23.4	Campeche	37.6
Veracruz	26.3	Morelos	39.5
Zacatecas	26.4	Hidalgo	39.6
Guanajuato	28.2	Sinaloa	41.6
Chihuahua	29.4	Sonora	42.6
Baja California	30.1	Nuevo León	45.9
Nayarit	30.6	Yucatán	49.6
Durango	31.2	Querétaro	50.4
San Luis Potosí	31.4	Valle de México[a]	55.4
Tlaxcala	31.5	Aguascalientes	60.8

a. Includes the state of México and Distrito Federal.
Source: Mexico, COPLAMAR (1982), table 4.13.

The relative weight assigned to the different kinds of IMSS benefits is shown in table 7-9. The largest share of resources is devoted to nonmonetary benefits. For example, during the entire period 1976–85 the latter represented over 70 percent of total expenditure incurred by the IMSS. With 60 percent of the nonmonetary benefits allocated to health-related services such as medical assistance and hospitalization and transport, over 40 percent of total IMSS expenditure is dedicated to health services.

According to Mesa Lago, the large weight of nonmonetary benefits reflects, in fact, part of the inefficiency of the system (1978, pp. 243, 244). These benefits include some items that he considers luxurious (vacations and recreational, sports, and training centers) and heavy administrative expenditures, devoted mostly to expansion of personnel and their remuneration but also to luxurious installations and costly equipment (often underutilized).

Education

Before the Revolution, education was a scarce commodity restricted to a few urban centers. There was no national university, and only a few schools existed for professional training in medicine, law, and engineering.

Table 7-9. Expenditures of IMSS, by Type of Benefit, 1980
(percent)

Type of benefit	Share of total
Benefits in kind	
Medical assistance	49.0
Hospitalization	9.6
Other	41.4
Total	100.0
As a share of all benefits	74.7
Benefits in cash	
Disability	5.3
Widowhood pensions	9.9
Old age pensions	27.7
Other	57.1
Total	100.0
As a share of all benefits	25.3

Source: Mexico, IMSS, *Memoria estadística* (various years).

The 1917 Constitution declared that primary education was to be compulsory and that the education system was to be lay and humanistic and designed to induce a nationalistic and democratic spirit. All education given by the state was to be free, and private educational institutions would have to be authorized to offer primary and secondary schooling.

In spite of high growth rates of both formal and informal education by 1980, 12 percent of the labor force still had no schooling, and only 24 percent had gone beyond primary school. There were between 6 million and 8 million people who could not read or write (15–21 percent of the population over the age of fourteen) and about 15 million who had not completed primary school.

One reason for this was the high rate of population growth (close to 3.5 percent for many years, which made it difficult for the supply of schooling to keep up with increasing demand); another was the relatively heavy weight of rural population (estimated at about 40 percent of the total) and the proportion of the population living in isolated places. About 30 percent of the total population lives in localities of less than 1,000 inhabitants (Urquidi 1982, p. 115). Rural poverty itself played a role in areas where child labor is important and schooling is a luxury that many families cannot afford. Though education is free and so are many of the basic textbooks, there are other complementary (and compulsory) expenditures on uniforms, notebooks, pencils, dresses for national festivities, and the like, as well as transportation costs that cannot easily be met by low-income families. Such reasons help to explain the high dropout rate, especially in rural areas.

Government spending on education expanded in the 1920s when José Vasconcelos, a prominent political and intellectual figure in the Revolution greatly concerned with the modernization of Mexico, was minister of education. During Cárdenas's government another push was given to education (including physical education). And between 1920 and 1940, emphasis was given to education in rural areas.

In the 1940s the share of resources going to education declined, reflecting a swing away from the leftist ideology of the Cárdenas era (table 7-10). Avila Camacho and Alemán were presidents who emphasized economic outlays in the richer regions of the country. The tendency was partially reversed by Ruiz Cortines in terms of the resources devoted to education; however, it was not until the presidency of López Mateos (1959–64) that educational policy became a serious concern—the result, it seems, of the pressure put on the system by popular (unmet) demand. This gave rise to development of a long-term plan for primary education, known as the "eleven-year plan," designed by Minister of Education Jaime Torres Bodet. The projections of demand and of the number of schools and trained teachers required to meet this demand resulted in an increase in budgeted allocations and the levying of a 1 percent tax on payrolls for education. In 1960 distribution of free textbooks to primary students began, and in two years more than 56 million books had been distributed and were available in all primary schools in the country. A strong urban bias in this first edition of free textbooks, however, meant that literacy in rural areas continued to lag (Nash 1965, pp. 53, 54).

Table 7-10. Public Current and Investment Expenditure on Education, Selected Years, 1935–80

Year	Current, on education	Investment, on education and research	Current expenditure as share of GDP (percent)
	Expenditures (millions of pesos)		
1935	38	2	0.9
1940	75	3	0.9
1950	314	29	0.8
1960	1,959	192	1.3
1970	7,817	1,060	1.9
1977	61,761	5,874	3.7
1980	131,130	9,809	3.5

Source: P. Aspe and J. Beristain in Aspe and Sigmund (1984), pp. 296–97.

The effort to expand education in this period was concentrated on the primary level, and by the mid-1960s the inadequacies of secondary and higher education became evident. During the Díaz Ordaz presidency, resources for primary and secondary levels expanded further, but it was not until Echeverría's administration that strong emphasis was put on development of technical schools and of higher education (table 7-11). Also, in the Echeverría presidency, despite opposition from the more conservative middle classes of the northern states and from the teaching profession on their content, a new set of free textbooks was prepared.

Since the 1982 crisis the share of national income devoted to education and the real per capita expenditure on it have declined (see Lustig 1987; Samaniego 1986). In 1983, expenditure fell by 38 percent, and the level in 1985 was slightly below that of 1978. It is hard to see the short-run effects of this crunch, but the average quality of teachers (given the further erosion in their real wages) will inevitably deteriorate, and the absence of new investment will eventually be reflected in shortages and deterioration of existing infrastructure.

One possible (but by no means sufficient) indicator of the quality of the educational system is the student-teacher ratio. At the primary level that ratio rose between 1950 and 1960 and afterward continuously declined, reaching 33.6 students per teacher in 1985.

At the secondary and higher levels there has been a rising student-teacher ratio as enrollment has increased over time (table 7-12). The numbers for 1950 are so small as to seem unreliable; there may have been measurement problems when the data were collected or later when they were reconstructed. The ratios for other years are not large by international standards (see Aspe and Beristain in Aspe and Sigmund 1984, table 10.28, for example).

Private education has been a significant factor in the perpetuation of social differences, though its prevalence has declined since 1970 (table

Table 7-11. Federal Educational Spending per Student, 1976
(pesos)

Item	Amount
Pre-school	785
Elementary school	577
Secondary school	1,376
Teacher training	6,383[a]
Higher education	43,947
Average	1,156

a. For 1975.
Source: Aspe and Beristain in Aspe and Sigmund (1984), p. 301.

Table 7-12. Number of Students per Teacher, Selected Years, 1950–81

Year	Primary school	Secondary school	Preparatory	Higher education
1950	44.7	7.8	5.3	4.9
1960	49.9	11.8	13.3	7.0
1970	47.7	16.2	14.2	10.8
1975	44.8	17.1	18.4	11.6
1981	37.5	18.0	17.0	13.4

Source: Mexico, INEGI (1984b).

7-13). In 1985, 5 percent of enrollment in primary schools was private and 9.5 percent of secondary enrollment. The quality of private secondary schools is notably better than that of government schools, where the student-teacher ratio is 50 percent higher. At the university level, about 16 percent of enrollment is in autonomous institutions that have mixed private and government funding.

Alongside the regular primary schools are other systems that either offer partial primary schooling or simultaneously serve other levels as well. There are also itinerant schools serving areas of very scant population; these *albergues* try to provide children from isolated communities with food and shelter in addition to schooling and other forms of community school services. In the 1970s over 13 percent of total enrollment in primary school was in schools of these kinds, especially those that did not have the complete cycle. Children in such schools are generally not able to finish primary education since, in the majority of cases, they live in isolated areas (Mexico, COPLAMAR 1982, pp. 18, 19).

Programs for adult education were not given high priority until the 1980s. In 1981 a literacy campaign was launched and an Institute for Adult Education was created. The most important action, however, was enactment of the Law of Schooling and Training, which obliges employers to train their workers (Mexico, COPLAMAR 1982, p. 66). It is not clear to what extent this law has actually been enforced.

Though primary public education is unrestricted and free, there are within the system (and also in private institutions) important differences in quality and in the conditions provided to finish the schooling cycle. The differences are reflected in variations in such measures as the rate of dropout or grade repetition within the system and in the qualification levels of students leaving the system. The inequality in opportunity is apparent, for example, in the distribution of schools that do not offer the complete primary cycle. In rural areas (those with fewer than 2,500 inhabitants) it was estimated that in 1973 about 75 percent of

Table 7-13. Share of Students and Teachers in Public and Private Educational Institutions, 1970 and 1985
(percent)

Category	Total	Federal	State	Private
Primary school				
1970				
Students	100.0	65.7	26.5	7.8
Teachers	100.0	63.4	26.8	9.8
1985				
Students	100.0	72.6	22.4	5.0
Teachers	100.0	73.8	21.3	4.9
Secondary school				
1970				
Students	100.0	51.8	20.1	28.1
Teachers	100.0	40.7	22.0	37.3
1985				
Students	100.0	71.5	19.0	9.5
Teachers	100.0	63.0	21.8	15.2
Higher education				
1970				
Students	100.0	19.6	66.4	14.0
Teachers	100.0	16.0	68.0	16.0
1985				
Students	100.0	14.1	70.1	15.8
Teachers	100.0	15.3	66.3	18.4

Source: For 1970, Mexico, INEGI (1984b); for 1985, de la Madrid (1986).

all primary schools were incomplete, in urban areas 10 percent. Moreover, there is a higher ratio of complete to incomplete schooling in rural areas in the richer northern states and the Federal District than elsewhere (see Aspe and Beristain in Aspe and Sigmund 1984, table 10.16).

Student enrollment at all levels has risen over time (Mexico, COPLAMAR 1982, tables 3.11, 3.14). And efforts were obviously made in the 1970s to reduce the variance among states since the largest increases occurred in states that had the lowest levels (which were in general the poorest states such as Chiapas, Guerrero, and Oaxaca).

According to Reyes Heroles (1976), the incidence of government expenditure on education is progressive at the primary level and regressive at the high school and higher levels. As the possibilities for completing school cycles or pursuing a higher (or technical) degree are linked, in general, to the economic condition of lower-income families, the poorer sectors of the population are unlikely to get a reasonable share of higher education without a skillfully administered and targeted scholarship system.

Health

Government concern for health was originally limited to regulation of hygienic standards, supply of some food products (milk, for example), provision of drinkable water, the fight against diseases such as rabies, and the like.

In the early 1960s the government began massive vaccination programs against polio, diphtheria, and other infectious diseases and in 1970 against measles. These campaigns resulted in a decline in mortality from infectious diseases, which accounted for 43 percent of all deaths in 1940 and 14 percent in 1980.

Health services now include the physical and mental health of the population; improvement of nutrition and hygiene; fight against pollution and prevention and control of diseases and accidents that affect public health; sanitary control of food and medical products, beverages, pesticides, and so forth; and campaigns against alcoholism and drug addiction. These services are under the control of the Ministry of Public Health and Welfare (Secretaria de Salubridad y Asistencia, or SSA), except that those in the areas of occupational health are linked to the Ministry of Labor.

Personal health services are provided by either public social security organizations, the public-governmental sector, or private medicine. The distribution of financial resources among the IMSS, the ISSSTE, and the SSA, the major public institutions in charge of health care, is quite unequal. For example, the two large social security agencies, IMSS and ISSSTE absorb about 90 percent of the budget allocated to the three, but they serve only 40 percent of the population. As a result, per capita expenditure by the health agency, SSA, is only a fraction of that on government employees and insured workers (table 7-14).

The evidence shows that resources are unequally distributed geographically as well. In fact, there has been a tendency for the poorer states (Oaxalca, Guerrero, Chiapas, Tlaxcala, Hidalgo, and México, for example) to be less well staffed than the states with higher per capita income (for example, Nuevo León, Coahuila, Chihuahua, Baja California Sur, Sonora, and, of course, the Federal District). The poorer states are also less well covered by health institutions in proportion to their population.

Since 1982, there have been substantial cuts in health investment and in the real salary level of health workers, but so far, physical standards

Table 7-14. Government Expenditure per Capita on Health, by Client Group, 1972, 1978, and 1983

Category	1972	1978	1983
Expenditure (1978 pesos)			
State employees (ISSSTE)	3,784	4,901	3,002
Insured workers (IMSS)	2,866	2,587	1,829
Uninsured population (SSA)	180	305	169
Ratio of state employee benefits to uninsured benefits	21:1	16:1	18:1

Source: Ward (1986), p. 112.

(doctors and beds per capita of population) have not fallen (Lustig 1987).

Housing

Initially, the government's response to the housing problem of the central-city poor was rent control (begun in 1942). As might be expected, there was a drop in information on what frozen rental units were available. The policies of renewal that were then established favored commercially developed housing. In addition, eviction as the response to land invasion was replaced by the designation of peripheral zones, especially in Mexico City, as low-income barrios.

The share of housing construction undertaken by the public sector rose from 5.4 percent in 1951–60 to 18 percent in 1970–74. Public participation was concentrated in Mexico City, and public sector employees were major beneficiaries. In both periods about 65 percent of housing consisted of ramshackle, owner-constructed dwellings (Garza and Schteingart 1978). Private construction by builders fell from 29 percent in 1951–60 to 17 percent in 1970–74.

The government has dealt with housing as if it were mainly a financial problem and has viewed public sector intervention mainly as a stimulus to private initiative. The reliance on private institutional lending has meant that only the top of the lower-income groups could be reached.

The Institute of National Funds of Housing for Workers (Instituto de Fomento Nacional para la Vivienda de los Trabajadores, or INFONAVIT), created in 1973, is the most important institution designed to meet housing demand. However, the conditions for loans are such that it covers only those in the formal labor market who are earning more than the minimum wage; and since the allocation of credit to individuals involves administrative discretion, some degree of favoritism is involved.

All in all, housing policies have concentrated mainly on the capital and to a smaller extent on other metropolitan areas. In the rural sector, housing policy is almost nonexistent.

Food Subsidies

The Mexican government began regulating the prices of food staples in the 1930s (Barkin and Esteva 1981). The objectives of this long-standing intervention were to protect small farmers in rural areas against speculators and to protect the purchasing power of poor consumers in urban areas against rising food prices. The government intervened by purchasing basic grains at guaranteed (support) prices; by maintaining price controls on staples; giving subsidies on some fundamental inputs (such as corn form tortillas) to the industries that produced them; and by participating directly in the production and marketing of basic foodstuffs.

The first agency in this field was the National Storage Houses (Almacenes Nacionales de Depósito, S.A., or ANDSA), founded by Cárdenas in 1936; its main objective was to stop speculation by providing a place to store crops and to provide cash in advance against the stored merchandise. In 1938 the Regulating Committee for Subsistence Markets was founded to participate in selling corn, wheat, rice, beans, sugar, and other staples. This committee was dissolved in 1941 and its functions were transferred to the Mexican Company for Exports and Imports (Compañía Exportadora e Importadora Mexicano, S.A., or CEIMSA). In 1961 CONASUPO took over CEIMSA's work; its objectives have been to regulate the market for basic staples as a means of guaranteeing a minimum price to agricultural producers and of ensuring supply at reasonable prices for urban consumers (Lustig and Martín del Campo 1985).

Between 1965 and 1982 CONASUPO's operations, on average, imposed an implicit tax on the average agricultural producer of corn (with the exception of the years 1967, 1968, 1982, and 1982), sorghum, and wheat (the guaranteed price was lower than the international price corrected for overvaluation of the exchange rate) (Norton 1984, pp. 2-14, 2-15, 2-16) and provided a subsidy for consumers (Martín del Campo 1987, table 4). CONASUPO's deficit, though large, has not exceeded 1.4 percent of GDP (table 7-15).

Since CONASUPO's principal subsidies are general (as opposed to targeted), the degree of progressiveness in their allocation can be judged by looking at the distribution of consumption expenditures on the particular items by income decile. The only foodstuff items on which the impact is progressive are (raw) corn and *piloncillo* (unrefined sugar), neither of which is subject to an explicit subsidy (although in the case of corn the implicit tax on producers could be viewed as a subsidy to net

Table 7-15. Fiscal Cost of Food Subsidies, 1969–82

Year	Operational deficit of CONASUPO (millions of pesos)	Transfers to CONASUPO as a share of total public expenditures (percent)
1969	1,198	1.7
1970	650	1.4
1971	665	1.5
1972	659	1.3
1973	1,828	0.8
1974	5,653	2.3
1975	8,731	1.7
1976	3,261	0.9
1977	7,424	1.3
1978	10,520	2.0
1979	6,778	1.6
1980	27,827	2.4
1981	80,374	2.8
1982	82,882	2.4

Source: Lustig (1986), pp. 17, 18.

buyers of corn in agricultural areas). The rest of the subsidies on basic staples tend to be distributed regressively. The strongest regressive impact was on rice and tortillas.

A much lower share of the CONASUPO subsidies goes to beans and rice (below 10 percent) than to maize. Over time the share going to the latter has declined while that going to sorghum and oilseeds has risen. Sorghum is a major input in the production of beef and poultry, both of which are more intensively consumed by higher-income groups (though a very high proportion of the amount spent for food by the poor may go to meat). This indicates that for some products the largest portion of the benefit of the general price subsidies is captured by higher-income groups. Thus a lot could be gained in terms of equity if the subsidies on food products were targeted to lower-income groups, as is the milk coupon program LICONSA (Leche Industrializada Conasupo S.A.) (see Lustig 1986; Martín del Campo 1987).

Faced with stringent budget goals, the government has recently made an effort to rationalize food subsidies and target them more carefully—as with the tortilla coupon program (Martín del Campo 1987). However, it is not yet clear whether savings under the new schemes are the result of rationalization or of sheer elimination of the subsidy on certain foodstuffs. Nor is it clear whether those who stop having access to subsidies are those who should be excluded on distributive grounds.

Overall Distributive Impact of Government Spending and Revenue

In 1982, when total government expenditure was 36.7 percent of GDP, expenditure or welfare (poverty relief in its pure form) was 2.1 billion pesos ($37 million) which, when rounded, was zero percent of GDP. (Table 7-16 shows the pattern of government expenditure.) The social security programs did not include unemployment benefit or family allowances, and their main beneficiaries were government employees, salaried employees, and workers in the formal sector. Health expenditure was even more heavily concentrated on government employees, and the uninsured population got virtually no benefits. The same was true of housing expenditure. The very high cost of subsidies (for products of public corporations, government food stores, and credit subsidies) was random or regressive in its impact, and foreign exchange subsidies went mainly to private firms to meet their debt payment commitments.

Table 7-16. Categories of Government Expenditure, 1975 and 1982

Category	1975 Billions of pesos	1975 Percentage of GDP at market prices	1982 Billions of pesos	1982 Percentage of GDP at market prices
Expenditure of local government[a]	5.1	0.5	49.8	0.5
Expenditure of state government[a]	32.5	3.0	436.3	4.6
Expenditure of central government	187.4	17.0	2,973.8	31.6
Defense	5.9	0.5	45.4	0.5
Education	29.4	2.7	369.5	3.9
Health	6.8	0.6	36.6	0.4
Social security	38.1	3.5	296.7	3.2
Welfare	1.8	0.2	2.1	0.0
Housing and social services	0.0	0.0	86.9	0.9
Subsidies	45.2	4.1	1,068.0	11.3
Public debt interest	13.6	1.2	417.3	4.4
Exchange subsidies	0.0	0.0	318.5	3.4
Capital expenditure[b]	37.7	3.4	638.6	6.8

a. Net of transfers to and from other levels of government.
b. Some of this is also included in other items.
Source: IMF (1985), pp. 575–80.

Table 7-17. Categories of General Government Revenue, Total Expenditure, and Overall Balance, 1975 and 1982

	1975		1982	
Category	Billions of pesos	Percentage of GDP at market prices	Billions of pesos	Percentage of GDP at market prices
Indirect taxes	68.0	6.2	967.2	10.3
Direct taxes	55.0	5.0	487.5	5.2
Social security contributions	24.4	2.2	215.0	2.3
Other net income	16.2	1.5	178.3	1.9
Total revenue	164.0	14.9	1,850.7	19.7
Total current and capital expenditure	227.1	20.6	3,459.9	36.7
Overall balance	−63.1	−5.7	−1,609.2	−17.1

Source: IMF (1985), pp. 575–80.

Table 7-18. Tax Incidence, by Level of Income, 1968

Family income (thousands of pesos)	Share of total (percent)		Tax as a share of income (percent)
	Families	Income	
Less than 2,100	2.80	0.21	15.15
2,100–2,700	1.51	0.18	18.81
2,700–3,60 0	2.78	0.34	12.14
3,600–4,800	5.78	0.94	10.95
4,800–6,360	8.41	1.85	10.89
6,360–8,400	9.39	2.60	9.82
8,400–11,400	13.74	5.34	12.23
11,400–15,000	11.31	5.61	12.71
15,000–20,400	12.42	8.17	13.19
20,400–26,400	7.32	6.38	13.40
26,400–36,000	8.25	9.94	13.74
36,000–48,000	5.30	8.45	14.11
48,000–62,400	3.58	7.36	14.45
62,400–84,000	3.10	9.05	18.29
84,000–110,400	1.53	6.08	16.04
110,400–151,200	0.98	5.35	17.62
More than 151,200	1.80	22.15	9.53
Total	100.00	100.00	13.28

Source: Reyes Heroles G. G. (1976), pp. 199, 239, 287, 289.

These redistributive expenditures therefore had a limited social impact, and many were the fruit of an etatist mania for a bureaucratic hand in resource allocation.

The major social or redistributive expenditure that provided some help for the poorer section of the population was education, which got 3.9 percent of GDP; education helped to increase access to better jobs for its recipients, increased the productivity of the labor force, and contributed to the productivity of the economy.

However, the coverage of primary education was incomplete, and the coverage of secondary education poor. A substantial proportion of better-off families still send their children to private schools, whose quality is considered to be better than that of government schools and whose teacher-pupil ratios at the secondary level are 50 percent higher than public schools'.

Table 7-19. Tax Incidence, by Type of Tax, 1980
(percent of income)

Income quintile[a]	Indirect taxes	Individual income tax	Payroll tax	Corporate income tax	Social security levies	Total
Bottom 5	5.20	0.000	0.043	1.026	1.256	7.53
5–10	5.07	0.000	0.068	1.130	1.872	8.14
10–15	5.45	0.000	0.071	1.041	2,062	8.61
15–20	5.74	0.000	1.001	1.226	2.845	9.91
20–25	6.41	0.000	0.141	0.708	3.539	10.84
25–30	5.41	0.016	0.147	0.880	4.162	10.60
30–35	6.08	0.035	0.176	0.938	4.712	11.93
35–40	6.79	0.098	0.130	0.794	3.800	11.61
40–45	6.26	0.173	0.155	0.664	4.451	11.69
45–50	6.52	0.344	0.114	3.235	3.145	13.35
50–55	6.45	1.352	0.185	2.591	5.203	15.78
55–60	6.76	1.741	0.166	5.955	4.764	19.28
60–65	6.08	3.208	0.220	3.206	5.773	18.32
65–70	6.88	3.026	0.176	7.470	4.653	22.12
70–75	6.49	4.499	0.207	3.753	5.888	20.84
75–80	6.87	6.543	0.201	4.043	5.361	23.01
80–85	7.22	7.930	0.274	2.509	7.163	25.06
85–90	7.92	7.209	0.222	4.137	6.330	25.86
90–95	8.04	5.582	0.286	4.253	7.253	25.41
Top 5	7.35	4.001	0.213	20.215	5.383	37.15

a. Official income figures were adjusted upwards by Gil Diaz to include unreported income.
Source: F. Gil Diaz in Aspe and Sigmund (1984).

208 Brazil and Mexico

Table 7-17 shows the breakdown of government revenue in 1975 and 1982. One striking point is the large deficits—already substantial in 1975 and horrendous in 1982. Another is the relatively small weight of direct taxes—5 percent of GDP—and the apparent inability to increase this proportion.

Table 7-18 shows that the incidence of taxation in 1968 was rather erratic. In fact, it exacted a higher share of income from the two lowest family-income groups than from the highest. It had little effect on the Gini coefficient, which was 0.580 before tax and 0.568 after tax (Reyes Heroles G. G. 1976).

Table 7-19 shows tax incidence in 1980 after substantial tax reforms. The picture is certainly different from that in 1968, with a fairly steady progression rising from 7.5 percent for the lowest half decile to 37 percent for the top half decile. However, these results are based on a household survey that contained no information on actual tax payments. The tax rates are imputed and represent the theoretical incidence.

Statistical Appendix

Reliability of GDP Estimates for Brazil

The available Brazilian estimates of GDP for 1920 onward are those prepared by Fundação Getúlio Vargas (the Vargas Foundation). These are indeed the official estimates, for it was only in 1987 that responsibility for the national accounts was transferred to the statistical office Fundação Instituto Brasileiro de Geografia e Estatística (FIBGE). The estimates are based wherever possible on the benchmark economic censuses covering major sectors of the economy; the estimates are less reliable for years between censuses and for measuring cyclical movements. Input-output tables are used to provide guidelines for ratios of value added to gross output.

Official practice is to reconstitute current price estimates of production by multiplying the volume figure by the general price deflator used by the Vargas Foundation. Given the persistence of inflation over the long term, the alternative technique of deflating current price figures to arrive at a volume estimate is not available. In terms of expenditure breakdowns, the accounts are crude, and the income breakdown is even weaker.

One major drawback of the official accounts is that between 1920 and 1980 the direct volume estimates only cover gross value added in agriculture, industry, commerce, and transport and communications; output in the rest of the economy was simply assumed to grow at the same rate as the total for the four measured sectors. The excluded sectors are financial intermediaries, government, rents, and other services; in 1980 those sectors amounted to 31.3 percent of GDP (before deduction of imputed financial services), and they accounted for 26.3 percent of employment in 1980 as shown in the demographic census.

In comparisons with Mexico, use of the official Brazilian figures would exaggerate Brazil's growth. Therefore this study assumes that half of the growth in "other services" in Brazil (mainly government services and related services from housing and other real estate) was at the rate of growth in the covered sectors and the other half at the rate of population growth.

The Brazilian national accounts make little allowance for informal activity not covered in the economic censuses. Therefore the official accounts understate the level of output in Brazil relative to Mexico, where elaborate estimates are made for the informal sector.

This can be seen most clearly in manufacturing. The industrial census is used by the official Brazilian statisticians to calculate the contribution of manufacturing to GDP with only a small addition for output outside census establishments. In 1980, the census establishments accounted for 98.8 percent of gross value added in the national accounts definition for manufacturing and only 1.2 percent was estimated to be produced by people working outside these census establishments. However, the 1980 demographic census recorded 6.9 million people who reported themselves to be working in manufacturing, compared with the 4.8 million recorded in the industrial census. Even after allowance for misreporting of area of activity, for exaggeration of activity by people who are really unemployed, and for the lower productivity of people in the informal sector, it seems clear that the national accounts understate manufacturing output substantially.

The proportionate discrepancy in manufacturing employment reported in the two types of census was similar in all the benchmark years, 1950, 1960, 1970, and 1980, so one should not infer that output growth is mismeasured. But, compared with Mexico, there is clearly an understatement of the level of manufacturing output in the Brazilian national accounts. For 1975, the Mexican national accounts estimated manufacturing value added to have been 44 percent higher than that reported in the Mexican industrial census.

There are problems in reconciling the demographic and economic census figures for employment. In all nonagricultural sectors, except hotels and restaurants, the economic censuses seem to omit a significant amount of activity. In commerce, for instance, the economic census reports only 3.1 million people as employed in 1980, compared with 4 million in the demographic census, but the national accounts assumed that 11 percent of 1980 output in this sector was produced by people working in the informal sector.

For the economy as a whole the national accounts estimate of informal activity in 1980 was about 10.5 percent of GDP. There is no discussion in the national accounts of the problem of reconciling the two main sources for employment and there is no attempt to measure labor productivity.

The fact that the Brazilian national accounts understate output levels has been stressed by Merrick and Graham (1979) who compared the demographic and economic censuses and referred to a survey by Merrick of informal activity in Belo Horizonte. Pfefferman and Webb (1979) also noted the understatement in the national accounts, as did the 1984 World Bank mission on improving the national accounts. A rough study for the Vargas Foundation estimates informal activity to be about 20 percent of GDP (including criminal activities) and points out the substantial incentives and possibilities for such activity (Melo Flores de Lima 1985; this was a study of the size of informal activity, some of it included in GDP; no detailed reconciliation with GDP was attempted). The fact that social charges paid by employers on labor in the formal sector have risen from 13.3 percent of wages in 1950 to 45 percent in 1982 encourages some employers to look for informal labor. In 1983, according to Melo Flores de Lima, only 65 percent of people working in Brazil were wage earners and 47 percent of these did not have a *carteiro de trabalho*, which would indicate their employer and wage level. In 1983, 52.3 percent of those employed were outside the social security system. Melo Flores de Lima suggests that the proportionate size of the underground economy increased relatively in the years of recession and slow growth in the 1980s. However, the evidence is rather that people had a greater need to supplement their income than that they succeeded in doing so. In order to deal with this problem in tables where income levels in Brazil and Mexico are compared, the benchmark comparison is converted by purchasing power parities rather than exchange rates and corrected for differences in coverage of the national accounts (see Maddison and van Ark 1989 for a discussion of this problem).

Table A-1. Brazilian Population, GDP, and GDP per Capita, Selected Years, 1900–50

Year	Midyear population (thousands)	GDP (millions of 1970 cruzeiros at factor cost)	Index of GDP (1950 = 100)	GDP per capita (1970 cruzeiros)
1900	17,984	7,091	14.07	394
1913	23,660	11,150	22.12	471
1920	27,404	14,492	28.75	528
1929	32,894	19,455	38.59	591
1938	39,480	29,250	58.02	741
1940	41,114	29,894	59.30	727
1950	51,941	50,412	100.00	971

Source: For population, IBGE (1960), p. 5. For GDP, 1900–20, indicators for industry, commerce, transport and communications from Haddad (1978), p. 7, and for agriculture from Haddad (1980), p. 24; 1920–50, for these sectors from Zerkowski and de Gusmão Veloso (1982). Half of the rest of economic activity was assumed to rise parallel with population, the other half parallel with the output movement in the covered sector; for 1900–50, the 1947 sector weights are from de Gusmão Veloso (1987).

Table A-2. Brazilian GDP, Population, and GDP per Capita, 1950–88

Year	GDP at factor cost Millions of 1970 cruzeiros	Annual change (percent)	Midyear population (thousands)	GDP per capita (1970 cruzeiros)	Annual change in GDP deflator (percent)
1950	50,412	6.1	51,941	971	9.2
1951	52,812	4.7	53,494	987	18.4
1952	55,961	6.0	55,093	1,016	9.3
1953	58,651	4.8	56,739	1,034	13.8
1954	62,533	6.6	58,435	1,070	27.1
1955	67,122	7.4	60,181	1,115	11.8
1956	68,089	2.9	61,980	1,099	22.6
1957	73,760	6.8	63,832	1,156	12.7
1958	80,447	9.1	65,740	1,224	12.4
1959	87,199	8.4	67,704	1,288	35.9

(continued)

Table A-2. *(continued)*

Year	GDP at factor cost Millions of 1970 cruzeiros	Annual change (percent)	Midyear population (thousands)	GDP per capita (1970 cruzeiros)	Annual change in GDP deflator (percent)
1960	94,450	8.3	69,739	1,354	25.4
1961	101,537	7.5	71,752	1,4 15	34.7
1962	107,728	6.1	73,823	1,460	50.1
1963	108,849	1.0	75,955	1,433	78.4
1964	112,522	3.4	78,147	1,440	89.9
1965	114,791	2.0	80,403	1,428	58.2
1966	121,981	6.3	82,724	1,475	37.9
1967	126,881	4.0	85,112	1,491	26.5
1968	138,198	8.9	87,569	1,578	26.7
1969	150,254	8.7	90,097	1,668	20.1
1970	165,030	9.8	92,759	1,779	16.3
1971	181,769	10.1	95,061	1,912	19.3
1972	201,359	10.8	97,419	2,067	19.9
1973	226,626	12.5	99,836	2,270	29.6
1974	244,490	7.8	102,312	2,390	34.5
1975	257,244	5.2	104,851	2,453	34.0
1976	281,458	9.4	107,452	2,619	41.4
1977	294,621	4.7	110,117	2,676	45.5
1978	309,393	5.0	112,849	2,742	38.2
1979	331,366	7.1	115,649	2,865	54.4
1980	360,604	8.8	118,518	3,043	90.3
1981	344,712	−4.4	121,458	2,838	108.1
1982	346,914	0.6	124,471	2,787	105.6
1983	334,891	−3.5	127,559	2,625	141.4
1984	352,012	5.1	130,723	2,693	215.0
1985	381,387	8.3	133,966	2,847	231.4
1986	410,299	7.6	137,288	2,989	143.8
1987	425,106	3.6	140,692	3,022	209.3
1988	423,935	−0.3	143,661	2,951	684.6

Source: For 1950–80, de Gusmão Veloso (1987); sectoral growth indicators for covered sectors at 1970 weights; half of the residual assumed to grow with population, half at the same pace as the covered sector. For 1981–88, supplied by FIBGE.

Table A-3. Brazilian Gross Domestic Product by Sector at Factor Cost, Selected Years, 1950–88

(millions of 1970 cruzeiros)

Year	Agriculture, forestry, and fishing	Industry	Commerce	Transport and communications	Other (residual)[a]	Gross domestic product[a]
1950	8,535	13,415	8,045	1,647	18,770	50,412
1960	13,248	31,617	16,290	3,753	29,542	94,450
1970	20,157	62,610	28,627	7,525	46,311	165,030
1980	32,024	141,846	61,908	26,859	97,967	360,604
1988	40,791	155,392	66,731	42,969	118,052	423,935

a. Net of intermediate financial services.
Source: Same as for table A-2.

Table A-4. Value of Brazilian Commodity Exports and Imports, Selected Years, 1950–87

	Current prices (millions of dollars)			Quantity indexes (1977 = 100)	
Year	Exports (f.o.b.)	Imports (c.i.f.)	Balance	Exports (f.o.b.)	Imports (c.i.f.)
1950	1,359	1,090	269	27.8	20.4
1960	1,268	1,462	−194	32.3	24.4
1970	2,739	2,849	−110	56.5	47.5
1971	2,904	3,701	−797	59.8	58.1
1972	3,991	4,783	−792	76.2	70.4
1973	6,199	6,999	−800	87.5	85.2
1974	7,951	14,168	−6,217	89.2	115.2
1975	8,670	13,592	−4,922	93.2	109.1
1976	10,128	13,726	−3,598	99.4	108.1
1977	12,120	13,257	−1,137	100.0	100.0
1978	12,659	15,054	−2,395	112.9	105.2
1979	15,244	19,804	−4,560	123.7	114.4
1980	20,132	24,961	−4,829	152.0	114.5
1981	23,293	24,079	−786	182.8	99.3
1982	20,175	21,069	−894	166.9	91.1
1983	21,899	16,801	5,098	191.3	76.2
1984	27,005	15,210	11,795	233.9	73.1
1985	25,639	14,332	11,307	238.4	72.1
1986	22,349	15,557	6,792	195.0	83.1
1987	26,224	16,581	9,643	—	—

— Not available.
Source: IMF, International Financial Statistics, except for import volume, 1950–70, CEPAL (1976).

Table A-5. Brazilian Exchange Rate, Internal and World Prices, and Real Exchange Rate, Selected Years, 1889–1967

Year	Exchange rate (units of national currency per dollar)[a]	GDP deflator (1929 = 100)	Exchange rate divided by GDP deflator	World export unit value dollar index (1929 = 100)	Real exchange rate
1889	1.87	21.9	8.55	70.6	6.04
1900	5.19	48.1	10.79	69.0	7.45
1913	3.09	40.5	7.63	79.4	6.06
1929	8.47	100.0	8.47	100.0	8.47
1930	9.34	87.6	10.66	85.7	9.14
1931	14.22	78.1	18.21	65.9	12.00
1932	14.04	79.3	17.70	52.4	9.27
1933	12.56	77.7	16.16	59.5	9.62
1934	11.86	82.6	14.36	73.0	10.48
1935	12.05	86.5	13.93	71.4	9.95
1936	11.67	87.9	13.28	73.0	9.69
1937	11.57	93.6	12.36	80.2	9.91
1938	17.11	99.3	17.23	75.4	12.99
1939	16.66	101.3	16.45	—	—
1940	16.51	108.1	15.27	—	—
1941	16.51	119.1	13.86	—	—
1942	16.51[b]	138.5	11.92	—	—
1943	16.50	—	—	—	—
1944	16.50	194.8	8.47	—	—
1945	16.50	223.9	7.37	—	—
1946	16.50	256.7	6.43	—	—
1947	18.38	279.9	6.57	—	—
1948	18.38	296.4	6.20	187.3	11.61
1949	18.38	320.4	5.74	—	—
1950	18.38	346.7	5.30	166.7	8.84
1951	18.38	410.5	4.48	202.4	9.07
1952	18.38	448.7	4.10	195.2	8.00
1967	2,660.00	36,303.4	7.33	198.4	14.54

— Not available.
a. Average for year.
b. Milreis became the cruzeiro on October 31, 1942.

Source: For exchange rates, U.S. Federal Reserve System, *Banking and Monetary Statistics*. For GDP deflator, to 1947, Goldsmith (1986); after 1947, supplied by FIBGE. For world export unit value, Maddison (1962).

Table A-6. Brazilian Multiple Exchange Rates, by Category, 1953–66
(old cruzeiros per dollar)

Year	Category 1	Category 2	Category 2	Category 3	Free
1953[a]	23.4	28.4	n.a.	n.a.	43.0
1954[a]	24.2	28.4	n.a.	n.a.	65.9
1955[a]	31.5	36.6	43.9	50.1	n.a.
1956[a]	n.a.	40.4	49.5	59.0	n.a.
1957[a]	n.a.	43.1	55.0	67.0	n.a.
1958[a]	n.a.	43.1	62.5	79.0	142.2
1959[a]	n.a.	n.a.	72.3	100.0	152.7
				Coffee rate [b]	
1960[a]	n.a.	n.a.	n.a.	100.0	189.6
1961	n.a.	n.a.	n.a.	(114.1)	270.0
1962	n.a.	n.a.	n.a.	(149.1)	390.0
1963	n.a.	n.a.	n.a.	(293.7)	580.0
1964	n.a.	n.a.	n.a.	(501.6)	1,250.0
1965	n.a.	n.a.	n.a.	(759.1)	1,900.0
1966	n.a.	n.a.	n.a.	(944.5)	2,220.0

n.a. Not applicable.

Note: Figures are average for year.

a. Until 1961, the official par value remained theoretically at 18.70 cruzeiros to the dollar.

b. For 1961–66 rate at end of year adjusted to an average for the year on the basis of the end-year relation to the free rate.

Source: For 1953–60, U.S. Federal Reserve System, *Banking and Monetary Statistics*; from 1961, IMF, *International Financial Statistics*.

Table A-7. Brazilian Exchange Rate, Internal and World Prices, and Real Exchange Rate, 1967–88

Year	Exchange rate (new cruzeiros per dollar)	GDP deflator (1970 = 100)	Exchange rate (divided by GDP deflator)	World export unit value dollar index (1970 = 100)	Real exchange rate
1967	2.66	56.5	4.71	93.0	4.38
1968	3.40	71.6	4.75	92.2	4.38
1969	4.07	86.0	4.73	95.6	4.52
1970	4.59	100.0	4.59	100.0	4.59
1971	5.29	119.3	4.43	105.6	4.58
1972	5.93	143.0	4.15	115.2	4.78
1973	6.13	185.4	3.31	141.9	4.70
1974	6.79	249.3	2.72	196.3	5.34
1975	8.13	334.1	2.43	213.7	5.19
1976	10.67	472.5	2.26	218.1	4.93
1977	14.14	687.4	2.06	237.8	4.90
1978	18.07	950.0	1.90	261.5	4.97
1979	26.95	1,466.8	1.84	309.3	5.69
1980	52.7	2,791.4	1.88	370.4	6.96
1981	93.1	5,808.9	1.60	366.7	5.87
1982	179.5	11,943.0	1.50	353.4	5.30
1983	577.0	28,830.4	2.00	334.8	6.70
1984	1,848.0	90,815.9	2.03	328.2	6.66
1985	6,200.0	300,964.0	2.06	323.0	6.65
1986	13,656.0	733,751.0	1.86	341.5	6.35
1987	39,230.0	2,269,500.0	1.73	364.5	6.30
1988	262,380.0	17,810,000.0	1.47	—	—

— Not available.

Note: The new cruzeiro (1 = 1,000 old cruzeiros) was introduced in 1967. The cruzado was introduced February 28, 1986 (1 = 1,000 new cruzeiros).

Source: For exchange rate and world export unit value, IMF, *International Financial Statistics.* For GDP deflator, supplied by FIBGE.

Table A-8. Active Labor Force and Labor Force with Monthly Earnings below One Minimum Wage, Selected Years, 1960–83

Year	Total labor force (thousands) (A)	Labor force with earnings (thousands) (B)	B/A (percent)	Labor force earning minimum wage or less (thousands) (C)	C/A (percent)
1960	22,750.0	18,969.5	83.4	13,295.2	58.4
1970	29,557.2	25,980.1	87.9	15,743.9	53.3
1977	41,132.2	35,863.7	87.2	14,067.8	34.2
1980	43,235.7	39,695.8	91.8	13,574.6	31.4
1981	47,488.5	40,951.0	86.2	13,170.0	27.7
1983	50,940.7	43,936.6	86.3	15,746.2	30.9

Source: FIBGE, *Censo demográfico* (1960, 1980); FIBGE, *Indicadores socials* (1979, 1984).

Reliability of GDP Estimates for Mexico

Figures in the tables in this appendix are from official sources. For 1895–1960 the official estimates, by the Bank of Mexico, are not adequately described. For 1895–1921 they are identical in movement with the estimates of E. Pérez López (in Pérez López and others 1967). He describes his estimates as provisional, and, as he assumed that service output (half of GDP) moved at the same rate in real terms as commodity output, his estimates probably overstate growth. The official Bank of Mexico series are very close to the estimates of Pérez López for 1939–60 but show lower growth than he does for 1921–39. Pérez López used a sophisticated technique from 1939 onward, and it looks as if the Bank of Mexico retained his results for 1939–60, changing the weights from 1950 to 1960, that they redid his estimates for 1921–39, and did not bother to modify his results for 1895–1921. Bank of Mexico (1963) contains the most detailed description of the pre-1960 figures.

From 1960 on, the official figures are from Mexico, INEGI (1987a). The INEGI series, now the official source for national accounts, is wider in coverage than the earlier Bank of Mexico estimates (about 6.1 percent higher in value terms in 1970). There is a detailed reconciliation of the Bank of Mexico figures and those of INEGI in Reyes Heroles G. G. and Sidaoui (1981).

The major problem with the new estimates is that they make extensive allowance for informal economic activity, so that their level is high by international standards and certainly by comparison with Brazil.

Table B-1. Mexican Population, GDP, and GDP per Capita, Selected Years, 1895–1950

Year	Midyear population (thousands)	GDP (millions of 1970 pesos)	Index of GDP (1950 = 100)	GDP per capita (1970 pesos)
1895	12,632	32,447	24.7	2,568
1900	13,607	36,210	27.6	2,661
1910	15,000	49,510	37.7	3,301
1921	14,895	53,302	40.6	3,579
1929	16,875	57,782	44.0	3,424
1932	17,790	47,609	36.3	2,676
1940	20,558	73,592	56.1	3,580
1950	27,376	131,293	100.0	4,796

Source: Population in 1895–1900 from Mexico, INEGI (1985a), table 9.1; in 1910 and 1921 from Greer (1966); in 1929–40, estimates from Mexico, INEGI (1985a) adjusted pro rata from Greer's 3 percent upward adjustment for 1921 to the 5.76 percent upward adjustment of CONAPO (Mexico, INEGI 1985d) for 1950. GDP from Mexico, INEGI (1985a), table 9.1.

Table B-2. Mexican GDP, Population, and GDP per Capita, 1950–88

Year	GDP Millions of current pesos	GDP Millions of 1970 pesos	Midyear population (thousands)	GDP per capita (1970 pesos)[a]
1950	42,163	131,293	27,376	4,796
1951	54,375	141,446	28,140	5,027
1952	60,993	147,071	28,954	5,079
1953	60,664	147,475	29,814	4,947
1954	73,936	162,216	30,720	5,280
1955	90,053	176,002	31,669	5,558
1956	102,920	188,035	32,662	5,757
1957	118,206	202,278	33,701	6,002
1958	131,377	213,036	34,784	6,125
1959	140,772	219,408	35,909	6,110

(continued)

Table B-2. *(continued)*

Year	GDP Millions of current pesos	GDP Millions of 1970 pesos	Midyear population (thousands)	GDP per capita (1970 pesos)[a]
1960	159,703	237,216	37,073	6,399
1961	173,236	246,716	38,273	6,446
1962	186,781	257,988	39,510	6,530
1963	207,952	277,263	40,790	6,797
1964	245,501	306,744	42,118	7,283
1965	267,420	326,679	43,500	7,510
1966	297,196	346,796	44,935	7,718
1967	325,025	367,385	46,418	7,915
1968	359,858	394,024	47,952	8,217
1969	397,796	416,899	49,538	8,416
1970	444,271	444,271	51,176	8,681
1971	490,011	462,804	52,884	8,751
1972	564,727	502,086	54,661	9,186
1973	690,891	544,307	56,481	9,637
1974	899,707	577,568	58,320	9,903
1975	1,100,045	609,976	60,153	10,140
1976	1,370,968	635,831	61,979	10,259
1977	1,849,263	657,722	63,813	10,307
1978	2,337,398	711,982	65,658	10,844
1979	3,067,526	777,163	67,518	11,511
1980	4,470,077	841,855	69,655	12,086
1981	6,127,632	915,707	71,305	12,842
1982	9,797,791	909,957	72,968	12,471
1983	17,878,720	871,773	74,633	11,681
1984	29,471,575	903,245	76,293	11,839
1985	47,402,549	926,570	77,938	11,888
1986	79,353,450	889,917	79,563	11,185
1987	195,614,800	902,660	81,163	11,122
1988	389,211,000	900,908	82,734	10,889

a. Derived from GDP and population figures.

Source: For GDP at current market prices to 1979, Bank of Mexico, *Indicadores económicos* (May 1986), thereafter, Mexico, INEGI (1988). For GDP at 1970 market prices in 1960–80, Mexico, INEGI (1987b), pp. 155–56; in 1980–88, Wharton (1989). For GDP movement in 1950–60, Bank of Mexico, *Indicadores económicos* (May 1986); in 1960–88, Mexico, INEGI (1988). For population, Mexico, INEGI (1985d).

Table B-5. Value Added per Person Employed in Selected Years, 1900–84
(pesos)

Year	Agriculture, forestry, and fishing	Mining	Manufacturing, construction, and utilities	Services	
At 1960 market prices					
1900	1,868	8,000	3,939	13,311	4,609
1910	2,105	14,855	5,718	17,760	5,813
1940	2,364	27,935	12,106	21,609	7,971
1950	3,282	43,361	12,743	22,860	9,983
At 1970 market prices					
1950	5,539	43,186	21,028	35,726	15,741
1960	8,013	51,859	29,659	43,179	23,227
1970	10,225	62,167	41,080	58,020	34,291
1980	13,411	57,423	54,660	55,945	43,305
1984	13,677	63,393	58,559	52,690	42,714

Source: Tables B-3, B-4.

Table B-6. Population by Age and Sex, Selected Years, 1950–80
(thousands)

Year and age	Male	Female	Total
1950			
Under 15	6,006	5,799	11,805
15–64	7,286	7,364	14,649
65–69	180	203	383
Over 69	245	293	538
Total	13,716	13,659	27,375
1960			
Under 15	8,615	8,297	16,912
15–64	9,365	9,541	18,906
65–69	244	279	523
Over 69	333	399	732
Total	18,557	18,516	37,073
1970			
Under 15	12,160	11,718	23,878
15–64	12,644	12,864	25,508
65–69	339	389	728
Over 69	482	580	1,062
Total	25,625	25,551	51,176
1980			
Under 15	15,780	15,233	31,013
15–64	17,851	18,063	35,914
65–69	439	510	949
Over 69	678	839	1,517
Total	34,748	34,645	69,393

Source: Mexico, SPP; Mexico, INEGI (1984a); Mexico, INEGI (1985d).

Table B-7. Economically Active Population in Mexico, by Age and Sex, 1950, 1960, and 1980
(thousands)

Year and age	Male	Female	Total
1950			
Under 15	412	89	501
15–64	6,398	989	7,387
65–69	160	23	183
Over 69	237	37	274
Total	7,207	1,138	8,345
1960			
Under 15	201	56	257
15–64	7,787	1,544	9,331
65–69	192	42	234
Over 69	316	75	391
Total	8,496	1,717	10,213
1980, census version			
Under 15	535	263	798
15–64	14,564	5,620	20,184
65–69	327	97	424
Over 69	499	161	660
Total	15,925	6,141	22,066
1980, Gregory's version[a]			
Under 15	513	204	717
15–64	13,963	4,370	18,333
65–69	313	75	388
Over 69	478	125	603
Total	15,267	4,774	20,041

a. Total male and female estimates distributed by age with census proportions.

Source: For 1950, Gregory (1986), derived from activity rates; 1960, Altimir (1974); 1980, census version, Mexico, INEGI (1984a); 1980, Gregory's version, Gregory (1986).

Table B-8. Mexican Activity Rates, by Age and Sex, 1950 and 1980
(percent)

Year and age	Male	Female	Total	Ratio of females to males in labor force
1950				
Under 15	6.9	1.5	4.2	21.6
15–64	87.8	13.4	50.4	15.5
65–69	88.9	11.3	47.8	14.4
Over 69	96.7	12.6	50.9	15.6
Ratio of labor force to total population	52.5	8.3	30.5	15.8
Ratio of labor force to population ages 15–64	98.9	15.5	57.0	15.8
1980, Gregory's version				
Under 15	3.3	1.3	2.3	39.8
15–64	78.2	24.2	51.0	31.3
65–69	71.3	14.7	40.9	24.0
Over 69	70.5	14.9	39.7	26.2
Ratio of labor force to total population	43.9	13.8	28.9	31.3
Ratio of labor force to population ages 15–64	85.5	26.4	55.8	31.3
1980, census version				
Under 15	3.4	1.7	2.6	49.2
15–64	81.6	31.1	56.2	38.6
65–69	74.5	19.0	44.7	29.7
Over 69	73.6	19.2	43.5	32.2
Ratio of labor force to total population	45.8	17.7	31.8	38.6
Ratio of labor force to population ages 15–64	89.2	34.0	61.4	38.6

Source: Derived from tables B-6, B-7.

Table B-9. Mexican Exports, Total and per Capita, and Exchange Rates, Selected Years, 1801–1988

Year	Total exports (millions of dollars)	Exchange rate (pesos per dollar)	Per capita exports (dollars)	Export volume (1929 = 100)
1801–10	16.0	1.00	2.7	—
1823	2.3	1.00	0.3	—
1877	29.6	1.10	3.1	9.0
1889	48.0	1.32	4.2	16.4
1910–11	140.0	2.01	9.2	63.6
1929	284.6	2.15	17.5	100.0
1938	186.3	4.52	9.8	50.0
1940	177.8	5.40	9.0	40.6
1950	532	8.65	20.6	53.8
1960	765	12.50	21.9	81.1
1964	1,031	12.50	25.4	95.3
1970	1,403	12.50	27.7	112.3
1973	2,261	12.50	41.0	141.0
1980	15,570	22.95	248.8	313.2
1984	24,407	167.83[a]	326.8	558.7
1985	22,112	256.87[a]	283.7	507.4
1986	16,347	611.77[a]	205.5	512.5
1987	20,887	1,378.20	257.3	568.8
1988	20,765	2,273.10	251.0	—

— Not available.

a. Principal rate, parallel market was 185.19 pesos in 1984, 310.17 pesos in 1985, 637.38 pesos in 1986.

Source: For export values and exchange rates, in 1801–10, Rosenzweig (1965); in 1823, Herrera Canales (1977); in 1877–10, Banco Nacional de Comercio Exterior (1960); after 1910, Maddison (1985), IMF and World Bank data. For volume index, in 1877–1910, Banco Nacional de Comercio Exterior (1960); in 1910–29 derived by using U.S. import unit values; in 1929–87, data from CEPAL.

Table B-10. Mexican Exchange Rates, Internal and World Prices, and Real Exchange Rates, 1950–87

Year	Exchange rate (pesos per dollar)	Exchange rate divided by GDP deflator	World export unit value dollar index (1970 = 100)	Real exchange rate
1950	8.64	25.57	78.1	19.97
1951	8.65	21.38	94.8	20.27
1952	8.63	19.78	91.5	18.10
1953	8.62	19.92	88.9	17.71
1954	11.04	23.02	87.4	20.12
1955	12.50	27.86	86.6	24.12
1956	12.50	21.71	88.9	19.30
1957	12.50	20.33	90.0	18.30
1958	12.50	19.26	87.0	16.76
1959	12.50	18.52	85.1	15.76
1960	12.50	17.65	87.0	15.36
1961	12.50	17.07	87.4	14.92
1962	12.50	16.57	86.7	14.37
1963	12.50	16.07	88.1	14.16
1964	12.50	15.21	89.3	13.58
1965	12.50	14.87	90.7	13.49
1966	12.50	14.30	93.0	13.30
1967	12.50	13.90	93.0	12.93
1968	12.50	13.58	92.2	12.52
1969	12.50	13.06	95.6	12.49
1970	12.50	12.50	100.0	12.50
1971	12.50	11.80	105.6	12.46
1972	12.50	11.11	115.2	12.80
1973	12.50	9.85	141.9	13.98
1974	12.50	8.02	196.3	15.74
1975	12.50	6.93	213.7	14.81
1976	15.43	7.16	218.1	15.62
1977	22.57	8.03	237.8	19.10
1978	22.77	6.94	261.5	18.15
1979	22.81	5.78	309.3	17.88
1980	22.95	4.52	370.4	16.74
1981	24.52	3.83	366.7	14.04
1982	56.40	5.48	353.4	19.37
1983	120.09	6.12	334.8	20.05
1984	167.83	5.38	328.2	17.66
1985	256.87	5.25	323.0	16.96
1986	611.77	7.17	341.5	24.49
1987	1,366.73	6.59	364.5	24.02

Source: For exchange rates, in 1950–60, U.S. Federal Reserve System; in 1960–84, IMF, *International Financial Statistics*. For GDP deflator, table B-11. For world export unit value index, in 1950–60, Maddison (1962); in 1960–87, IMF, *International Financial Statistics*.

Table B-11. **Mexican GDP Deflator, Selected Years, 1950–88**

Year	Deflator (1970 = 100)	Annual change (percent)
1950	33.79	5.4
1951	40.45	19.7
1952	43.64	7.9
1953	43.28	−0.8
1954	47.96	10.8
1955	53.84	12.3
1956	57.59	7.0
1957	61.49	6.8
1958	64.89	5.5
1959	67.51	4.0
1960	70.84	4.9
1961	73.23	3.4
1962	75.43	3.0
1963	77.77	3.1
1964	82.20	5.7
1965	84.09	2.3
1966	87.39	3.9
1967	89.94	2.9
1968	92.08	2.4
1969	95.74	4.0
1970	100.00	4.4
1971	105.88	5.9
1972	112.48	6.2
1973	126.93	12.8
1974	155.77	22.7
1975	180.34	15.8
1976	215.62	19.6
1977	281.16	30.4
1978	328.29	16.8
1979	394.71	20.2
1980	507.98	28.7
1981	640.05	26.0
1982	1,029.85	60.9
1983	1,961.86	90.5
1984	3,121.13	59.1
1985	4,894.23	56.8
1986	8,530.64	74.3
1987	20,729.46	143.0
1988	41,334.55	99.4

Source: Mexico, INEGI (1985a), table 9.1; Bank of Mexico, *Indicadores económicos* (May 1986); World Bank data.

Table B-12. Mexican GDP per Capita, by State, 1970, 1975, and 1980

(pesos)

State	1970	1975	1980
National total	9,094	19,268	63,827
Arguascalientes	7,175	15,558	50,153
Baja California	13,262	26,408	81,637
Baja California Sur	12,607	26,230	80,483
Campeche	7,606	15,616	48,288
Coahuila	10,948	23,980	72,877
Colima	7,826	19,296	57,951
Chiapas	4,520	10,078	55,530
Chihuahua	9,279	19,823	60,091
Distrito Federal	17,634	36,692	121,590
Durango	6,576	13,596	45,993
Guanajuato	6,516	13,733	41,298
Guerrero	4,723	10,701	33,739
Hidalgo	4,918	10,886	41,705
Jalisco	9,502	20,175	64,103
México	9,718	20,606	61,546
Michoacan	4,809	11,055	35,267
Morelos	7,658	15,822	48,660
Nayarit	6,916	14,137	45,163
Nuevo León	15,181	30,936	100,160
Oaxaca	3,237	7,573	25,348
Puebla	5,680	12,150	41,346
Querétaro	7,153	17,200	54,566
Quintana Roo	8,900	25,592	75,794
San Luis Potosí	5,344	10,951	37,087
Sinaloa	8,528	17,699	48,134
Sonora	12,661	23,656	68,976
Tabasco	6,617	20,476	159,420
Tamaulipas	9,599	19,693	65,390
Tlaxcala	4,165	10,995	35,057
Veracruz	7,418	14,429	46,036
Yucatán	6,543	16,682	45,546
Zacatecas	4,730	9,275	29,967
Ratio of highest to lowest state GDP per capita (percent)	5.4	4.8	6.3

Source: Mexico, INEGI (1985c).

Bibliography

The word "processed" describes informally reproduced works that may not be commonly available through library systems.

Abranches, S. M., and others. 1980. *Empresa publica no Brasil: Uma abordagem multidisciplinar*. Brasilia: Instituto de Pesquisas Econômica e Social.

Abreu, M. P. 1977. "Brazil and the World Economy, 1930–45." Ph.D. dissertation, Cambridge University, England. Processed.

Ahluwalia, Montek S., Nicholas G. Carter, and Hollis B. Chenery. 1979. *Growth and Poverty in Developing Countries*. World Bank Reprint Series 118. Washington, D.C..

Altimir, Oscar. 1974. "La medición de la población económicamente activa de México, 1950–70." *Demografía y economía* 8 (1): 50–83.

―――. 1982. *The Extent of Poverty in Latin America*. World Bank Staff Working Paper 522. Washington, D.C.

Aspe, P., and P. E. Sigmund. 1984. *The Political Economy of Income Distribution in Mexico*. New York: Holmes and Meier.

BACEN (Banco Central do Brasil). Various issues. *Boletim do Banco Central*.

Baer, Werner. 1969. *The Development of the Brazilian Steel Industry*. Nashville, Tenn.: Vanderbilt University Press.

―――. 1985. *A industrialização e o desenvolvimento econômico do Brasil*. 6th ed. Rio de Janeiro: Vargas Foundation.

Banamex. 1986. *México social 1985–86*. México, D.F.

Banco Nacional de Comercio Exterior. 1960. *Comercio exterior de México 1877–1911*. México, D.F.

Banco do Brasil. Various years. *Relatorio anual*.

Bank of Mexico. 1963. "Informe sobre la revisión preliminar de las estimaciones del producto nacional de México para los años de 1950 a 1962." *Comercio Extérior* (September).

―――. 1969. *Cuentas nacionales y acervos de capital 1950–1967*. México, D.F.

―――. 1974. *La distribución del ingreso en México: Encuesta sobre los ingresos y gastos de las familias*. México, D.F.

―――. Various issues. *Indicadores económicos*. México, D.F.

_____. Various years. *Informe anual.* México, D.F.

Barkin, David, and Gustavo Esteva. 1981. "El papel del sector público en la comercialización y fijición de precios de los productos agricolas." MREEX/1051. CEPAL, Santiago. Processed.

Bazant, Jan. 1968. *Historia de la dueda exterior de México 1823–1946.* El Colegio de México. México, D.F.

Bergsman, Joel. 1970. *Brazil: Industrialisation and Trade Policies.* London/New York: Oxford University Press.

_____. 1980. *Income Distribution and Poverty in Mexico.* World Bank Working Paper 395. Washington, D.C.

Beteta, Mario Ramon. 1951. *Tres Áños de politica hacendaria.* Mexico, Secretaria de Hacienda y Crédito Público. México, D.F.

Bethell, Leslie, ed. 1984. *Cambridge History of Latin America,* vols. 1 and 2. New York: Cambridge University Press.

Borges, U., H. Freitag, T. Huntiene, and M. Nitsch. 1985. "PROALCOOL–Economia política e avaliação sócio-econômica do programa brasileiro de biocombustiveis." Instituto de Estudos Latinomericanos, Berlin. Processed.

Brasil, Conselho Nacional de Comércio Exterior. 1944. *Dez anos de atividades.* Rio de Janeiro.

Brasil, IPEA/IPLAN (Instituto de Planejamento do Instituto de Planejamento Econômico e Social). 1984. *Política de financiamento do sistema de saúde brasileiro: Uma perspectiva internacional.* Série estudos para o planejamento 16. Brasília.

Brasil, Ministério da Fazenda. *Comercio exterior do Brasil 1929–30.* Rio de Janeiro.

_____. *Comercio exterior do Brasil (por mercadorias) 1948–52.* Rio de Janeiro.

Bueno, G. M. 1987. "Policies on Exchange Rate, Foreign Trade, and Capital." Background paper. México, D.F. Processed.

Camp, R. A. 1985. *Mexico's Leaders: Their Education and Recruitment.* Tucson: University of Arizona Press.

CELADE (Centro Latinoamericano de Demografia). *México: Estimaciones y proyecciones de población, 1950–2000.* México, D.F.

CEPAL (Comision Economica para America Latina y el Caribe). 1976. *America Latina: Relacion de precios de intercombio.* Santiago.

_____. 1984. *Anuário estadístico de America Latina.* Santiago.

_____. 1986. *Los efectos de la crisis de 1982–86 en las condiciones de vida de la población en México.* México, D.F.

Coale, Ansley J., and Edgar M. Hoover. 1958. *Population Growth and Economic Development in Low-Income Countries.* Princeton University Press.

Coatsworth, J. H. 1976. "Anotaciones sobre la producción de alimentos durante el Porfiriato." *Historia mexicana* 26 (2).

_____. 1981. *Growth against Development: The Economic Impact of Railroads in Porfirian Mexico.* De Kalb: Northern Illinois University Press.

Collier, Paul, and Deepak Lal. 1986. *Labor and Poverty in Kenya, 1900-80.* Oxford: Clarendon Press.

de Humboldt, Alexander. 1978. *Ensayo político sobre el reino de la Nueva España.* México, D.F.: Porrúa.

de Mello e Souza, Alberto. 1979. *Financiamento da educacão e accesso a escola no Brasil*. Rio de Janeiro: Institito de Pesquisas do Instituto de Planejamento Econômico e Social.

de Gusmão Veloso, Maria Alice. 1987. "Brazilian National Accounts, 1947–85." Paper presented to the International Association for Research in Income and Wealth, Rocca di Papa, Italy. Processed.

de la Madrid, Miguel. 1986. *Cuarto informe de gobierno*. México, D.F.

Dean, Warren. 1969. *The Industrialisation of Sao Paulo, 1880–1945*. Austin: University of Texas Press.

Delfim Netto, Antonio. 1986. *So o politico pode salvar o economista*. Rio de Janeiro: Edicão do Autor.

Denison, Edward F. 1985. *Trends in American Economic Growth, 1929–82*. Washington, D.C.: Brookings Institution.

Denslow, David, Jr., and William G. Tyler. 1983. *Perspectives on Poverty and Income Inequality in Brazil: An Analysis of Changes during the 1970s*. World Bank Staff Working Paper 601. Washington, D.C.

Derossi, Flavia. 1971. *The Mexican Entrepreneur*. Paris: OECD Development Centre.

Diaz-Alejandro, Carlos F. 1983. "Some Aspects of the 1982–83 Brazilian Payments Crisis." *Brookings Papers on Economic Activity* 2: 515–52.

Diez-Canedo, Juan, and Gabriel Vera. 1982. *Distribución del ingreso en México, 1977*. Serie Cuadernos de Análisis Estructural. México, D.F.: Banco de México.

El Colegio de México. 1960. *Comercio exterior de México. 1877–1911*. México, D.F.

Eris, Ibrahim, C. C. C. Eris, D. K. Kadota, and N. R. Zagha. 1983. "Distribuicão de renda e o sistema tributário no Brasil." *Finanças públicas*: 259–316.

FAO (Food and Agriculture Organization of the United Nations). 1980. *Food Balance Sheets, 1975–77 Average*. Rome.

FAO. Various years. *Production Yearbook*. Rome.

Fernandes, Florestan. 1969. *The Negro in Brazilian Society*. New York: Columbia University, Institute of Latin American Studies

FIBGE (Fundação Instituto Brasileiro de Geografia e Estatística). Various years a. *Anuário estatístico do Brasil*. Rio de Janeiro.

———. Various years b. *Censo demográfico—Brasil*. Rio de Janeiro.

———. Various years c. *Indicadores sociais—tabelas seleccionadas*. Rio de Janeiro.

Fields, G. S. 1977. "Who Benefits from Economic Development: A Reexamination of the Brazilian Experience." *American Economic Review* (September): 570–82, and comments on the article in 1980 *Review* (March): 257–62.

Fishlow, Albert. 1972a. "Brazilian Size Distribution of Income." *American Economic Review* 62 (May): 391–402.

———. 1972b. "Origins and Consequences of Import Substitution in Brazil." In L. E. di Marco, ed., *International Economics and Development*. New York: Academic Press.

Freyre, Gilberto. 1959. *New World in the Tropics*. New York: Knopf.

FUNCEX. 1986. *Balança comercial e outros indicadores conjunturais* (August).

Fundação Getulio Vargas. Various issues. *Conjuntura*. Rio de Janeiro.

Furtado, Celso. 1963. *The Economic Growth of Brazil*. Berkeley: University of California Press.

Garcia de Oliveira, L. E., R. M. Porcaro, and T. C. N. Araujo. 1985. *O lugar do negro na força de trabalho*. Rio de Janeiro: Fundação Instituto Brasileiro de Geografia e Estatística.

Garza, G., and M. Schteingart. 1978. *La acción habitacional del estado en México*. México, D.F.: El Colegio de México.

Goldsmith, Raymond W. 1966. *The Financial Development of Mexico*. Paris: OECD Development Centre.

_____. 1985. *Comparative National Balance Sheets*. University of Chicago Press.

_____. 1986. *Brasil 1850–1984: Desenvolvimento financeiro sob um seculo de inflação*. São Paulo: Harper and Row.

Gordon, Lincoln, and Englebert L. Grommers. 1962. *United States Manufacturing Investment in Brazil*. Cambridge, Mass.: Harvard University Press.

Greer, R. G. 1966. "The Demographic Impact of the Mexican Revolution 1910–21." Master's thesis. University of Texas. Processed.

Gregory, Peter. 1986. *The Myth of Market Failure*. Baltimore, Md.: Johns Hopkins University Press.

Haddad, C. L. S. 1978. *Crescimento do produto real no Brasil 1900–1947*. Rio de Janeiro: Vargas Foundation.

_____. 1980. "Crescimento econômico do Brasil, 1900–76." In Paulo Neuhaus, ed., *Economia brasileira: Uma visâo historica*. Rio de Janeiro: Campus.

Herrera Canales, I. 1977. *El comercio exterior de México 1821–1875*. México, D.F.: El Colegio de México.

Hewlett, Sylvia, and Richard S. Weinert. 1982. *Brazil and Mexico: Patterns in Late Development*. Philadelphia: ISHI Press.

Hicks, J. R. 1979. *Causality in Economics*. Oxford: Blackwells.

Hicks, James F., and David M. Vetter. 1983. *Identifying the Urban Poor in Brazil*. World Bank Staff Working Paper 565. Washington, D.C.

Hoffmann, Helga. 1984. "Poverty and Property in Brazil: What Is Changing?" Columbia University, Institute of Latin American and Iberian Studies, New York. Processed.

IAA (Instituto do Açúcar e do Alcool). Various years. *Anuário açucareiro*.

IBC (Instituto Brasileiro do Café). Various years. *Anuário estatístico do cafe*.

IBGE. (Instituto Brasileiro de Geografia e Estatística) 1960. *O Brasil em Numeros*. Supplement to *Anuário estatístico do Brasil–1960*. Rio de Janeiro.

_____. 1983. *Censo demográfico*, Vol. 1, tomo 5, no. 1. Rio de Janeiro.

_____. Various years a. *Anuário estatístico do Brasil*. Rio de Janeiro.

_____. Various years b. *Sinopse preliminar do censo agropecuario*. Rio de Janeiro.

IDB (Inter-American Development Bank). 1982. *External Debt and Economic Development in Latin America*. Washington, D.C.

_____. 1986. *Economic and Social Progress in Latin America* Washington, D.C.

IMF (International Monetary Fund). 1985. *Government Finance Statistics Yearbook*. Washington D.C.

_____. Various years. *International Financial Statistics Yearbook.* Washington, D.C.

King, Timothy. 1970. *Mexico: Industrialization and Trade Policies since 1940.* London/New York: Oxford University Press.

Kravis, Irving B., Alan Heston, and Robert Summers. 1982. *World Product and Income: International Comparisons of Real GDP.* Baltimore, Md.: Johns Hopkins University Press.

Kuznets, Simon. 1955. "Economic Growth and Income Inequality." *American Economic Review* 45 (March): 1–28.

Lamartine Yates, Paul. 1978. *El Campo Mexicano.* 2 vols. México, D.F.: Ediciones El Caballito.

Langoni, C. G. 1973. *Distribuição da renda e desenvolvimento econômico do Brasil.* Rio de Janeiro: Expressão e Cultura.

_____. 1974. *As causas do crescimento econômico do Brasil.* Rio de Janeiro: APEC.

Lecaillon, Jacques, and others. 1984. *Income Distribution and Economic Development.* Geneva: International Labour Organisation.

Leff, N. H. 1982. *Underdevelopment and Development in Brazil.* 2 vols. London: Allen and Unwin.

Lewis, Oscar. 1964. *The Children of Sánchez.* London: Penguin.

Little, I. M. D., Tibor Scitovsky, and Maurice Scott. 1970. *Industry and Trade in Some Developing Countries.* London/New York: Oxford University Press.

Lustig, Nora. 1986. *Food Subsidy Programs in Mexico.* Working papers on Food Subsidies 3. Washington, D.C.: International Food Policy Research Institute.

_____. 1987. "Crisis económica y niveles de vida en México." In *Estudios Económicos.* México, D.F.: El Colegio de México.

Lustig, Nora, and A. Martín del Campo. 1985. "Descripción del funcionamiento del sistema CONASUPO." *Investigación economica* 173 (July/September).

Maddison, Angus. 1962. "Growth and Fluctuation in the World Economy 1780–1960." *Banca Nazionale del Lavoro Quarterly Review* (June): 3–71.

_____. 1984. "Origins and Impact of the Welfare State, 1883–1983." *Banca Nazionale del Lavoro Quarterly Review* (March): 55–87.

_____. 1985. *Two Crises: Latin America and Asia 1929–38 and 1978–83.* Paris: OECD Development Centre.

_____. 1989. *The World Economy in the Twentieth Century.* Paris: OECD Development Centre.

Maddison, Angus, and Bart van Ark. 1989. "International Comparison of Purchasing Power, Real Output, and Labour Productivity: A Case Study of Brazilian, Mexican, and U.S. Manufacturing, 1975." *Review of Income and Wealth* (March): 31–55.

Martín del Campo, A. 1987. "Notas sobre la evolución reciente de los subsidios a productos básicos alimenticios." Centro Tepotzlán. Processed.

Melo Flores de Lima, B. 1985. *Criptoeconomia ou economia subterranea.* Rio de Janeiro: Vargas Foundation.

Merrick, T. W., and D. H. Graham. 1979. *Population and Economic Development in Brazil: 1800 to the Present.* Baltimore, Md.: Johns Hopkins University Press.

Mesa Lago, Carmelo. 1978. *Social Security in Latin America*. Pittsburgh, Pa.: University of Pittsburgh Press.

Mexico, COPLAMAR (Coordinación General del Plan Nacional de Zonas Deprimidas y Marginadas). 1982. *Necesidades esenciales en México: Salud*. Vol. 4. México, D.F.: Siglo Veintiuno.

Mexico, IMSS (Instituto Mexicano del Seguro Social). Various years. *Memoria estadística*. México, D.F.

Mexico, INEGI (Instituto Nacional de Estadistica Geografia e Informatica). 1977. *Encuesta nacional de ingresos y gastos en las hogares*. México, D.F.

_____. 1983. *Sistema de cuentas nacionales de México: principales variables macroeconómicas: periodo 1970–82*. México, D.F.

_____. 1984a. *X censo general de población y vivienda, 1980, resumen general abreviado*. México, D.F.

_____. 1984b. *Anuario estadístico de los Estados Unidos Mexicanos*. México, D.F.

_____. 1984c. *Sistema de cuentas nacionales de México, 1981–83*. México, D.F.

_____. 1985a. *Estadísticas históricas de México*. 2 vols. México, D.F.

_____. 1985b. *Sistema de cuentas nacionales de México, cuentas de producción del sector público, 1975–83*. México, D.F.

_____. 1985c. *Sistema de cuentas nacionales de México, estructura económica regional: producto interno bruto por entidad federativa 1970, 1975 y 1980*. México, D.F.

_____. 1985d. *Proyecciones de la población de México y las entidades federatives: 1980–2010*. México, D.F.

_____. 1987a. *Sistema de cuentas nacionales de México: cuentas consolidadas de la nación, oferta y utilización, producto interno bruto, 1980–86*. México, D.F.

_____. 1987b. *Sistema de cuentas nacionales de México, 1960–85*. México, D.F.

_____. 1988. *Sistema de cuentas nacionales de México, cuentas de producción del sector público, 1980–86*. México, D.F.

Mexico, Ministry of Agriculture. Various years. *Annual Crop Production Report*. México, D.F.

_____. Various years. *Annual Livestock Report*. México, D.F.

Mexico, SECOFI (Secretaría de Fomento y Comercio Industrial). Various years. *Dirección general de inversiones extranjeras*. México, D.F.

Mexico, SPP (Secretaría de Programación y Presupuesto). Various years. *Censo general de población*. México, D.F.

Miller, S. M. 1960. "Comparative Social Mobility." *Current Sociology* 9.

Mollo, M. L. R. 1983. "Politica de garantia de preços minimos: Uma evaliaçao." *Anàlise e Pesquisa*. 29 (August).

Montoro, A. F., and C. N. Porto. 1982. *Previdência social e previdência complementar*. São Paulo: Fundação Instituto de Pesquisas Econômicas.

Morley, S. A. 1982. *Labor Markets and Inequitable Growth*. New York: Cambridge University Press.

Mosk, Sanford A. 1954. *Industrial Revolution in Mexico*. Berkeley: University of California Press.

NAFINSA (Nacional Financiera S.A.). 1978. *La economía mexicana en cifras*. México, D.F.

Nash, Charles. 1965. *Education and National Development in Mexico*. Research Report Series 106. Princeton University, Industrial Relations section.

Norton, Roger. 1984. "Policy Issues in Mexican Agriculture." World Bank, Washington, D.C. Processed.

OECD (Organisation for Economic Co-operation and Development). 1975. *Education, Inequality and Life Chances*. Paris.

_____. 1979. *Demographic Trends 1950–90*. Paris.

_____. Various years a. *Labour Force Statistics*. Paris.

_____. Various years b. *National Accounts*. Paris.

Oliveira, F. E. B., and others. 1985. *Tendências a médio prazo da previdência social brasileira: Um modelo de simulacão*. Rio de Janeiro: Instituto de Pesquisas do Institito de Planejamento Econônomico e Social.

Pastore, Jose. 1979. *Disigualdade e mobilidade social no Brasil*. São Paulo: Queiroz.

Pastore, Jose, Helio Zylberstajn, and Carmen S. Pagotto. 1983. *Mudança social e pobreza no Brasil 1970–80*. São Paulo: Fundação Instituto de Pesquisas Econômicas.

PEMEX (Petróleos Mexicanos). Various years. *Memoria de labores*. México, D.F.

Pérez Lopéz, E., ed. 1967. *Mexico's Recent Economic Growth*. Austin: University of Texas Press.

Pfeffermann, Guy P., and Richard Webb. 1979. *The Distribution of Income in Brazil*. World Bank Staff Working Paper 356. Washington, D.C.

Reyes Heroles G. G., Jesus. 1976. "Política fiscal y redistribución del ingreso: Estimación de la incidencia del sistema fiscal mexicano en 1968." Licenciado thesis, ITAM, México, D.F. Processed.

_____. 1987. "Financial Policies and Income Distribution in Mexico." México, D.F. Processed.

Reyes Heroles G. G., Jesus, and J. J. Sidaoui, D. 1981. "Cuentas nacionales y análisis macroeconomico." Document 38. Bank of Mexico, México, D.F. Processed.

Riding, Alan. 1985. *Distant Neighbours*. New York: Knopf.

Roett, Riordan, ed. 1972. *Brazil in the Sixties*. Nashville, Tenn.: Vanderbilt University Press.

Ronfeldt. D. 1984. *The Modern Mexican Military: A Reassessment*. San Diego.

Rosenblat, Angel. 1945. *La población indigena de América desde 1492 hasta la actualidad*. Buenos Aires: ICE.

Rosenzweig, F., ed. n.d. "Fuerza de trabajo y actividad económica por sectores, estadístícas económicas del Porfiriato." El Colegio de México, México, D.F. Processed.

Rosenzweig, F. 1965. "El desarrollo económico de México de 1877 a 1911." *El Trimestre Económico* (July–September).

Samaniego, N. 1986. "Los efectos de la crisis de 1982–86 en las condiciones de vida de la población en México." CEPAL/LC/R.539. México, D.F. Processed.

Sawyer, Malcolm. 1976. *Income Distribution in OECD Countries.* OECD Occasional Studies. Paris.

Selowsky, Marcelo. 1967. "Education and Economic Growth: Some International Comparisons." Ph.D. dissertation, University of Chicago.

Simonsen, Mario H., and Roberto de Oliveira Campos. 1974. *A nova economia Brasileira.* Rio de Janeiro: Olympio.

Smith, P. H. 1979. *Labyrinths of Power.* Princeton University Press.

Stein, S. J. 1957. *The Brazilian Cotton Manufacture.* Cambridge, Mass.: Harvard University Press.

Stepan, Alfred. 1971. *The Military in Politics: Changing Patterns in Brazil.* Princeton University Press.

ten Kate, Adrian. 1988. *La estructura de la protección effectiva en México: 1984–86 informe preliminar.* México, D.F.: Secretaría de Comercio y Fomento Industrial.

Thomas, Vinod. 1982. *Differences in Income, Nutrition, and Poverty within Brazil.* World Bank Staff Working Paper 505. Washington, D.C.

Titkin, M. 1984. "Deficit presupuestal, crecimiento, inflación y balanza de pagos: El caso de México: 1965–82." *Cuadernos de planeación hacendaria.*

Trejo, Saul. 1987. *El futuro de la política industrial en México.* México, D.F.: El Colegio de México.

UN (United Nations). 1977. *Statistical Yearbook.* New York.

———. Various issues. *Monthly Bulletin of Statistics.*

Urquidi, Victor L. 1982. "Technical Education in Mexico: A Preliminary Appraisal." *Prospects* 12 (1).

US (United States), Federal Reserve System. Various years. *Banking and Monetary Statistics.* Washington, D.C.

van Ginneken, Wouter. 1980. *Socioeconomic Groups and Income Distribution in Mexico.* London: Croom Helm.

Van Ooststroom, Harry, and Angus Maddison. 1984. "An International Comparison of Levels of Real Output and Productivity in Agriculture in 1975." Memo 162, with revisions. University of Groningen, Institute of Economic Research. Processed.

Vernon, Raymond, ed. 1964. *Public Policy and Private Enterprise in Mexico.* Cambridge, Mass.: Harvard University Press.

Villalpando Hernández, L. H., and J. Fernández Moran. 1986. "La encuesta de acervos, depreciación y formación de capital del Banco de México, 1975–85," (with 6 diskettes). Bank of Mexico, México, D.F. Processed.

Villela, Annibal V., and Werner Baer. 1980. *O setór privado nacional: problemas e politicas para seu fortalecimento.* Rio de Janeiro: Instituto de Planejamento Econômico e Social.

Villela, Annibal V., and Wilson Suzigan. 1975. "Crescimento da renda durante a II guerra mundial, 1940–45." In F. R. Versiani and J. R. Mendonça de Barros, eds. *Formacão econômica do Brasil.* São Paulo: Saraiva.

———. 1977. *Government Policy and the Economic Growth of Brazil, 1889–1945.* Brazilian Economic Studies 3. Rio de Janeiro: Instituto de Planejamento Econômico e Social.

Ward, Peter M. 1986. *Welfare Politics in Mexico*. London: Allen and Unwin.

Wharton Economic Forecasting Associates. 1989. "Perspectivas éconómicas de México." CEMIEX-WEFA, México, D.F. Processed.

Wilkie, James W. 1970. *The Mexican Revolution: Federal Expenditure and Social Change since 1910*. Berkeley: University of California Press.

Wilkie, James W., and Kenneth Ruddle. 1977. *Statistical Abstract of Latin America*. Supplement 6. Los Angeles: UCLA Latin American Center.

Williamson, John, ed. 1983. IMF *Conditionality*. Washington, D.C.: Institute for International Economics.

World Bank. 1982. *Brazil: A Review of Agricultural Policies*. Washington, D.C.

———. 1983. *Brazil: Industrial Policies and Manufactured Exports*. Washington, D.C.

———. Various years. *World Tables*. Washington, D.C.

Zerkowski, Ralph M., and Maria Alice de Gusmâo Veloso. 1982. "Seis decadas de economia brasileira atraves do PIB." *Revista brasileira de economia* 36 (3, July–September): 331–36.

Index

Agencia Especial de Financimento Industrial (FINAME), 77
AGF. Aquisicaes do Governo Federal, 70
Agrarian Reform Act of 1915 (Mexico), 161
Agriculture in Brazil: alcohol program and, 71; financial credit for, 67–69; food subsidies and, 70–71; government policies toward, 63–71; land reform and, 65–67; minimum price program for, 70; research and extension programs of, 67. *See also names of specific crops.*
Agriculture in Mexico, 161–76; concentration of poverty in, 188–89; crop yields and, 170–71; economy and, 173–76; farm capital and inputs of, 167–69; investments in improving, 168–69; irrigation and, 170; labor force for, 164–67; land reform and, 161–64; livestock and, 171; price policy and, 171–73. *See also names of specific crops.*
Alemán, Miguel, 125, 197; contribution to education by, 127; enmity toward Vicente Lombardo Toledano, 126–27; irrigation program of, 170; social security expanded by, 192
Alliance for Progress, 129–30; Committee of Nine, 130
Altos Hornos de Mexico, 124
American Federation of Labor, relations with Mexican unions by, 118
American and Foreign Power Company, 178
ANDSA. National Storage Houses (Mexico), 203
Apprenticeship training in Brazil, 52
Aquisicaes do Governo Federal (AGF), 70

Balance of payments in Brazil, oil shock of 1979 and, 37–38
Banco de México, 124, 126, 137; devaluation of the peso by, 128; estimate of agriculture growth by, 174; FICORCA established by, 139; response to oil shocks by, 133–34
Banco do Brasil, 26; agricultural credit and, 67
Banco Nacional de Desenvolvimento Econômico (BNDE), 27–28, 76; incentives offered by, 77; Plano de Metas prepared by, 28–29
Banco Nacional de Habitação, 33; housing in Brazil and, 106
Banks, Mexico's nationalization of, 9–10, 159
BEFIEX. Comissão para Concessão de Beneficios Fiscais a Programas Especiais de Exportação, 77
Beteta, Ramón, 125, 127
Birth rate in Brazil, 51, 82
BNDE. *See* Banco Nacional de Desenvolvimento Econômico
Bodet, Jaime Torres, "eleven-year plan" by, 197
Branco, Humberto de Alencar Castelo, 23, 24, 31, 34
Brasileiro, Frente Negra, 91
Brazil: access to foreign technical knowledge by, 53–55; agriculture policies of, 63, 65–71; civilian government returned to in 1985, 40, 42; colonial period of, 19; comparing growth outcomes and policy to Mexico, 4–7; crisis of 1980s effect on, 7–10; distributive impact of the fiscal structure of, 106–08, 110; eco-

Brazil *(continued)*
nomic structure of, 46–49; education in, 101–04; effect international migration on, 58–59; emperor rule of, 19; external finance used by, 55, 57–58; first republic of, 19; foreign investment in, 44; growth accounts of, 43–46; health services in, 104–05; housing in, 105–06; income distributions in, 79–80, 82–95; industry and services policies of, 71–78; international trade by, 59, 61–63; investment effort of, 49–50; job patronage in, 20–21; labor inputs of, 51–52; lack of factional conflicts in, 24; land reform in, 65–67; Mexico's debt moratorium effect on, 38; Mexico's income distribution compared with, 10–16; military officer class of, 23; natural resources as a growth factor of, 52–53; politics and macroeconomic policy of, 25–40, 42; slavery in, 19; social security system of, 96–101; suffrage in, 20

Brazilian Agricultural Research Enterprise (EMBRAPA), 67
Brazilian Coffee Institute (IBC), 67
Brazilian labor party, 21–22
Bulhões, Octavio Gouveia de, 24, 31

Calles, Plutarco Elias, 113
Camacho, Manuel Avila, 117, 123–24, 197; national unity policy of, 123; new economic order of, 122–27
Campaign to Abolish Adult Illiteracy (Brazil), 102
Campos, Roberto de Oliveira, 24, 31
Capital in Mexico, mobilization and allocation of, 150–51
Capital productivity in Brazil, 46
Capital stock in Brazil, measuring the growth of, 50
Cárdenas, Lázaro, 113, 163, 197; National Storage Houses established by, 203
Carteira Industrial, 26
Castro, Fidel, 129
CEIMSA. Mexican Company for Exports and Imports, 203
CELPAC. Executive Commission for the Planning of Cocoa Cultivation (Brazil), 67
CEMIG. Centrais Elétricas de Minas Gerais, 73
Centrais Elétricas Brasileris. *See* ELECTROBRAS

Centrais Elétricas de Minas Gerais (CEMIG), 73
Centro Internacional de Mejoramiento de Maíz y Trigo (CIMMYT), 171
CFP. Commissão de Financiamento da Produção, 70
CIMMYT. Centro Internacional de Mejoramiento de Maíz y Trigo, 171
Clayton, William, 125
Cocoa cultivation, planning of (Brazil), 67
Coffee: Brazil's over reliance on, 5, 61; government policy toward, 63–65; government purchase of, 26; as percentage of Brazilian exports, 48; São Paulo stabilization program for, 20; share of agriculture credit, 68
Comissão para Concessão de Benefícios Fiscais a Programas Especiais de Exportação (BEFIEX), 77
Commissão de Financiamento da Produção (CFP), 70
Companhia de Financiamento da Produção, 70
Companhia Siderúrgica Nacional (CSN), 73–74
Companhia Vale do Rio Doce (CVRD), 74, 75
Compañía Nacional de Subsisténcias Populares, 16, 172, 203–04
Computer industry, development of Brazilian, 54
CONASUPO. Compañía Nacional de Subsisténcias Populares, 16, 172, 203–04
Confederación de Cámaras Industriales, 119
Confederación de Trabajadores de México (CTM), 118
Conselho de Desenvolvimento Econômico, 35
Conselho Federal de Comércio Exterior, 26
Coordinación General del Plan Nacional de Zonas Deprimidas y Marginadas (COPLAMAR), 193
Cortines, Adolfo Ruiz, 197, 130; irrigation program of, 170; macroeconomic policies of, 128–29
Cotton, Brazilian government policy toward, 64–66
Crop yields in Mexico, 170–71
Cruzado plan, 40
CSN. Companhia Siderúrgica Nacional, 73–74

CTM. Confederación de Trabajadores de México, 118
CVRD. Companhia Vale do Rio Doce, 74–75

Debt: delinquency by Brazil, 57; moratorium by Mexico, 38, 57. *See also* Public debt
Departamento Administrativo do Serviço Público, 21
Diaz, Porfirio, 113
Dornelles, Francisco N., 40
Dutra, Eurico Gaspar, 22, 27

Echeverría, Luis, 117, 192; policies during the administration of, 132–35; "shared developmenté strategy of, 132; technical schools emphasized by, 198;
Economic growth, comparing Brazil and Mexico, 4–7
Education in Brazil, 101–04; average levels of, 43, 87; Campaign to Abolish Adult Illiteracy and, 102; comparison of education in Mexico with, 10–13; expenditure per capita for, 103; inequalities of, 87–88; sources of funds for, 101–02; work force quality and, 51–52
Education in Mexico: adult education programs and, 199; comparison of education in Brazil with, 10–13; government aid to the spread of, 190–91; government policy toward, 195–201; labor force average levels of, 152; Miguel Alemán's contributions to, 127; redistributive expenditures and, 207–08; status of intellectuals in, 120–21
EGF. Empréstimos do Governo Federal, 70
Ejidatarios of Mexico, 119, 162–06; output per hectare of, 175
Ejidos, 162–66, 175
Electric utilities in Mexico, 178
ELECTROBRAS, 27, 73, 75
EMBRAER. Emprésa Brasileira da Aeronáutica S.A., 78
EMBRAPA. Brazilian Agricultural Research Enterprise, 67
Emprésa Brasileira da Aeronáutica S.A. (EMBRAER), 78
Empréstimos do Governo Federal (EGF), 70
Energy development: nuclear energy in Brazil, 54; sugar-based alcohol, 54
Eris, Ibrahim, 107

Estado novo, 22, 25; minimum wage as part of, 86
Estatuto do Trabalhador Rural, 66
Ethnicity in Brazil, income distributions and, 90–91
Executive Commission for the Planning of Cocoa Cultivation (CEPLAC) (Brazil), 67
Export-Import Bank, creation of, 28
Exports by Brazil: aid for manufactured, 77–78; changing patterns of, 47–48; earning growth of 1964–67, 33; effect of the crisis of 1980s on, 38–39
External finance, Brazilian use of, 55, 57–58

Farm credit in Mexico, 169
Federal Electric Commission (Mexico), 178
Fernandes, Florestan, 91
FGTS. Fundo de Garantia por Tempo de Servico, 33, 97–98
FIBGE. Fundação Instituto Brasileiro de Geografia e Estatística, 108
FICORCA, established, 139
Figueiredo, João Baptista de, 24, 36
FINAME. Agencia Especial de Financiemento Industrial, 77
Financial services: Brazilian government intervention in, 49; growth of Brazilian, 48–49
Fiscal structure of Brazil, distributive impact of, 106–08, 110
Flores, Antonio Carrillo, 128
Food subsidies in Mexico, 203–05
Freyre, Gilberto, 90
FUNABEM. Fundação Nacional do Bem-Estar do Menor, 97
Funaro, Dilson, 40
Fundação Getúlio Vargas foundation, 35; measuring of Brazilian capital stock growth by, 50
Fundação Instituto Brasileiro de Geografia e Estatística (FIBGE), 108
Fundação Nacional do Bem-Estar do Menor (FUNABEM), 97
Fundo de Garantia por Tempo de Serviço (FGTS), 33, 97–98
Furor legiferandi, 31
Furnas Centrais Elétricas S.A., 73

Galicia, Joaquin Hernandez, 118
Gas utilities in Mexico, 178
Geisel, Ernesto, 24

General Agreement on Tariffs and Trade (GATT), decision of Mexico to join, 125, 154, 180
General Office of Civil Pensions, 192
Gortari, Carlos Salinas de, 117
Goulart, João Belchior Marques, 22, 31, 85
Gross domestic product in Brazil, the crisis of 1980s effect on, 7, 38
Gross domestic product in Mexico: the crisis of 1980s effect on, 7; growth of during 1950–70, 131
Gudin, Eugenio, 24

Health services: comparison of Brazilian and Mexican, 15; Brazilian government policies toward, 104–05; Mexican government policies toward, 201–02
Herzog, Jesús Silva, 124, 137
Housing: comparison of Brazilian and Mexican, 15; Brazilian government policies toward, 105–06; Mexican government policies toward, 202–03

IAA. Sugar and Alcohol Institute (Brazil), 67
IBC. Brazilian Coffee Institute, 67
IDB. Inter-American Development Bank, 137
Illiteracy in Brazil, Campaign to Abolish Adult 102
Immediate Action Plan, 129–30
Immigration, benefits to Brazil through, 44, 58–59
Imports by Brazil: computers barred as, 77–78; effect of the crisis of 1980s on, 38; Law of Similars and, 76; substitution of, 59, 61–62
Imports by Mexico, government intervention in, 154–56
IMSS. Mexican Institute of Social Security, 192–96, 201
INAMPS. See Instituto Nacional de Assistencia Médica da Previdencia Social (INAMPS)
Income distribution in Brazil, 79–80, 82–95; causes of inequality controversy about, 83–84; compared with Mexico, 10–16; effect of social mobility on, 93–94; effect of taxes, transfers, and government spending on, 93; ethnicity and, 90–91; Langoni view of, 86–89; minimum wage effect on, 85–86; poverty and, 94–95; property inequality and, 91–93; wage spreads, 89–90

Income distribution in Mexico: compared with that in Brazil, 10–16; inequality of, 185–91
Income tax in Brazil, regressive nature of, 106–08, 110
INCRA. Instituto Nacional de Colonização e Refoma Agrária, 67
Industry in Brazil, government policies toward, 71–78. *See also specific kinds of industry.*
Industry in Mexico: foreign investment in, 181–82; government policy toward, 176–83; government protection of, 180. *See also specific kinds of industry.*
Inflation in Brazil: crisis of 1980s effect on, 7–8; effect of oil shock of 1979, 37–38; policy of the military regime toward, 31–32
Inflation in Mexico, 158
INFONAVIT. Institute of National Funds for Housing for Workers, 202
INPS. Instituto Nacional de Previdencia Social, 96, 98, 100, 104
Institute for Adult Education (Mexico), 199
Institute of National Funds of Housing for Workers (Mexico), 202
Institute of Social Security and Services of State Employees (Mexico), 192
Instituto Agronômico de Campinas, 67
Instituto Brasileiro de Reforma Agrária (IRBA), 66–67
Instituto de Administração Financeira de Previdencia e Assistencia Social (LAPAS), 97
Instituto Nacional de Assistencia Médica da Previdencia Social (INAMPS), 97, 98, 100, 104–05; principal elements of, 105
Instituto Nacional de Colonização e Refoma Agrária (INCRA), 67
Instituto Nacional de Previdencia Social (INPS), 96, 98, 100, 104
Instituto Panamericano de Alta Dirección de Empresa (IPADE), 120
Inter-American Conference on Postwar Economic and Financial Problems, 125
Inter-American Development Bank (IDB), 137
International Center for Maize and Wheat Research (Mexico), 171
International Monetary Fund (IMF): effect of the devaluation of the peso on, 128; Juscelino Kubitschek refuses to borrow from, 22; rescheduling of Mexican pub-

lic debt by, 139–40
International trade, Brazil and, 59, 61–63
IPADE. Instituto Panamericano de Alta Dirección de Empresa, 120
IRBA. Instituto Brasileiro de Reforma Agrária, 66–67
Irrigation in Mexico, 170
ISSSTE. Social Security and Services of State Employees (Mexico), 192–94, 201

Kaldor, Nicholas, 129

Labor force in Brazil: cost of, 71–72; education of, 51–52; as percentage of total population, 51; suppression of unions and, 71–72
Labor supply in Mexico, growth and allocation of, 151–54
Labor unions in Brazil, suppression of, 71–72
Land reform: in Brazil, 65–67; comparison of land reform in Brazil and in Mexico, 10, 12; 1964 law of, 66
Landholders in Mexico, protected from expropriation (1946), 126
Langoni, C. G., study of income inequality in Brazil by, 86–89
LAPAS. Instituto de Administração Financeira de Previdencia e Assistencia Social, 97
Law of Schooling and Training (Mexico), 199
Law of Similars (Brazil), 29, 76
Law of Tariffs (Brazil), 29
Legiao Brasileira de Assistencia (LBA), 97
LICONSA, 204
Livestock in Mexico, 171
Lozano, Raúl Salinas, 130

Macroeconomic policy in Brazil: conservative period, 1946–51, 27; development policy of in 1951–64, 27–31; disequilibrium of (1970–82), 158–61; military regime of 1964–85 and, 31–36; the "miracleé years of 1967–79 and, 34–36; world crisis and, 25–27; World War II and, 25–27
Macroeconomic policy in Mexico, 122–37, 139–41; adjustment policies period for (1982–88), 139–41; Avila Camacho's new economic order and (1940–52), 122–27; destabilizing policies and (1970–76), 132–35; development of price stability (1958–70), 129–32; oil boom and bust period and (1965–82), 135–37; Ruiz Cortines (1952–58) and, 128–29
Madrid, Miguel de la, 117, 137; policies of 1982–88 by, 139–41, 160–61
Magón, Enrique Flores, 162
Manufacturing in Brazil, foreign owned firms and, 54
Manufacturing in Mexico: government policy toward, 178–82; poverty in, 190
Margain, Hugo B., 132
Mateos, López, 129, 130–31, 151; emphasis on education by, 197; social security expanded by, 192
Medici, Emilio Garrastazu, 34
Mena, Ortiz, 132, 151; retained by Díaz Ordaz as minister of finance, 131
Mexican Company for Exports and Imports, 203
Mexican Entrepreneur, 119–20
Mexican Institute of Social Security (IMSS), 192–96, 201
Mexican Light and Power, 178
Mexican Oil Workers' Union, 118
Mexico: agricultural policies of, 161–76; Brazil's income distribution compared with, 10–16; class structure of, 121; colonial period in, 113; comparing growth outcomes and policy to that of Brazil, 4–7; the crisis of 1980s effect on, 7–10; dimensions of income inequality and poverty in, 185–91; distributive impact of government spending and revenue, 205, 207–08, education in, 195–201; effect of debt moratorium on Brazil, 38; exercise of power in, 113–21; food subsidies in, 203–05; growth accounts of, 143, 145, 147–61; health services of, 201–02; housing programs in, 202–03; ideology of, 113–21; industry and services policies of, 176–83; intellectual climate of, 120–21; interest groups of, 116–21; makeup of political elite of, 116–17; politics and macroeconomic policy of, 122–37, 139–40; power of the presidency of, 115; revolution of 1910–20 in, 113–14; role of the military in, 117–18; social security program in, 191–95
Migration, from Mexico, 13–14, 153–54
Milagre brasileiro, 34

246 Index

Military in Mexico, political role of, 117–18
Military regime in Brazil: macroeconomic policies in 1964–85, 31–36; officer class in, 23
Minimum wage in Brazil: effect on income distribution and, 85–86; establishment of, 21
Minimum wage in Mexico, 153, 191
Mining in Mexico, government policy toward, 176–78
Ministry of Public Health and Welfare (SSA), 201
Movimento Brasileiro de Alfabetização (MOBRAL), 88, 102

Nacional Financiera (NAFIN), 124, 126, 179
National Development Study (Mexico), 136
National Investment Commission (Mexico), 130
National Plan for Land Reform (Brazil), 67
National Rural Credit Bank (Mexico), 169
National Social Security Institute (Mexico), 127
National Storage Houses (Mexico), 203
National Study on Family Expenditures (ENDEF) (Brazil), 107–08
National System of Rural Credit (SNCR) (Brazil), 67
National Workers Housing Institute (Mexico), 137
Nationalization of Mexico's banks, 9–10, 159
Natural resources in Brazil, growth resulting from, 52–53
Netto, Antonio Delfim, 24, 34, 35, 83; indexed bonds created by, 39; response to inflation of, 7–8; response to oil shock of 1979 of, 37
Neves, Tancredo, 31
Nobréga, Mailson Ferreira da, 42
NUCLEBRAS, 36
NUCLEP, 36
Nutrition in Brazil, 51

OAS. Organization of American States, 131
Obregón, Alvaro, 115
Obrigacoes readjustaveis do Tesouro Nacional (ORTN), 33
Oil in Mexico: boom and bust period (1976–82), 135–37; discovery of, 135; effect of shock on, 7–8, 133, 136–37; government overreliance on, 5; price decline effect on, 140
Oil shock in Brazil: effect of, 7–8, 35, 36; policy development after, 36–40
Oliveira, Juscelino Kubitschek de, 22, 28
Ordaz, Gustavo Díaz, 131, 151; aid to education by, 198; social security and,192
Organization of American States (OAS), 131
ORTN. *Obrigacoes readjustaveis do Tesouro Nacional*, 33

Partido Accion Nacional (PAN), 120
Partido Nacional Revolucionario (PRN), 113–14, union section of, 119
PASEP. Programa de Formação do Patrimonio do Servidor Público, 34
Patronage in Brazil, 19, 20
PEMEX. Petróleos Mexicanos, 115, 133, 177
Pereira, Luiz Carlos Bresser, 42
Peso, devaluation of, 128, 156
Petróleo Brasileiro S.A. (PETROBRAS), 36, 73, 74; creation of, 27, 75
Petróleos Mexicanos (PEMEX), 115, 133, 177
PGPM. Política de Garantia de Precos Minimos, 70
PIS. Programa de Integração Social, 34
Plano de Metas, 28–29
Policy development, in Brazil after second oil shock, 36-40
Política de Garantia de Precos Minimos (PGPM), 70
Political economy, types of, 3
Porfiriato: foreign purchase of land during, 161; mining under, 176–77; utilities under, 178; village farmland loss during, 162
Portillo, José López, 115, 117, 120–21, 134, 156; effect of oil discovery in Mexico on, 135–37; macroeconomic mismanagement by, 159; promotion of rural area development by, 193; public borrowing by administration of, 158
Poverty in Brazil, income distribution and, 94–95
Poverty in Mexico, 185–91
PASEP. Programa de Formação do Patrimonio do Servidor Público, 34
PRI. Partido Revolucionario Institucional
Prices in Mexico: agriculture policy and,

171–73; government manipulation of, 158
Private sector in Brazil: emphasis between public sector and, 74–76; promoting investments in, 76
PRN. Partido Nacional Revolucionario, 113–14
PROAGO, 68–69
PROALCOOL, 36, 71
Product markets in Mexico, inefficiency in, 154–58
Productivity: of Brazil and Mexico compared, 11; growth of in Mexico, 148–51
Programa de Formação do Patrimonio do Servidor Público (PASEP), 34
Programa de Integração Social (PIS), 34
Programa Nacional de Alcool, 36
Property in Brazil, inequality of ownership of, 91–93
Public debt: effect of the crisis of 1980s in Brazil on, 39; in Mexico, 139
Public enterprises in Mexico, pricing policy of, 156–58
Public health services in Brazil, 104–05
Public sector in Brazil, emphasis between private sector and, 74–76
Punta del Este Charter, 129

Quadros, Janio da Silva, 22; anti-inflation measures of, 30–31

Regional inequality, of Brazil and Mexico compared, 13
Regulating Committee for Subsistence Markets, 203

Salazar, Antonio de Oliveira, 22
Second National Development Plan, Brazilian balance of payments deficit and, 35
SENAC, 102
SENAI. Serviço Nacional de Aprendizagem Industrial, 88, 102
Services in Mexico, government policy toward, 176–83, 182–83
Serviço Nacional de Aprendizagem Industrial (SENAI), 88, 102
SIDERBRAS, 75
Silva, Arthur da Costa e, 34
Simonsen, Mario, 7, 24, 35, 36
Simonsen, Roberto, 22, 24
SINPAS. Sistema Nacional de Presidencia e Assistencia, 97

Sistema Financeira de Habitaço, 106
Sistema Nacional de Previdencia e Assisencia (SINPAS), 97
Slavery, in Brazil, 19
SNCR. National System of Rural Credit (Brazil), 67
Social mobility in Brazil, income distribution and, 93–94
Social security: of Brazil and Mexico compared, 14–15; Brazil's system of, 96–101; distributive impact of in Mexico, 191–95; establishment of in Mexico, 127
Social Security and Services of State Employees (ISSSTE) (Mexico), 192–94, 201
Social welfare programs: distributive impact of in Brazil, 96–106; distributive impact of in Mexico, 191–95
SSA. Ministry of Public Health and Welfare, 201
State enterprises in Brazil: creation and expansion of, 73–74; government policy toward, 72–73
Steel plant, Tubarção, 36
Suárez, Eduardo, 124
Subsidies: of Brazil and Mexico compared, 15–16; for food in Mexico, 203–05
SUDENE. Superintendência para o Desenvolvimento do Nordeste, 30, 76
Sugar and Alcohol Institute (IAA) (Brazil), 67
SUMOC. Superintendency of Money and Credit (Brazil), 28
Superintendência para o Desenvolvimento do Nordeste (SUDENE), 30, 76
Superintendency of Money and Credit (SUMOC) (Brazil), 28
Survey on Household Budget (Brazil), 108

Tariffs: imposed by Brazil, 59, 61; Law of, 29
Taxes in Brazil: effect on income distribution, 93; regressive nature of income, 106–08, 110
Technocrats, influence on the government in Mexico by, 117, 122
Telecommunicações Brasileiras S.A. (TELEBRAS)
Tello, Carlos, 137
Tlaltelolco massacre of 1968, 117
Toledano, Vicente Lombardo, 118, 126–27
Tubarão steel plant, 36

UNCTAD. United Nations Conference on Trade and Development, 133
Unions in Mexico, 118; suppression of by Brazil, 71–72
United Nations Conference on Trade and Development (UNCTAD), 133
Utilities in Mexico, government policy of, 178

Vargas, Getúlio Dornelles, 21–22, 25; elected president, 27; military rebellion led by, 21; suppression of political parties by, 91
Vasconcelos, José, 197
Velasquez, Fidel, 118
Velloso, João Paulo dos Reis, 35

Villegas, Daniel Cosío, 124
Voz da raça, 91

Wages in Brazil: adjustment rules for in 1980s, 39–40, income distribution and, 85–86; minimum, 21, 85–86; spreads of, 89–90
Wages in Mexico, minimum, 153, 191
Work force. *See* Labor force World Bank: creation of BNDE and, 28; loans to Nacional Financiera by, 179
World Crisis, Brazilian macroeconomic policy during, 25–27
World War II, Brazilian macroeconomic policy during, 25–27

The complete backlist of publications from the World Bank is shown in the annual *Index of Publications,* which contains an alphabetical title list and indexes of subjects, authors, and countries and regions. The latest edition is available free of charge from the Publications Distribution Unit, Office of the Publisher, The World Bank, 1818 H Street, N.W., Washington, D.C. 20433, U.S.A., or from Publications, The World Bank, 66 avenue d'Iéna, 75116 Paris France.